The Dynamics of Hutterite Society

The Dynamics of Hutterite Society

An Analytical Approach

Karl A. Peter

 The University of Alberta Press

First published by
The University of Alberta Press
Athabasca Hall
Edmonton, Alberta, Canada
T6G 2E8

Copyright © The University of Alberta Press 1987

ISBN   0-88864-108-7 cloth
        0-88864-109-5 paper

Canadian Cataloguing in Publication Data

Peter, Karl A. (Karl Andreas), 1924–
The dynamics of Hutterite society

Bibliography: p.
ISBN 0-88864-108-7 (bound). — ISBN
0-88864-109-5 (pbk.)

1. Hutterite Brethren. 2. Hutterite
Brethren – Social conditions. I. Title.
BX8129.H8P48 1987   289.7'3   C86–091338–4

Printed by D. W. Friesen & Sons Ltd.,
Altona, Manitoba, Canada

Permissions

Chapter 1: Karl A. Peter. "The Survival and Institutional Evolution of Hutterite Society." Published with the permission of the author.

Chapter 2: Karl A. Peter. "The Certainty of Salvation: Ritualization of Religion and Economic Rationality Among Hutterites." *Comparative Studies in Society and History: An International Quarterly* 25, no. 2 (April 1983): 222-40. Reprinted with the permission of Cambridge University Press, New York, New York.

Chapter 3: Karl Peter, Edward D. Boldt, Ian Whitaker, Lance W. Roberts. "The Dynamics of Hutterite Defection." *Journal for the Scientific Study of Religion* 21, no. 4 (December 1982): 327-37. Reprinted with the permission of the authors and first printed in the *Journal for the Scientific Study of Religion*.

Chapter 4: Karl Peter. "The Hutterite Family." In *The Canadian Family*, edited by K. Ishwaran, pp. 248-62. Toronto: Holt, Rinehart and Winston of Canada, Ltd., 1971. Also appeared in *The Canadian Family*, second edition (1976), on pp. 289-303. Reprinted with the permission of the author.

Chapter 5: Karl A. Peter. "Childhood and Adolescent Socialization Among Hutterites." In *Childhood and Adolescency in Canada*, edited by K. Ishwaran, pp. 344-65. Scarborough, Ontario: McGraw-Hill Ryerson Limited, 1979. Reprinted with the permission of the publisher.

Chapter 6: Karl A. Peter. "Problems in the Family Community and Culture of Hutterites." In *Canadian Families: Ethnic Variations*, edited by K. Ishwaran, pp. 221-36. Scarborough, Ontario: McGraw-Hill Ryerson Limited, 1980. Reprinted with the permission of the publisher.

Chapter 7: Karl Peter and Ian Whitaker. "Hutterite Perceptions of Psycho–physiological Characteristics." *Journal of Social and Biological Structures* (1984): 1-8. Reprinted with the permission of Academic Press Inc. (London) Ltd.

Chapter 8: Karl Peter. "Toward a Demographic Theory of Hutterite Population Growth." *Variables* 5 (Spring 1966): 28-37. Reprinted with the permission of the author.

Chapter 9: Karl A. Peter. "The Decline of Hutterite Population Growth." *Canadian Ethnic Studies* 12, no. 3 (1980): 97-110. Reprinted with the permission of the author and *Canadian Ethnic Studies*.

Chapter 10: Karl Peter and Ian Whitaker. "The Acquisition of Personal Property Among Hutterites and Its Social Dimensions." *ANTHROPOLOGICA* 13, no. 2 (1981): 145-55. Reprinted with the permission of *ANTHROPOLOGICA*, Laurentian University, Sudbury, Ontario.

Chapter 11: Karl Peter and Ian Whitaker. "The Hutterite Economy: Recent Changes and Their Social Correlates." *ANTHROPOS* 78 (1983): 535-46. Reprinted with the permission of *ANTHROPOS*, St. Augustin, West Germany.

Chapter 12: Karl Peter and Ian Whitaker. "The Changing Roles of Hutterite Women." *Prairie Forum* 7, no. 2 (Fall 1982): 267-77. Reprinted with the permission of *Prairie Forum*, Canadian Plains Research Centre, Regina, Saskatchewan.

Chapter 13: Karl A. Peter. "Hutterite and Ethnic Relations." Published with the permission of the author.

_____TO
LYDIA
&_____
KARL GOTTLIEB PETER

CONTENTS

ACKNOWLEDGMENTS

For several years Drs. Ed Boldt and Lance Robert from the University of Manitoba, and Dr. Ian Whitaker and myself at Simon Fraser University have collaborated in a number of research aspects concerning Hutterites. It is therefore my duty and my pleasure to acknowledge coauthorship of Chapter 3, *Contemporary Dynamics of Religious Defection*, with these three individuals. In particular those readers who are familiar with the writings of Dr. Ed Boldt will detect his fine conceptual and linguistic skills in this chapter. Dr. Whitaker is coauthor of chapter seven which was originally titled "Hutterite Perceptions of Psycho-physiological Characteristics." The three chapters concerned with contemporary social changes among Hutterites are the result of recent field work conducted by Dr. Ian Whitaker and myself. Again I must acknowledge the contributions which Dr. Whitaker made in putting our observations down on paper. He was also the first who suggested to have this volume published.

Several chapters contained in this volume have appeared as articles in various journals or have been previously published in books. I am grateful to these journals and publishers for permission to reprint these articles. All chapters previously published were revised, updated, and to some extent rewritten to facilitate a fluent reading of this volume. I must express my gratitude to

Mrs. Norma Gutteridge, director of the University of Alberta Press, who undertook a complete editing of the book. She detected all the repetitions, ambiguities, and conceptual uncertainties which I was unable to see.

My wife Franziska has been an active participant in all research projects that I undertook among Hutterites. She is a much better observer than I am and her social skills and genuine affection for Hutterite individuals have helped me immensely to perceive patterns of behavior which I would not have seen without her. Her substantive contribution to anthropological data and her constant critical assessment of my writings were invaluable throughout.

Dr. Robert Brown, Dean of the Faculty of Arts at Simon Fraser University made financial contributions toward the first draft of this volume. Barbara Barnett in the Dean's office skillfully produced the final version. My thanks to these individuals who assisted me in putting this book together. The task of writing and rewriting is such an anxiety producing activity that the competent typing of a manuscript not only makes a substantive contribution but also helps to maintain the author on a psychological even keel.

Finally I must acknowledge the many Hutterite individuals who over the years facilitated my research. I can not single out any individual out of fear of offending others who made equitable contributions. Hutterites are a trusting people if they have gained the impression that one deserves such trust. Many pieces of information were offered to me because of such a trusting attitude and I hope I have repaid this trust by refraining from any frivolous, sensational, or unethical disclosure. Whatever mistakes have been made nevertheless, are no one's fault but my own.

INTRODUCTION

The Hutterites, members of an Anabaptist sect inhabiting parts of the western plains region of Canada and the United States, are largely seen by the general public as a social problem. Due to their spectacular demographic increase and accompanying physical expansion as agriculturalists, they are perceived as an "invading minority" by a considerable sector of the farm population. Although this feature has interesting dimensions for social scientists which we shall develop in Chapter 13 on the ethnic relations of Hutterites, there are other characteristics of Hutterite society and culture that make them a unique sociocultural laboratory. Their history has been fairly well recorded over the past 450 years and this offers a rare dimension in anthropological and sociological research. What is often perceived as a relatively static society which, as some observers have remarked, "has changed little for the last few centuries," is in reality a highly dynamic social group. Indeed Hutterites today can best be understood in terms of the historical changes which the sect has undergone throughout its history. It is this fact that leads to my title *The Dynamics of Hutterite Society*. I attempt to capture the Hutterite phenomenon as an ongoing sociocultural entity constantly adapting to environmental, political, and social circumstances and at the same time realizing the opportunities which their particular cultural configuration offers.

The existing sociological and anthropological literature on Hutterites is predominantly descriptive. Much of this writing has followed a chronological development; other studies have been arranged according to traditional ethnographic schema. John Hostetler's *Hutterite Society* (1974) is a very good descriptive study utilizing a wealth of historical and contemporary data. John Bennett's excellent study, *Hutterite Brethren* (1967), utilizes the theoretical framework of cultural ecology. The present monograph deviates from these approaches and instead presents a collection of analytical studies that address themselves to questions which are derived from unexpected Hutterite data.

For example, Hutterites have existed under mediaeval feudalism, under Catholic absolutism, and under Muslim rule; they have become subject to East European nationalism, have weathered the Industrial Revolution, and for the last 100 years have existed in North America in the midst of rapid technological modernization under capitalist conditions. How did they do it? Obviously one cannot offer a definitive explanation on such a complex phenomenon but in Chapter 2, "The Certainty of Salvation: Ritualization of Religion and Economic Rationality among Hutterites," an attempt is made to come to terms with the sociocultural elements that possibly have played major roles in the evolution and adaptation of Hutterites. Another baffling question has to do with the Hutterites' "community of goods" (*Guetergemeinschaft*). This institution, which forms the centre of the Hutterite value system in that it symbolizes and behaviourally manifests the group's relation to God, disappeared twice and was recreated twice — after lapses of eighty and fifty years respectively. How is that possible?

Under what circumstances can a human group go back to previously discarded social structures and make them work in an entirely new environment with a new generation of members that had no personal experiences of these early structures? In Chapters 1 and 2, "The Survival and Institutional Evolution of Hutterite Society" and "The Certainty of Salvation: Ritualization of Religion and Economic Rationality Among Hutterites," an attempt is made to come to grips with these questions. What made Hutterites survive whereas others perished? Or better yet, why did the "community of goods" disappear twice in the social history of Hutterites only to be revived after prolonged interregna? Read in conjunction with each other these two chapters should throw some light on these questions and possibly make some theoretical contributions while doing so.

Hutterites are world champions in having maintained one of the highest reliably recorded rate of natural increase in the world for nearly one hundred years, and yet they have been able to finance every successive generation to obtain the highest technological level of agricultural production. Moreover, all their earnings, profits, and capital were generated through agricultural work. No other similar population in the world even comes close to such an achievement. How can they do it?

What mode of production, what restrictions on consumption are required to make such an achievement possible? How are individuals motivated to participate in this task where the fruits of individual labour are constantly reinvested for the survival of the next generation? These are some of the questions which are pursued in this monograph and although there is no pretence of fully answering them, at least the attempt is made to contribute toward their resolution.

An important feature of recent Hutterite life that has not been generally discussed by other authors is the modification of the traditional colony through the replacement of mixed farming by specialization in one or two crops. This process involves the acquisition of the most sophisticated agricultural equipment, calling into play new skills which, in turn, modify the old hierarchical colony structure, and ultimately also contribute to a complete revision of the gender-based division of labour. There is, for example, the gradual erosion of the traditional attitudes towards the possession of private property. The role of women in Hutterite communities is also changing. The modernization of the traditional housing patterns now emphasize family privacy. Traditional female occupations that have been discontinued are causing corresponding changes in the female work group and thereby modifying interpersonal relations between women. The relatively greater emphasis on affective ties between husband and wife and the possibility of expressing marital discontent more openly than before, are transforming husband-wife relations and these, in turn, are allowing women to express themselves in ways previously unknown among Hutterites.

A monograph organized around important sociological or anthropological topics must present sets of data which are relevant. Given the interrelationship of social data it becomes therefore unavoidable to repeat parts of the data in several of the topical treatments. This has the advantage that each of the topics can be read separately as an independent study. Its disadvantage lies in the repetition of data with which the reader might already be familiar. An attempt has been made to strike a balance between data that are necessary for the understanding of any topic while keeping their repetition to a minimum.

The reader who searches for a single theoretical model in this monograph will be disappointed. Theoretical purity is not necessarily a virtue when one approaches a complex sociocultural group from the point of view taken by this monograph. Any attempt to analyse a historical as well as contemporary sectarian movement will sooner or later encounter the difficulty of capturing the multi-dimensionality of cultural and societal affairs through only one interpretative framework. But to say that no single theoretical model is applied does not mean that theoretical perspectives are absent. Any analysis needs some theoretical anchorpoint and the present contribution is no exception. The guiding principle was, however, to utilize that kind of theoretical perspective which contributes most to the explanation and understanding of the phenomenon in question.

There is probably no social group which better fits Max Weber's definition of a "sect" than the Hutterites. The emergence of the group as part of the Anabaptist movement during the Reformation is conceptualized in Weber's *The Protestant Ethic and the Spirit of Capitalism* (1958), although in fact the Hutterites did not subscribe to the notion of predestination which played such an important part in the thought of Calvinists and Puritans. Their belief system depended on a behaviouristic validation in the "community of goods" (*Guetergemeinschaft*), to which a corresponding psychological state had to be attained: *Gelassenheit* (a state of mind of submission to the will of God).

The "community of goods" brought heaven down to earth, and the early Hutterites called their communities the "vestibule of heaven." Karl Mannheim claims (1936: 212) that the decisive turning point in modern history came when the idea of the millenial kingdom became transformed into the activist movements of specific social strata. The "spiritualization of politics," which emerged in the utopian mentality of the oppressed strata during the Reformation, gave direction and purpose to politics, and these contrasted sharply with the fatalistic acceptance of events as they were. This process gave rise, albeit very slowly, to an awareness of the social and political significance of the lower classes, and thereby facilitated the development of modern politics.

The founders of the Hutterite movement were far ahead of most of their contemporaries in their social and political awareness, and this cognizance was typically codified in religious ideas. The basic religious concept of Hutterites, the "community of goods" as a unit of production and consumption based on the pooling of communal efforts and the satisfaction of basic individual needs, is only passingly supported by the Bible. The major impetus for this institution came from the preceding social structures prevalent in Central Europe, such as the agricultural institution of the commons and the manufacturing organization of the Guilds, before the latter became transformed by mercantilism and early capitalism.[1] It was this ancient memory of a communal self-determining way of life destroyed by feudalism that found its expression in the religious ideas of Hutterites. The convincing logic in the days of the Reformation was religious, and social concerns or demands could only be expressed in religious terms. There existed a desperate and unswerving belief in God, and His commands were seen as belonging to the social sphere as well as the spiritual. The utopian mentality, as Mannheim calls it, was not so utopian after all. It was a simmering mentality of resistance against feudalism, mercantilism, and the beginnings of capitalism, searching for a language through which this resistance could be expressed. The Reformation and the early writings of Luther provided such a language, and the Hutterites, among many other groups, seized the opportunity to propel themselves into the public forum where social claims and demands could be made in the name of religion.

The Anabaptist movement, of which Hutterites were a part, was a diverse social development associated with such charismatic leaders as Thomas Muentzer, Hans Hut, Balthasar Hubmaier, and John of Leiden, to mention only four of the more outstanding individuals that engaged in social action. It developed in contrast both to the Reformation of Luther, whose policies shifted in favour of the territorial prince, and to Zwingli and Calvin, whose interest centred around the urban powers of the guilds. Anabaptists, on the whole, were recruited from the educated peasants and the journeymen of the crafts, the latter having been organized in associations that assisted them in their travels throughout Europe. The emergence of the Hutterites as a distinct socioreligious Anabaptist group can be traced to the Zwinglian reformation in Zurich. Zwingli's reformation of the city-state was based on the powers of the guilds and was affected by essentially bureaucratic means; it led to a reduction of the powers of the Church, confiscation of its property in favour of the state, dissolution of the monasteries, and in the process it also achieved a reduction in the political influence of the patricians, the hereditary ruling class with whom the guilds were in a power struggle for almost two centuries.

At the same time, a third force, in the form of peasants and village craftsmen, emerged from the hinterland of the city-state and presented Zwingli with a number of sociopolitical demands. The nature of those claims provides a key to our analysis of the Hutterites. Weber (1961: 68) recognizes clearly that the peasant wars of the sixteenth century in Germany were waged primarily against the usurpation of communal rights and properties contained in the common mark (*Markgenossenchaft*) and in the common pasture (*Almend*). These rights provided access to unsettled land, hunting, fishing, lumber, water, and pasture. Under Feudalism, the nobility had wrested these rights from the peasants. When the peasantry rose and presented their demands to the city-state of Zurich, or in the later peasant wars to the local nobility, these demands were not directed so much against the nobility's exaction of excessive dues, although that played a part, as in protest of the original usurpation of communal rights and properties.

The city-state of Zurich, from the time it became a full member of the Swiss Confederation in 1351, had acquired from the peasantry of the surrounding countryside their communal rights and properties. In the latter part of the fifteenth century and the beginning of the sixteenth, the city-state attempted to facilitate a more central administration of these possessions. It simplified the civil and criminal codes and subjected the various economic branches, such as agriculture, viticulture, and forestry, to standardized regulation, thus eliminating all trace of the communal rights enshrined in the common mark.

While the peasants' pursuit of communal rights and property quickly resulted in their employment of military means, which in Germany led to the peasant war of 1525, the Tyrolean uprising of 1525-27 and the conquest of the city of Muenster in 1535 — all of which eventually failed — the Anabaptists of Zurich attempted to achieve restoration of former rights through rational persuasion in the form of religious disputations. It is characteristic of the Reformation that all social classes followed Wycliff's teachings that the Bible was the supreme guide to the lifestyle of a Christian, and to a large degree they proceeded to codify their sociomaterialistic interests in religious terminologies selectively abstracted from the Bible. In the spirit of learning and the admiration for wisdom associated with the Renaissance, it was initially believed in Zurich that conflicting Biblical interpretations could be reconciled in public disputations between learned men.

The early Anabaptist leaders in Zurich, therefore, engaged in such religious disputations with Zwingli, and the main topic of these debates was child baptism versus adult baptism. From the time of European conversion to Christianity, civil and religious society had presented a unity and baptism was a ritualistic confirmation of this unity. Now adult baptism offered congregationalism as an alternative, thus challenging the very core of citizenship. As might be expected, the Anabaptists were not permitted to prevail. Not until 250 years later with the creation of the United States of America would changes in social conditions make it possible for such a challenge to succeed. Following the failure of public disputations and the subsequent suppression of the Anabaptist movement in Zurich, the centre of activity shifted to the Tyrol. Feudalism there coexisted with remnants of a freeholding peasantry. In addition, since prehistoric times, copper mining had been conducted as an organized communal enterprise, only recently coming under feudal dominance as copper metallurgy obtained importance for warfare. The gallant uprising of Michael Gaissmaier, although not an Anabaptist, reached for the impossible: the total transformation of society from a feudal state to a theocratic–religious–communistic society. While it is true, that Gaissmaier did not pursue the realization of communal property as found later among Hutterites, he nevertheless aimed at the control of both production and the market and thereby tried to regulate consumption on an egalitarian basis. Gaissmaier published his constitution of the theocratic state in 1526 but his movement soon suffered defeat at the hands of the Austrian feudal forces. Only after this military attempt had been crushed did the formation of the Hutterite social movement get under way in the Tyrol. This is not to say that Anabaptist ideas developed as a result of Gaissmaier's defeat. On the contrary, literary versions of Anabaptism were proclaimed by a number of individuals and groups in southern Germany, Switzerland, and Austria either before and after the Gaissmaier affair. The inference, however, can be made that as long as the Gaissmaier movement absorbed the discontent of the Tyrolean citizenry there was no need to form clandestine religious groups expressing the same general sentiments. Only when the futility of the military overthrow of the feudal hierarchy became evident did the formation of an underground Hutterite movement proceed. But Gaissmaier's defeat had demonstrated that a societal change was impossible under the circumstances of the times. Thomas Muentzer and Balthasar Hubmaier provided the same lesson either in the failure of the Peasants War of 1525 or the eventual surrender of the city of Waldshut. Thus the realization of a new order based on Christian-communistic principles could not be achieved militarily, but if at all, only on a small pacifistic scale. This realization set the emergent Hutterite movement on a course of separation from the world, rejection of existing churches, social isolation, noncooperation with worldly authorities, rejection of civil duties, and selective membership. These socioreligious principles form a large part of the religious-ideological framework of Hutterites which over the next fifteen years became solidified in a set of "confessions of faith." At the same time these ideas were transformed in the institutions of living Gemeinschaft groups that Tyrolean and other migrants began to form in Moravia. Chapters 1 and 2 contain an elaboration of these processes.

If one realizes that Weber traces the spirit of capitalism in its rational Western form to the psychological effects of the Reformation and Karl Mannheim attributes the rise of socialism to the Anabaptist movement as does Kautsky (1897), one gets an impression about the antithetical developments that can follow from a singular source. Perhaps this realization makes the reluctance to apply a single theoretical perspective even more understandable. Indeed there is one other factor which makes sociohistorical inquiry bothersome at times: historical accidents. Crucial accidental events are not explainable in terms of any logic or theoretical framework. How can one explain the accidental meeting of Lutheran refugees and persecuted Hutterites in Transylvania in the 1750s when the former injected new life and new initiatives into a dying sectarian movement and thereby carried it on? Theories are more or less deterministic systems as they have to be. They do not explain historical accidents. Yet an understanding of Hutterites must take into account accidental occurrences and their short range or long range effects on the culture.

The experiences and the accumulated wisdom of the group on the other hand is such that they have learned how to deal with, avoid, or endure hostile majorities. At the same time they have managed to confine themselves to those economic pursuits which allowed them to maintain their communities. Such a decision requires sacrifices on the part of the individual who must confine himself to those opportunities that are offered by the group and forego others that are attainable only outside the group; and the group must see to it that the individual finds it worthwhile to stay. Given the relatively low defection rate, Hutterites seem to have succeeded so far in maintaining their membership more effectively than any other ethnic group. Chapter 3 on religious defection among Hutterites, written in conjunction with Drs. Edward Boldt, Lance Roberts, and Ian Whitaker, points to the ongoing dynamics between the power of retention of Hutterite religion and social life and the religious attraction to which some Hutterites expose themselves.

In Part III, the demographic dynamics of the Hutterite population are explored through the presentation of two papers written in 1966 and 1980, respectively. There seems to be a major shift in the demographic behavior of the group and these papers, presented as Chapters 8 and 9, do seem to reflect these changes not only in terms of demographic data but in terms of their social correlates as well. Since the last of these papers was written additional data have been uncovered and these data are presented in a postscript to Chapter 9.

There is one other element which at this time can only be hinted at. It is biology. I am not suggesting the adoption of recent theories of sociobiology where a calculus of genetic attributes is meant to account for the behaviour of individuals and groups. But there is the possibility that selective mechanisms in a population can lead to a higher concentration of certain mental traits, and a very high coefficient of inbreeding can lead to psychosocial characteristics which could set such a population apart from the general population from which it originated. The chapter on the psychophysiological observations of the Hutterites points in the direction of such possibilities.

The old saying that "if one has seen one Hutterite colony one has seen them all" is quite wrong. There are not only significant social and traditional differences between the three "Leut" but there are differences from one community to the other and of course from one individual to another. Under the camouflage of uniform dress and identical housing, there is a surprising variety of behavioural and material manifestations.

Part IV of this book which deals with contemporary social changes among Hutterites not only attempts to delineate these changes but also tries to elicit some variables with which these changes might be associated. There is a distinct possibility that the highly uniform development which characterised the sect in the past has come to an end. It is replaced by variable streams of development taking into account different social and economic conditions.

Hutterites like to portray themselves as a "saintly" people and a number of social scientists in the past have done their best to perpetuate this image. As effective as such an image might have been and still is in a struggle against prejudice and discrimination, Hutterites are no more saintly or unsaintly than other sectarian groups. In their present form they are first and foremost a "Bauernvolk," a folk of peasants in the traditional European sense of a folk society. They "work and they pray" and find this satisfactory, as have so many folk societies through the ages. In this folk society Hutterite individuals grow up as sturdy practical human beings who suffer from the failings of some cultural traits as much as they enjoy others. Hutterite life has as many frustrations, interpersonal conflicts, and injustices as most other societies. To the outsider it is not a very attractive lifestyle owing to its restrictions on individual freedom, the required high degree of conformity, and the communal presence in the private affairs of individuals. However, my task is not to judge Hutterites but to analyse their social and economic life. Their co-operation in this enterprise over the last twenty-five years has been exceptional. Although they have long become used to the fact that they elicit curious responses from outsiders wherever they go, they have not grown tired of answering my questions or assisting me to see things which I would be unable to perceive without their help. There was and still is an element of trust in such behaviour which I hope to repay by presenting the results of my inquiries to their own scrutiny. Perhaps they will choose to learn a little from it as I have learned much from them.

PART I

Religion and History

ONE

The Survival and Institutional Evolution of Hutterite Society

The question "What makes the Hutterite communal system survive while others perish?" was first addressed by Lee Emerson Deets in 1939. He found peacefulness, social harmony, and social cohesion to be the main variables contributing to the persistence of the group.

A decade later Joseph W. Eaton (1952) coined the term "controlled acculturation." It was designed to explain the survival technique of the Hutterian Brethren with references to their persistent cultural autonomy and social distinctiveness. Forces of social change, either originating in the outside society or generated inside the Hutterite social system, were seen by Eaton to be subject to the conscious control of Hutterite leaders, who were assumed to possess the foresight and the social skills to manipulate their communal system in such a way that the cultural integrity of the group endured. Preconditions for the exercise of such controls were the homogeneous nature of the Hutterite folk culture; the presence of religion as a major cohesive force; the relative isolation of the group from outside influences; the communal system of sharing property and the fruits of labour; and the principles of austere simplicity and self-sufficiency in a *Gemeinschaft*-setting. Eaton claimed that the strong communal organization of Hutterites enabled the leadership not only to prevent undesirable cultural traits from spreading but also allowed it to define those areas in which social change was acceptable. The problem with Eaton's formulation is that the preconditions that he lists, and which supposedly make controlled acculturation possible, must also be explained. Why is religion among Hutterites such a cohesive force? How is the relative isolation from outside influence maintained? What does it take to perpetuate a system of simplicity and self-sufficiency where the fruits of labour are shared communally?

John Hostetler, while addressing himself to the same problem, observes that the social system of Hutterites is by no means free of crises and problems. He explains that Hutterite colonies have not survived by avoiding the troubles that plague other communally living groups, but by having more than sufficient resources to weather the disasters common to communal societies. Among these resources he mentions an uncompromising belief system; comprehensive socialization; the reconciliation of delinquents; biological vitality; and the management of innovations. Through the thoughtful and flexible manipulation of these resources, Hutterites are seen to have preserved a communal way of life which for them "constitutes the practice of total Christianity" (Hostetler 1974: 285-302).

Hostetler confines himself to an enumeration of factors which might have a bearing, but like Eaton he does not refer to any theoretical framework, nor does he state why these phenomena exist in this setting.

John Bennett has ascribed the persistence of the Hutterite communities to an efficient institutional and managerial system with emphasis on the rational organization both of decision-making and of economics. He sees an additional factor in what he terms "the managed democracy of Hutterites," the dual system of a Hutterite being subjected to colony discipline and his knowledge that others will be disciplined also. This creates an atmosphere of equality and provides personal gratifications that facilitate group persistence (Bennett 1974: 193).

Working from the perspective of economic materialism within anthropology, Bennett tries to explain Hutterite persistence without emphasis on ideological or theological factors. While no doubt the efficiency of Hutterite institutions does contribute to their persistence, this efficiency also requires explanation; if this is attempted merely on the basis of economic factors, it would seem to be insufficient.

Bennett's approach is supplemented by an evolutionary analysis of Hutterite data developed by Paul Diener (1974: 601-18). This analysis formed part of a prolonged debate carried on in various anthropological journals, primarily concerned with the relative utility of evolutionary or ecological explanations in that discipline. Diener's presentation of Hutterite data is unfortunately somewhat cursory due to his reliance on secondary and tertiary sources. He does, however, trace the Hutterites through a series of historical situations where they occupied a unique evolutionary niche: the rural frontier regions of expanding capitalism. In a subsequent article, Vayda and McCay (1975) assess recent developments in ecological anthropology and, in considering Diener's paper, stress the utility of ecological explanations in considering developments in Hutterite history. The debate was continued between these protagonists in an article in *Current Anthropology* (Diener & Robkin 1978), but no serious further explanatory formulation relating to the Hutterites emerged.

The writers that we have considered so far have enumerated a number of important factors which seem to have some bearing on Hutterite continuity. These variables are, with the exception of Bennett and Diener, merely listed; there is no attempt to develop a theoretical paradigm. However, Rosabeth Kanter has, in her study of early utopian communities in America, provided a theoretical model which may be utilized for the understanding of Hutterite cultural survival. Her investigation focusses on the commitment mechanisms present in communal societies. Commitment, she states, arises as a consideration at the intersection between the organizational requisites of groups, and the personal orientations and preferences of their members. It thus refers to the willingness of people to do what will help maintain the group because it provides what they need. Commitment links self-interest to social requirements, such that the individual perceives no conflict between its requirements and his own needs (Kanter 1972: 66).

Kanter distinguishes among three types of commitment each of which contributes to aspects of social systems such as retention of members, group cohesion, and social control. A person's *cognitive* or *instrumental commitment* relates to a profit and cost evaluation. If a participant finds that "the costs of leaving the system would be greater than the costs of remaining," his continued participation can be assumed to be a commitment to a "social system role." *Affective commitment*, according to Kanter, involves primarily a person's emotional bond to other members of the group and entails the gratification that stems from the involvement with these members. Affective commitment increases solidarity and cohesiveness, qualities which help a group to withstand threats to its existence. Under *moral commitment*, Kanter understands a person's evaluative orientation towards the authority, values, and norms of the group. The demands made by the system are evaluated as right, moral, and just, and obedience to these demands becomes a normative necessity. Upholding norms, obeying the authority of the group and supporting its values, are processes that show the degree of integration between the individual's conception of self and the requirements of the social system. As such, moral commitment refers to an internalized value orientation.

Groups in which people have formed instrumental commitment should manage to hold their members; groups in which people have formed affective commitments should report more mutual attraction and interpersonal satisfaction; groups in which members have formed moral commitment should have less deviance, challenge to authority or ideological controversy. Rosabeth Kanter predicts that: "Groups with all three kinds of commitment, that is, with total commitment, should be more successful in their maintenance than those without" (Kanter 1972: 66-68).

There is a certain similarity between these types of commitment and Weber's categories of "associative social relationships" (1965: 115). Kanter's *instrumental commitment* is virtually identical to Weber's purposive-rational (*zweckrational*) orientation, as it designates a means/end mentality. The concept of *moral commitment* is contained in Weber's "value-rational" (*wertrational*) concept and the *affective commitment* appears in Weber as "affective rationality" designating communal social relations based on sentiments. Notably absent in Kanter's enumeration of commitments but present in Weber's catalogue of social relations, is tradition. Weber defines traditional authority as "a system of imperative co-ordination if legitimacy is claimed for it and believed in on the basis of the sanctity of the order and the attendant powers of control as they have been handed down from the past" (1965: 341). Kanter treats tradition as a transcendence-facilitating mechanism. The nineteenth century American utopias Kanter was concerned with successfully maintained themselves by facilitating transcendence through institutionalized awe, mystery, programming, ideological conversion, and tradition (Kanter 1972: 123). She agrees with Weber that tradition defines "what is" in terms of "what should be," and therefore pre-empts the ability of potential innovators to offer alternatives and suggest changes. Probably it is Kanter's preoccupation with relatively short-lived nineteenth century communal societies that induced her to include tradition under the label of a transcendence-facilitating mechanism rather than seeing it on par with the rest of Weber's "associative social relationships."

There is a further difficulty in comparing Weber and Kanter. Communal relations (*Vergemeinschaftung*) according to Weber rest on a mixture of *wertrational*, affective, and traditional associate relationships. The very nature of these determine the total involvement of the individual to the group, which he assumed to be a *Gemeinschaft*. Kanter steps outside the reasoning of this framework, and claims that commitment in part is determined by a cost benefit assessment of the individual, who rationally evaluates the organizational requisites of the group in terms of his personal needs.

The focus of her theory is an individual confronted with a choice of joining or not joining, staying with, or leaving a communal group. Weber's theories do not take such a possibility into account. The element of choice is of course crucial in the consideration of newly–formed groups. This is, however, not the case or at least much less the case in long-standing traditional groups where members are born in and socialized within the system. An instrumental (*zweckrational*) evaluation of the traditional group by an individual is antithetical to *Gemeinschaft* relations and characteristic of *Gesellschaft* relations. Kanter's emphasis on cognitive or instrumental commitment therefore seems to proceed from the assumption that a *Gesellschaft*-oriented individual constantly assesses his personal needs relative to the demands of the communal system, and on that basis decides whether to continue his participation or not. If such an assumption can be justified when analyzing contemporary communal groups, where the individual who joined a communal group has conceptual and practical alternatives at his disposal, it seems inapplicable to traditional communal systems. In the latter, individual needs are shaped by the communal experiences in the first place, and as the group is successful, these needs are adequately satisfied. Indeed inculcating limiting individual needs and proceeding to satisfy these in all members, regardless of how socially stratified the group might be, seems to characterize the successful communal group.

If in a *Gemeinschaft* setting a situation arises where a group member defines his needs in terms different from those instilled by socialization, and when this individual begins to assess these needs relative to the organizational requisites demanded of him, group survival is at stake. A cost benefit evaluation on the part of group members, as Kanter proposes, designates the border-line beyond which the survival of a communal group becomes problematic. As Coser remarks, while investigating the claim of the sect in regard to the allegiance of members:

> The morality of the sect is a morality of extremes, it cannot tolerate reservations. Allegiance is expected to be total, and hence, hesitation, an act of deliberation and reflection, is suspect (Coser 1974: 105).

Coser approves of the remarks of Bossuet who defined a "heretic" as "a man who has personal ideas." "From the point of the sectarian," to continue Coser's quote:

> ... a man who reflects for himself is indeed a dangerous man since he asserts a right to personal examination of conduct in an organization which is based on a rejection of the right to establish personal standards (Coser 1974: 105).

Kanter's cognitive or instrumental commitment therefore seems to have no explanatory value for traditional *Gemeinschaft* groups if one assumes that such commitment might retain members. The opposite seems to be the case. The cost benefit assessment of the individual, relative to communal benefits and demands, seems to constitute the seedbed of discontent and disintegration for the *Gemeinschaft*. The utility of this concept, therefore, is to measure the degree to which a communal group has already deviated from its *Gemeinschaft* foundation. The survival of a communal group depends on the successful elimination of such a mental orientation, or better still does not *allow the formulation of a mental orientation which asserts the right to personally examine the organization and conduct of the group.* Among Hutterites, as among sects in general, this principle facilitates the survival of the system. The individual in the sect must be precluded from formulating alternative ideas or if he has them should regard them as unworthy, evil, or undesirable. Part of the secret of Hutterite survival therefore must be sought in the nature and interrelationship of its institutions which prevent individuals from making their commitment to the sect dependent on a cost benefit analysis.

Kanter's theory has a social psychological focus. Her initial unit of analysis is the individual member, who, subject to certain group pressures, will form commitments of this or that type. In a next step she applies such commitments to the survival of groups which might or might not elicit appropriate commitments. Weber's theoretical formulations in contrast must be understood against the background of the ideal types of *Gemeinschaft* and *Gesellschaft*. Intermediate groups, he seems to imply, could only be transitory and by their very nature appear to be unstable because they incorporate contradictory orientations. The *zweckrational* instrumental cost benefit evaluation of an individual's participation in the *Gemeinschaft* is antithetical to *wertrational* moral and affective orientations. A *wertrational* commitment implies that the individual will be committed to the group in spite of instrumental disadvantages. If he entertains *zweckrational* instrumental ideas, these are incompatible with the *wertrational* demands of the group, as Coser has pointed out so clearly. But Weber also showed that in the process of

Vergesellschaftung a *Gemeinschaft* must undergo a change from a predominantly *wertrational* orientation to one that includes emergent interests of the membership and these might be of a *zweckrational* nature. The survival of such a group might be at stake, when an unchanging *wertrational* institutional framework becomes subject to *zweckrational* considerations of its membership.

In fact Hutterite history shows that during periods when individual *zweckrational* orientations did emerge, the individuals involved remained in the group, but their contradictory orientation in the end destroyed the very essence of the social system of which they were a part.

It becomes highly plausible now that our original question, "What made Hutterites survive whereas other communal groups perished?" has something to do with the group's institutionalized attempt to eliminate individual *zweckrational* instrumental orientations and to concentrate on the *wertrational* moral, affective, and traditional orientations of the ideal *Gemeinschaft*. The historical data on Hutterites make it possible to study these processes by assessing the disintegration of the *Guetergemeinschaft*. One could formulate the following hypothesis: The *Guetergemeinschaft* (community of goods) among Hutterites disintegrated everytime when members of the sect were allowed to develop a *zweckrational* mentality which allowed them to assess their participation in the sect on a cost benefit basis.

A short historical overview should establish the framework within which this hypothesis might be studied. The sect was founded between 1527 and 1535 and its basic institution the *Guetergemeinschaft* disintegrated for the first time 150 years later in 1685. It was reinstated after an interval of eighty years and disappeared a second time around 1818. After a further interregnum of fifty years a number of attempts to recreate the *Guetergemeinschaft* were made and three of these succeeded when the sect migrated to North America in the 1870s. During the last century the *Guetergemeinschaft* has proved to be an extremely viable institution in spite of an unprecedented growth pattern that has increased the number of communities from four to two hundred and sixty-plus in one century. It is important to remember, however, that when the *Guetergemeinschaft* was absent, the Hutterite religion and some communities continued although experiencing drastic declines in membership as well as in the number of communities.

These various phases of establishing communal institutions and seeing them decline form the basis of the present analysis. Applying Weber's four associate relationships to these processes some insights into the viability of our hypothesis should be obtained.

The founders of the Hutterite sect ascribed to an overpowering *wertrational* orientation, as attested by the thousands of martyrs who paid with their lives for the retention of their faith. The religious tenets to which they confessed made the distinction between the "flesh" and the "spirit." The former, if not completely subdued nevertheless had to be controlled through a variety of institutionalized means. The supposed dominant part in the actions of man, the "spirit" was attainable only through the unconditional surrender to the word of God and as such signified the union of God and man. This union was obtainable in a mental state called *Gelassenheit* which characterized an unqualified oneness with God to the total exclusion of all worldly concerns. It meant forsaking all selfishness and one's own will and surrendering to God's guidance even unto death (Friedmann 1961: 83). *Gelassenheit* served as the guidance in the construction of Hutterite institutions such that all social relations yielding to the "flesh" were as far as possible eliminated, while all aspects and social relations which signified man's relations with God were emphasized, encouraged, sanctified, and enforced.

Accordingly, husband and wife were not to love each other and get married as fleshly human beings but were guided to love each other through their mutual union with God. The sect, claimed the right to "put together" marriage partners according to its own criteria. Affective ties, therefore, were transformed by this *wertrational* orientation. The community of goods likewise incorporated the sharing of God's spirit with man as well as the sharing of material goods between men. Access to scarce resources were regulated on the basis of need. Pregnant women, working men or women, or the aged all had different needs and these needs were defined by the sect. The Brotherhood strove to satisfy these "temporal" needs but regarded them as inferior to the spiritual ones which received precedence. The spiritual gifts which the *Guetergemeinschaft* bestowed on the individual justified the expectation that every member would engage in labour and thereby contribute to the common good to the full extent of his mental and physical capacities. The individual who joined the sect, therefore, did so on the basis of *wertrational* sacrifice which required him to forego personal freedom, material goods, and worldly affections. Foregoing material interests was part of this sacrificial package. But sacrifice alone did not earn salvation for the individual involved. It constituted nothing more than acting on the word of God. It was an act of obedience. Obtaining a mental state of *Gelassenheit* required that the individual engaged in an active struggle against himself and his carnal nature. Only when he reached a mental state where the temptations of the world had become meaningless — when he could look at the world and his own carnal desires in a cool detached and utterly controlled way — was he ready to receive God's gift — faith. The institutions of the sect existed to aid man in this struggle. The legitimacy and the justification of these institutions which were purposively created rested on *wertrational* considerations throughout. This orientation also formed the basis of the individuals participation in these institutions, and this participation was an exercise in asceticism.

One hundred and fifty years later when the last community of goods had disintegrated, contemporary Hutterite observers attributed the failure to religious indifference, laziness, adultery, prostitution, nepotism, theft, fraud, private gain and private greed, disobedience, vanity, and conceit (Zieglschmid 1947: 201-28). The community ordinances (*Gemeindeordnungen*)[1] that were issued during this century and a half show a relentless decrease in the *wertrational* religious orientation of the sect and an ever increasing *zweckrational* instrumental tendency among the members (Peter and Peter 1980).

The key to this transformation must be sought in the failure to perpetuate the mentality of the founders. The educational ideal of *Gelassenheit* aimed to attain a personality structure consisting of sober, detached, controlled, obedient individuals who would willingly and rationally participate in the *Gemeinschaft*. Collective orientations rather than self assertions were emphasized; patience and sacrifice rather than spontaneity were valued.

The institutional means to achieve such a personality included abolishing the family as a socializing agent and confining its functions strictly to procreation. But the group institutions in the form of nursing homes for the very young and kindergartens and schools for the older children soon came into competition with parents who nevertheless were emotionally attracted toward their own offsprings. The result was a contradictory socialization process where the institutions of the sect attempted to inject discipline, submission, spiritual rationality, and austerity into the children while the family of procreation tried to undercut these efforts by emphasizing emotional ties and bestowing material advantages on them. As time went on these two positions became more extreme. Harsher discipline on the part of the school authorities was countered by the families particularly when the parents had obtained positions of status, power, and authority in the sect. The inevitable result of this conflict was a personality structure which institutionally learned how to circumvent the system. The failure of the Hutterite socialization processes is clearly spelled out in the "General Ordinance of 1651" which in part reads:

> We see how many ill-mannered children we receive from our schools; children which become a burden for the *Gemeinschaft*, many of which are getting lost in the world; converting to bad individuals heading toward a shameful end (Zieglschmid 1947: 519-32).

It appears that the institutional nature of the *Guetergemeinschaft* created by the first generation was indeed greatly unbalanced in favour of extreme *wertrational* demands. The socialization process explicitly designed to perpetuate such an orientation however failed. The denial of individuality and the suppression of emotional responses created strains and anxieties which eventually translated themselves into social pathologies. To teach *Gelassenheit* to succeeding generations proved to be impossible under the institutional structures that were adopted. Monastic lifestyles that have maintained such forms of human denial for centuries nevertheless are based on memberships which are selectively recruited from a wider society and therefore can show characteristics amenable to the continuation of such *wertrational* orientations. Hutterites formed a group with all the varieties of human temperament and personality by which continued groups are characterized. Moreover, this group had to perpetuate itself biologically and therefore had to engage in procreation, parenting, and socialization, all of which gave rise to a set of deep–seated human emotions. The suppression of these emotions and their substitution through sacrifice proved to be impossible in succeeding generations under conditions quite different from the fervour of the Reformation.

The concept which serves best to understand this transformation is Weber's term "elective affinity" (*Wahlverwandtschaft*). It appears in Parson's translation of *The Protestant Ethic and the Spirit of Capitalism* (Weber 1958: 91) as "certain correlations between forms of religious beliefs and practical ethics." By choosing this concept Weber tried to point out that although ideal and material interests govern the conduct of man, the respective emphasis on ideal or material interests is not necessarily equally distributed at all times during the lifetime of a religious group. In fact "elective affinity" was intended to demonstrate a change in the relative contribution of ideal and material interests, which in the case of the Protestant sects moved from the dominance of the first to a more equal contribution of both. The initial "ideal" nature of Hutterite institutions it seems was derived from insights into the Biblical universe leading to a very particular formulation of ideas. As Weber says:

> However incisive the social influences, economically and politically determined, may have been upon a religious ethic in a particular case, it receives its stamp primarily from religious sources, and, first of all, from the content of its annunciation and its promise (Gerth and Mills 1958: 269-70).

There is no question that the social conditions of feudalism and the religious-political strife of the Reformation greatly influenced the individuals who were to become members of the Hutterite sect. But the nature of their institutions and consequently the nature of their conduct was primarily influenced by the religious insights that they had formulated. This institutional one-sidedness became problematic when suppressed emotions and human desires, the material and emotional interests of generations removed from the fervour of the Reformation, aimed at modifying these institutions. However, since these original institutions rather than any written collection of scriptures and doctrines were the embodiment of the ideal interests of the sect an affinity between these and the emergent interests of these later members could not be found. The result was the disintegration of the communal framework of the Hutterite sect. The numerical decline of the group which began as the result of persecution but continued when the Brotherhood progressively lost its grip on the membership is indicative of this process, that already had begun around 1600. The inability to attract converts is noticeable at the same time and indicates further that an affinity between the ideal and material interests of these later generations was lacking. Unable to change the institutions' intentionality, which would have meant the behavioural negation of important religious values, the leadership resorted to exhortations and admonitions in the form of community ordinances (*Gemeindeordnungen*) which postponed the final day of disintegration but could not prevent it.

Perhaps at this point it is appropriate to shortly return to our original theoretical considerations. Rosabeth Kanter links self-interest to social requirements such that the individual perceives no conflict between these requirements and his own needs. This process assumes a balance between self-interest and social requirements which Kanter judges by the criteria of assessing the costs of leaving the system or staying with it. Kanter's thesis is in essence a reformulation of Weber's concept of "elective affinity" although the criterion of staying with a system or leaving it is only applicable in special cases. What more often seems to prevail is the emergence of affinitives which change the institutional setting to make it more amenable to the emergent ideal and material interests. In the case of Hutterites such affinities could not come into play because the incorporation of the emergent interests of the members would have destroyed the very nature of the ideal institutions that were supposed to govern the conduct of the sect. Unable to accommodate the new interests through institutional change, the sect went down the road of progressive disintegration until the community of goods was undermined and plundered into an empty shell. In terms of our hypothesis the sect indeed failed to eliminate a *zweckrational* instrumental mentality in successive generations and being unable to change its institutional configuration to accommodate such an instrumental mentality disintegrated. It is interesting to see that the second disappearance of the community of goods in 1818 demonstrates that the same forces were at work. The Russian official Fadjeew who investigated the affairs of Hutterites at the time reported:

> The masters which headed the various economic branches of the community demanded independence. Each withdrew from the common treasury and opened businesses of their own. They bought raw material and sold the goods independently. Instead of handing over the revenues to the community, they just presented the invoices (Klaus 1887: 67).

The undistributed wealth which the sect had accumulated over a number of decades suddenly transformed the behaviour of its members. As the same observer commented:

> With the increase in the material wealth of the group the tendency toward idleness increased. The trend to enjoy the good life on account of the common affluence took deep roots and paralyzed the activities of all members. It brought apathy, hostility, envy, and dissatisfaction into the *Gemeinschaft* and step by step caused the disintegration of the group.

The first breakdown of the communal structure of Hutterites can predominantly be attributed to the overpowering demands of an inflexible *wertrational* ascetic system: unconditional surrender, self–denial, and obedience. Competition over wealth, although by no means absent during the first period, only became dominant toward the end of the disintegration process. This was largely due to the fact that earlier the central authority of the

Hutterite sect legitimately absorbed community profits and stacked them away for emergency purposes, thereby removing them from competition. There is no evidence of adultery, prostitution, etc., the second time around, just plain competition over undistributed wealth. There were individuals who discovered that they could live comfortably in a social system that redistributed goods according to individual needs and not according to efforts. There were those that did expend effort and then felt deprived by receiving the same as everybody else. The *wertrational* orientation was not strong enough to compel the former toward expending more effort, nor could it educate the latter into accepting an unequal cost benefit distribution in the name of *wertrational* convictions.

On the basis of the foregoing discussion we might indeed have reason to accept our hypothesis. A *wertrational ascetic Gemeinschaft* based on obedience and sacrifice which built its *wertrational* substance into the very nature of its institutions, had to eliminate any *zweckrational* cost benefit analysis among its members if it wanted to survive.

We are now in a position to interpret the first and second breakdown of the *Guetergemeinschaft* as a result of the antagonistic interaction of *wertrational* and *zweckrational* mentalities acted upon in an institutional system with limited variability. This limited ability for institutional change made it impossible to accommodate the "elective affinities" of later generations. Unable to change, the institutions increasingly came under attack and disintegrated. But surprisingly they were recreated after several decades. The disintegration and the reintroduction of the *Guetergemeinschaft* must be seen in conjunction with each other. We seem to be dealing with a process where a continuous group of religious believers is first shedding an obsolete set of institutions followed by the recreation of a more fitting and more acceptable version of this institution. This process seems to be analogous to that of a social reform. Like a snake shedding its outgrown skin a sectarian group might shed its outgrown institutions underneath which a better fitting set of institutions has grown. Such a process allows for change where change is impossible to implement on dogmatic *wertrational* grounds. But this process puts the social group at great risk because the hiatus between the institutional disintegration and its re-establishment can easily lead to the total disappearance of the social system. As we explain in the next chapter the re-establishment of new institutions was only possible after the group had eliminated its dissatisfied membership and shrunk to a size where spontaneous collective behaviour again became possible. It also received at this stage new initiatives from converts. Responding to persecution or crisis imposed on it from the outside might also have facilitated such spontaneous behavior. This was the case in the second founding of the *Guetergemeinschaft*. The recreation of a more fitting institutional setting therefore is contingent on the maintenance of the religious faith among a small group of dedicated believers who in a crisis might act spontaneously to re-establish a new institutional model containing an updated *wertrational* orientation.

How this can be done is best shown in method and content when the *Guetergemeinschaft* was re-established by Hutterites in the 1860s and 1870s. There was a distinct threat of persecution under Alexander II of Russia who no longer was prepared to accept the pacifistic stance of Hutterites and other ethnic groups living in that country. In a series of social experiments groups of Hutterites who either shared some geographic area or some social characteristics such as wealth or kinship ties banded together and adopted a new *Guetergemeinschaft*. The emphasis in these experiments was clearly on social compatibilities among the members. This explains why a number of these experiments failed and others succeeded. Those individuals that failed tried again in the context of another group and many of these, after a series of false starts, gave up all together. Those three groups that succeeded were eventually helped to form a cohesive group by the migration experience to the United States of America. There is a world of difference between the soul–searching trembling individuals who during the Reformation often left their families and their properties behind in order to join the "Community of Saints" and the Hutterites who 340 years later leisurely experimented with the *Guetergemeinschaft* in a migratory crisis for which the individual alone was ill–prepared. As to the content: gone was the ascetic struggle between the "flesh" and the "spirit" with the respective alternatives of damnation or salvation. The individual's participation in the community of goods was now sufficient to obtain the certainty of salvation. Hutterites therefore were relieved of the internal turmoil that characterized the original *wertrational* orientation. They were now safely anchored to the institutionalized ability of the community of goods to save them. Salvation became spiritually effortless; what it demanded was behavioural participation in the community not spiritual struggle. Moreover the *wertrational* orientation of the sect had become traditionalized and ritualized. Religious scholarship ground to a halt around 1660 and had not been revived. Due to the ritualization of the *wertrational* ideology, few conceptual and intellectual demands were made on the individual. Traditional images and customary sayings sufficed. There was no more struggle for *Gelassenheit*, in fact the term is largely forgotten today. The suppression of kinship ties and emotions were no longer needed. Asceticism was largely read out of consideration. Kinship relations were strengthened. Due to inbreeding, Hutterites had become one great kinship group. Husband and wife were allowed to court each other and marry on the basis of affection. The family had become a central institution and was recognized in terms of housing, socialization, affection, and the redistribution of goods. It was only denied an economic base. The movements of individuals were no longer as circumscribed as they formerly were. There was a greater variety of accepted individual role performances and expressions which altogether avoided the excessive demands of "total surrender" which symbolized the first model. The enormous expansion of the group during the last century that led to a doubling of the population every seventeen to twenty years absorbed all the wealth for legitimate purposes. Therefore individual competition over accumulated capital was not possible because all profits were immediately reinvested for expansion. Agricultural technologies have led to a centralization of the division of labour in Hutterite colonies, including a central accounting system supervised by an outside accountant and subject to tax assessments. Individual access to monetary resources therefore were all but eliminated. These latter two features remove the competitive dangers inherent in the second model. The socialization process aimed at *Gelassenheit* which failed during the first phase is now geared toward the inculcating of concrete visible role models. The high technological standard and the social status associated with them make these models very attractive. The enormous expansion of the group assures the attainment of these role models due to the enlargement of the labour force that comes with expansion.

Hutterites do not depend on strong charismatic leaders any longer as, in fact, their elderly bishops are usually incapable of displaying charismatic traits. They depend on strong community leaders who, on the whole, are very pragmatic and economically rational individuals. Almost all communal societies investigated by Kanter depended on the charisma of one leader. The continuation of this charisma or its succession most often proved to be problematic and contributed to the disappearance of the communal group. Hutterites maintain an "institutionalized charismatic" leadership in the form of their community preachers. These are "found" in an election which involves the "charismatic disciples" (all preachers) and the community members (Weber 1965: 365). The preacher's office is recognized as the legitimate representation of the *wertrational*-traditional authority. But this authority is transferable to others and the transfer is institutionally regulated.

Hutterite culture has become a culture of work performance. Work is central to all its activities. Work offers the individual the possibility of expending his energies and directing his interests and aspirations. Hutterites speak of work as a "duty" which they understand very much in the same way as Weber defined the "calling" (1958: 77-92). They seem to regard it as something sanctified and justified by their *wertrational* orientation. But the notion of work as a commodity of exchange for certain material benefits is foreign to their mentality. Young men who occasionally are "lent" from one colony to another without any exchange of goods or money show no differences in interests or work efforts. The performance of work is a major source of individual pride and satisfaction. The sect still suppresses aesthetic expression in the form of music, graphic representations, radios, T.V.s, paintings, furniture, and dress. And of course it disallows emotional development toward material possessiveness and territoriality although these have changed greatly as well. These blocked emotional outlets are channelled into the performance of work roles and ultimately contribute to the importance which the hierarchical structure in the division of labour attains in the Hutterite community.

The planning of work patterns and the execution of such work is central to the mentality of all members of the sect. The role of the individual and the value of the hierarchical structure of the community are based on performing certain work patterns to the individual's and the community's satisfaction. Under these circumstances a cost benefit analysis of labour input and benefit output would indeed constitute a strange way of reasoning. By what kind of calculus can a Hutterite individual assess the certainty of salvation, his kinship ties, the psychological effects of ritual and labour relative to the individual efforts necessary for participation? This calculus is a qualitative one throughout, containing values which in the *wertrational* sense need to be realized without reference to costs. A Hutterite cannot set himself apart from his community and formulate a conception of what his individual needs are and then assess whether or not his needs are being satisfied by the group. In a well-functioning community such an instrumental assessment would not only be impossible but outright frivolous. The individual is part of the group not because he looks forward to the satisfaction of his needs but because he perceives his contribution as a necessary element in the realization of the *wertrational* nature of the sect. This qualitative package that we find in present-day Hutterite society is not without its weak points, but these are not to be found primarily in the instrumental assessment of the individual but in the possibility that one or the other element in this institutional configuration can be removed from its contextual position.

In Chapter 3 "The Contemporary Dynamics of Religious Defection" my coauthors and I demonstrate that this qualitative package can be dissolved through changing the religious awareness of sect members. There is also the continuing danger that accumulated wealth once again might become subject to competition and individual appropriation leading to the situation found during the second phase of communal living. An economic decline coinciding with population pressures in communities poses similar dangers. There is also the danger of cultural dilution. Colonies are becoming more unlike each other as their numbers and geographic distances between them increase. Different forms of adaptation to a variety of environmental conditions already have profound influences. All this is to say that the institutional configuration of the Hutterite community of goods as it can be observed today is no guarantee that the sect has eliminated instrumental assessments by individual members for all time. It constitutes a survival mechanism for today's internal and external conditions and there are already some ominous signs indicating that the system is becoming progressively unbalanced again.

Several summary conclusions can be drawn from these inquiries. First the *wertrational* structure of Hutterite institutions and the fact that these institutions were the embodiment of religious tenets pre-empted the possibility of changing these institutions in accord with the changing ideal and material interests of later generations. Secondly, the *wertrational* institutions at the inception required a corresponding *wertrational* personality structure on the part of the membership which under changing societal conditions could not be maintained either through socialization or exhortation among successive generations. Thirdly, a rigid *wertrational* institutional system populated by persons with incongruent personalities became subject to individual *zweckrational* manipulations resulting in a collective exploitation of these institutions causing their eventual disintegration. This third conclusion supports our hypothesis. Fourthly, the disintegration of the institutional system eliminated the *zweckrational* personalities from the group such that the residual population in the course of time was able to develop a new *wertrational* conception which in a spontaneous collective act led to the re-establishment of a modified *wertrational* communal system. The shedding of the old and the recreation of the new communal institutions brought about a new congruency between institutions and the mentality of its members. Both of these referred to orientations different from the previous ones, yet previous dysfunctional *zweckrational* orientations were eliminated. We seem to be dealing with a process similar to Weber's concept of "elective affinity" but applied to a rigid social system which, unable to suffer institutional change, had to shed its institutions in order to have them reappear in modified form.

Our initial question "Why did Hutterites survive while others perished?" can now be answered. They survived because they were able to modernize their institutional configuration from time to time in order to bring their institutions in line with the contemporary mentality of their members. This mentality as reflected in their ideal and material interests modified the institutions and made them viable again. The shedding of the old and the re-establishment of the new institutions created a hiatus during which the survival of the sect was at great risk. More than once it was a stroke of luck (the providence of God, as they claim) that prevented the sect from disappearing altogether. The repetition of processes of disintegration followed by processes of institutional renewal over a period of more the 450 years nevertheless indicates that we are dealing with important longitudinal social process which might be of relevance to a number of social phenomena.

TWO

The Certainty of Salvation

Ritualization of Religion and Economic
Rationality Among Hutterites

Hutterite society today is characterized on the one hand by a traditional social order but also by the pursuit of rationally–structured economic activities. How is it possible to combine these seemingly contradictory characteristics in the daily life of communities whose populations hardly exceed 140 members? Would it not be much more reasonable for Hutterites not only to uphold their traditional social order, but also to follow conservative economic practices as some of the Old Order Amish do? How is it possible that a Hutterite individual can at one moment give detailed technical instructions for repair of a complicated machine over shortwave radio and an hour later expose himself to a religious sermon, the text of which has not changed for 350 years?

We will return once more to Max Weber's thesis (1958) that the Protestant ethic facilitated the rationalization of the everyday life of the Puritans, Calvinists, and Baptists. Is it possible that, under certain conditions, the Protestant ethic might facilitate the traditionalization of the life of some sects and the rationalization of the conduct of others? Or, is it possible that the Protestant ethic might facilitate the traditionalization of some societal institutions and the rationalization of others?

The present study suggests that the routinization of the certainty of salvation among Hutterites is correlated with the ritualized nature of their religion and the traditional ordering of their society. The rationalization of economic activities among members of this sect seems to have originated as an adaptive response to secure their survival within a given host society. In other words, I suggest that the ideal interests of Hutterites became traditionalized, while their material interests underwent a process of rationalization. The theoretical framework through which this analysis is conducted borrows from Weber's attempt to correlate certain religious doctrines of Calvinism with the economic conduct of the Calvinistic individual. The classic study in regard to this correlation is Weber's essay, "Die Protestantische Ethik und der Geist des Kapitalismus," first published in 1904 and 1905 in the *Archiv fuer Sozialwissenschaften und Sozialpolitik.* That work was intended to be a first step towards a comparative study to determine the influence of certain religious sanctions on the development of an economic spirit. In 1920 the incomplete results of this study were presented in Weber's book, *Gesammelte Aufsaetze zur Religionssoziologie.*

As much as Weber was concerned with the association that seemed to exist between religious affiliation and a particular type of economic conduct, he nevertheless saw this correlation in a much wider framework. He says, "We are interested in the influence of those psychological sanctions[1] which, originating in religious belief and the practice of religion, gave a direction to practical conduct and held the individual to it" (Weber 1958: 97). The relationship between religious belief and practical conduct in the case of the Calvinists and the Puritan sects was traced by Weber to the workings of Protestant asceticism. He found that, "protestant asceticism ... created the force which was alone decisive for its effectiveness; the psychological sanction of it (faithful labours) through the conception of labour as a calling, as the best, often in the last analysis the only means of attaining certainty of grace" (Weber 1958: 178). The active self-control which the individual derived from Protestant asceticism, and which he applied to the conduct of his economic activities, however, could be generated in different ways.

Weber recognized that all Baptist communities desired to be pure churches, in the sense that the conduct of their members be blameless. A sincere repudiation of the world and its interests, and an unconditional submission to God, as speaking through the conscience, were the only unchallengeable signs of true rebirth. Thus a corresponding type of conduct was indispensable to salvation. Inasmuch as each Baptist sect spelled out in some detail its understanding of the particular form to be taken in the unconditional submission to God, the repudiation of the world, and the blameless conduct of its members, one can see the specific psychological sanctions at work in those sects that gave direction to the practical conduct of their members.

We have also seen in the previous chapter that as a group moves away from the religious preoccupation and fervour of its founders, and begins to struggle for survival within a larger society, it must adjust itself to the conditions of that society. The nature of these societal conditions, interacting with religious doctrines, ultimately determines the final relationship between the psychological sanctions that are felt by the individual and the practical conduct which is directed by them. Weber summarized this process in his concept of "elective affinity."

The present chapter attempts to show that the attainment of salvation among Hutterites changed from being a spiritual phenomenon speaking through the individual conscience (psychological sanctions, in Weber's terminology) to being a gift bestowed on the individual as a consequence of faithful participation in the group life. The *Guetergemeinschaft* (community of goods) became the means by which salvation was achieved, and the Hutterite individual received the certainty of partaking in salvation through participation in this community of goods. The ritualization of the religious institution and the retention of traditional order in the social relations of the community of goods can be seen as attempts to preserve intact this precious storehouse which bestowed salvation on its participants.

Economic activities, in contrast, initially had no eternal value for Hutterites whatever. Regarded as temporary necessities, they had certain religious restrictions imposed upon them, mainly in the areas of consumption, financing, and distribution. The membership was, however, free to develop a rational approach towards production. The structural freedom allowed in the conduct of production made it possible for Hutterites to use economics as their principal means in establishing mutually beneficial relations with their host societies, thereby enhancing the probability of survival for the group.

The Hutterite repudiation of the world shortly after the Reformation took an extremely radical form not shared by many other Baptist sects. The rejection of infant baptism by the Anabaptists amounted to a challenge to mediaeval civil society based on the unity of religious and societal membership. The abolition of feudalism and the establishment of a classless society without private property had already been the principal aims of the Taborites who had formed the radical wing of the Hussite movement a hundred years earlier. The Hussites, in turn, were greatly influenced by the teachings of John Wyclif, whose doctrine that the scriptures were supreme authority in all matters concerning the Christian way of life, provided the foundation from which the Anabaptist argument against feudalism and the Church proceeded. In an atmosphere of intense persecution in the Tyrol following the defeat of Michael Gaissmaier in 1527 (see Introduction), it was impossible to organize religious congregations, so individuals attracted by Anabaptist ideas migrated to Moravia to take advantage of the religious toleration offered there. In this relatively protected territory there assembled an amorphous group of religious dissidents, part of which developed into a highly organized socioreligious community between 1527 and 1535 known as the Hutterites. The mechanism by which this group-forming process occurred can be described as a form of doctrinal drift. From a large number of Anabaptist religious ideas, sequential factions of individuals chose some which they regarded as being central to their concerns. Successive repetition of this process eventually produced a final doctrinal system associated with a close-knit group of adherents.

The doctrinal drift began with a controversy about militarism and pacifism, which eventually was decided in favour of the latter. The second controversy concerned communal versus private ownership, which was resolved by the adoption of communal property. The third issue centred on the authority and legitimacy of competing charismatic leaders, and resulted in the recognition of Jacob Hutter, a Tyrolean, as undisputed leader. In the end, Hutterites were united in regard to the strictest pacifism, the *Guetergemeinschaft*, separation from the world, rejection of worldly office, refusal to swear the oath, rejection of established churches, nonpayment of taxes for war, and of tithes for churches. Both spiritually and practically the Hutterites had eliminated feudalism, the state, and the established churches for their members.

Quite clearly some of these doctrines and practices had their antecedents in the immediate experiences of the Tyroleans who had learned through the recent failure of the Tyrolean uprising that a true Christian Theocracy could not be formed within the framework of the existing political order. Hence separation from this order and political noncooperation with it were necessary to realize a true Christian Community. The idea of communal property again had its antecedents in the long struggle of the peasants for the reinstatement of the communal privileges that had been usurped by the nobility, the city-state, and the Church. The formation of a true Christian communal society, therefore, was an attempt to return to the state of affairs which existed before feudalism progressively destroyed the communal institutions of the *Markgenossenschaft* and the *Almend* (Commons).

A similar and equally strong argument can be made for the wish to restore the social conditions prevalent in the early guilds. Before the emergence of larger markets facilitated the capitalistic transformation of the guilds, the organization of a craft aimed at maximizing egalitarianism among its members. The supply of raw materials, use of technologies, and access to markets were organized and administered as cooperative activities. Little distinction existed between masters and journeymen at the place of work other than those arising from skills and experience. The mobility structure from apprentice to journeyman and master was open, and occupational inheritance, which later blocked the social advances of the journeymen and thereby created the first European proletariat, was absent. The appeal for restoration of old cooperative rights and privileges was as powerful for the journeymen of the fifteenth and sixteenth centuries as for the peasants. The composition of the Hutterite sect, largely conscious and well-educated peasants and journeymen, reflected these socioeconomic and political interests. As we will see later, the interests of these social strata were also reflected in the economic ethic of the Hutterite sect.

The manifestations of the psychological sanctions which Weber detected in Protestant asceticism among the Calvinists and Baptists took a very different form among Hutterites. The active self-control which the Calvinist individual derived from Protestant asceticism was essentially a tool to overcome the uncertainty of having been saved or not, assuming that his fate had been predestined by God. The individual had to detect in himself the certain signs of having been saved which were obtained by introspection. The Calvinist who in this way detected in himself and his actions the appropriate spiritual and behavioural characteristics of the elect could then justifiably overcome his doubts and regard himself as having been saved. Protestant asceticism and the active self-control that derived from it therefore constituted a mental and behavioural mechanism to deal with the uncertainty surrounding one's salvation.

Hutterites achieved the certainty of salvation in a different way. There was first the attainment of a mental state called *Gelassenheit*, a term already referred to in Chapter 1. Second, there was the appropriate participation in the *Guetergemeinschaft* or community of goods. *Gelassenheit*, as a state of mind, was entirely spiritual and potentially could be learned by any human being. In conjunction with participation in the community of goods, it formed a mental and behavioural unity that signified the attainment of the "vestibule of heaven" (Vorhof des Himmels) here on earth. That attainment carried with it the certainty of salvation. The combination of *Gelassenheit* and *Guetergemeinschaft* constituted the realization of the ideal and material interests of these sectarian believers. *Gelassenheit* was intended to set the individual free from the fear of extinction as well as rescuing him from the enslavement of his material desires. But there was still another dimension to *Gelassenheit*, although it was the individual who was supposed to attain this state of mind, he was to do so only in the context of a collectivity.

Hutterites were not lonely martyrs; they were a significantly group–oriented people. The proliferation of epistles composed in prison and the multitude of "confessions of faith" written by the condemned and addressed to their brothers and sisters, testify to their group orientation. Hutterites were required to share, in the fullest meaning of the word, the goods of this world and the rewards of the next. Attainment of salvation, therefore, was possible only in the group context, which in its purest form was implemented in the *Guetergemeinschaft*. Salvation as a group phenomenon imposed responsibilities for each other's conduct on every individual. This collective responsibility made it legitimate and mandatory to be concerned with every other person's most intimate thoughts and activities. To watch over each other and to assist each other was seen as an expression of the most valued form of love (Rideman [1542] 1950: 132). In the context of the *Guetergemeinschaft*, the spirit of God, the material resources of men, and the attainment of eternal grace were shared equally and simultaneously by all members. The individual, his work, and his eternal future were unalterably welded to the state of the total community. To the extent that he was saved only if the total community were saved, each individual, in turn, had to do his share to make such communal salvation possible. In his own state of mind and in his daily actions, the individual carried the burden of saving his neighbour, his kin, and himself.

The extraordinary persistence of the Hutterite *Guetergemeinschaft* and the reinstatement of communal property after the principle had twice been abandoned can be understood only if the powerful psychological sanctions implanted in the functioning of this institution are fully appreciated. The mental state of *Gelassenheit* acted out in the *Guetergemeinschaft* constituted the highest form of self-discipline and self-denial for Hutterites and as such marked the attainment of the certainty of salvation.

As we have seen already in Chapter 1 as time passed and the character of the sect changed from a voluntary affiliation to a hereditary one, the fervour and intense spiritual demands of *Gelassenheit* could not be maintained. A change occured that shifted the emphasis from the state of mind of *Gelassenheit* to the performance of appropriate behaviour in the *Guetergemeinschaft*. It meant a shift from self-control of the individual through the individual's own conscience, to social control of the group through an emerging network of traditions, norms, customs, and regulations.

This change was greatly facilitated by the increasingly ritualized nature of the religious institution. The religious spiritual creativity, which so characterized the first generation of

Hutterites, steadily declined in successive generations, and disappeared altogether around 1660, some 130 years after the founding of the sect (Peter 1967: 127-254). The *Lehren* (lectures, sermons) which consisted of explaining Bible chapters sentence by sentence, were originally nothing more than verbal explanations and interpretations of the Bible by various learned individuals. But under these circumstances it was unavoidable that different individuals would give different explanations of a given Biblical passage. To avoid theological strife within the sect, it became necessary to standardize these interpretations and commit them to writing. A series of written *Lehren* from the hands of elected "servants of the word" easily gave rise to a liturgical calendar, since some scriptural passages and their explanations were more fitting for certain occasions than others. Celebrations of the sacraments retained by Hutterites — adult baptism, marriage, and the Lord's supper — likewise needed a standardized format, and progressed from relatively freely conducted ceremonies to highly structured ones.

The demand for spiritual and material sharing exerted an enormous pressure on the group members towards singlemindedness and conformity. Consequently, appropriate means were needed to assure such conformity, and these were created by ritualizing the entire religious institution. With ritualization came traditionalization, in the sense that authority and value were assigned to religious observances. Traditionalization had an inhibiting effect on the religious creativity of Hutterites. In the face of what had been said by the "forefathers" — that is, those who were willing to die for their faith — the descendent Hutterites could not muster sufficient courage to come up with new Biblical interpretations. Nor would the Hutterite audience readily accept such new interpretations from living individuals. A visitor to a Hutterite church sermon today will participate in the *Lehr*, the main element of the service, which was written at least three hundred years ago, as were the songs intoned by the congregation. Hutterite preachers do not write their own sermons, but faithfully copy the old ones. Almost the entire religious literature of Hutterites was created by members of the first and second generations.

We can see that starting with the second generation the type of conscious self-control that had been the result of *Gelassenheit* slowly abated. Without the state of mind of *Gelassenheit*, the individual conscience could not be spiritually appealed to in its earlier form, and the psychological sanctions originating in this conscience, and holding the individual to his conduct, faded away. Their place was taken by the value which participation in the community of goods acquired. It was no longer the conscience of the Hutterite which assured his salvation, but his actions. Attainment of salvation then came routinely to all who participated in the *Guetergemeinschaft*. Self-control, originally directed toward an examination of one's innermost thoughts, motives, and desires followed by behavioural restrictions, was rechannelled in a way which de-emphasized examination of the spiritual individual and concentrated on the conforming individual. But conforming behaviour did not require critical self-examination; it could rely on the forces of social control in the community. Hutterites could depend, therefore, on the social control mechanism of the community to assure their appropriate participation in the group, which in turn bestowed salvation on them as a matter of routine. By the time that social controls in the form of positions, customs, norms, regulations, and so forth, had become traditionalized, the mental preoccupation of Hutterites had shifted from an active, value-oriented, conscientious direction to a passive, traditionally defined, group conformity, which had the added advantage of securing their place in eternity.

The fading away of *Gelassenheit*, however, could not fully be compensated by social controls. Hutterite sermons after 1660 complain bitterly about the deterioration of the *Guetergemeinschaft*; its disappearance followed a decade or two later. The disorganization of the *Guetergemeinschaften* as reflected in these complaints (see also Chapter 1) clearly indicate the erosion of the Hutterite *wertrational* orientation codified in *Gelassenheit*.

Some congregations of Hutterites in Hungary and Transylvania, however, managed to survive, although their membership shrank considerably during the next eighty years. The absence of the *Guetergemeinschaft* was by now subjecting the Hutterite believer to considerable doubt regarding his eternal fate, and there were various individual attempts to cope with this situation. Some converted to Catholicism and thereby dropped out of the socioreligious development of the sect. Others attempted to alter the religious doctrine by omitting most references to the *Guetergemeinschaft*, albeit with small success, since little was left when the *Guetergemeinschaft* was taken out. The rest confined themselves to teaching but not practicing the *Guetergemeinschaft*, thereby maintaining the hope of an utopia that might soon again be realized. When a new wave of religious persecution of the Hutterites started around 1740, it initiated a degree of religious awakening among them. The immediate result, however, was the enforced conversion to Catholicism of most communities such that by 1760 only a handful of individual believers was left. By accident, they came in contact with a group of religious dissidents recently deported from Carinthia for adhering to Lutheranism. In an act of spontaneous defiance these deportees joined the Hutterite faith and adopted the community of goods, thereby reinstating most if not all of the customs, traditions, and regulations previously in force in the *Guetergemeinschaft*. Although these new Hutterites were religiously highly motivated, they were nevertheless unable to capture the original spiritual content of *Gelassenheit*. The socioreligious background which had given rise to *Gelassenheit* at the time of the Reformation was no longer present. By 1770, the sect was settled in Russia, and in 1818, shortly after the last of the founding members of the new *Guetergemeinschaft* had died, the institution disappeared again, under similar circumstances of internal disorder, as observed previously. Between 1854 and 1875 the remaining Hutterites in Russia conducted a number of communal experiments, most of which failed. It was only in connection with the migration of 1874-79 to North America that the communal ventures then in progress succeeded. The harsh and unfamiliar environment of the frontier settlement certainly played a major part in the initial success of these early *Guetergemeinschaften* in America.

Against this now familiar religious background let us analyse the economic ethic and practices of the Hutterite sect. The economic ethic of Hutterites has a traditional orientation derived from the communal rights of peasants and the cooperative activities of the early guilds. As such it stood in marked opposition to the mercantile spirit that emerged with the creation of markets and the capitalistic tendencies created by the flow of money and credit.

Paul Diener's suggestion (1974) that the communal system of the Hutterites might be traceable to large-scale farming methods of the nobility and the monasteries is untenable. The feudal nobility consisted of warriors, not of farm managers or agricultural organizers (Weber 1961: 66). Monasteries followed the feudal example and were supported largely from dispersed peasant holdings from which dues were exacted. In addition, the Dominicans and the Franciscans engaged in organized begging. Although roughly one-third of the agricultural land at the end of the fifteenth century was in the hands of the Church, no widespread communal agricultural model could be derived from the administration of these holdings. In part this was due to the absence of markets; but even where markets emerged, as in the case of urban centres like Zurich, binding the peasant to these markets and forcing him to sell his products in a designated place proved to be an efficient means of exploitation. Large-scale farming methods were, therefore, not employed. Besides Hutterites were predominantly craftsmen although they tended to maintain an agricultural base.

For the sect, the development of economic practices was extremely difficult. To reject the political and religious order was one thing, to survive under it in spite of this rejection was another. Hutterites certainly would have perished as did dozens of similar movements had they not built into their doctrines the possibility of accommodation with the world. Politically this was done by stripping the worldly authorities of all rights of spiritual interference on the one hand, but acknowledging the necessity of their existence on the other. "Government authority hath been ordained by God because of the turning aside of the people, in that they turn away from him and walked according to the flesh" (Rideman [1542] 1950: 102). As "a rod of God to punish evil doers," government was seen as having grown from the wrath of God. Since men had turned away from God, government was necessary and its actions justified. Every Hutterite therefore was to obey the government save for matters of the spirit. "Since Government authority is ordained by God and hath its office from him, the payment of taxes for this purpose is likewise ordained and commanded ... For this reason we, likewise, willingly pay taxes, tribute or whatever men may term it, and in no way oppose" (Rideman [1542] 1950: 109).

An exception was made in the refusal to pay taxes for the purpose of war. Hutterites made a fine point in interpreting a passage of Paul: "Render therefore to all their dues: tribute to whom tribute is due." This they claimed did not mean "render whatsoever and however much they want," but "render their dues." And it went without saying that the distinction between what was "due" and what might be regarded as "whatsoever and however much" was rightfully made by the true Christians, which they believed they were. Potentially this attitude could have resulted in arbitrary refusals, but in the emerging practice Hutterites took no evasive action when tax collectors confiscated movable property (like cattle, sheep, or horses) in lieu of cash payments for "whatever" tax purposes were issued at the time. Such practices at the worst were a minor nuisance for the authorities but not reason enough to withdraw toleration from the group. In any case, the economic viability of the Hutterite communities was a guarantee that the authorities would receive their taxes one way or another.

The possibility of accommodation in the area of taxation and submission to government authority had opened the door for some form of economic practice. That this practice had to be compatible with the traditional content of the Hutterite economic ethic went without question. Hutterites regarded the activities of merchants and traders as sinful and even today do not engage in them. The regulation of prices through supply and demand was rejected and the taking of interest forbidden. As Peter Rideman formulated it in 1542, "Therefore do we allow no one to buy to sell again, as merchants and traders do. But to buy what is necessary for the needs of one's house or craft, to use it and to sell what one by means of his craft hath made therefrom, we consider to be right and not wrong" (Rideman [1542] 1950: 126).

Wages were to be set to allow a decent living for those who applied their work to a product, and prices were to reflect costs plus wages. (Hutterites of course did not receive wages, but occasionally they paid wages to persons rendering services to them.) The economic ethic of Hutterites was first and foremost an ethic of workmanship on the one hand and of fair distribution on the other. The Bible, which Hutterites claimed to be their guide in economic matters, in fact offers next to no guidance regarding a system of consumption — save for the principle of "each according to his needs" — and no direction whatsoever on a system of production. The sect therefore had to elaborate on traditional social ethics and develop its economic practices in conjunction with its striving for survival under given political and economic conditions.

Two distinct processes can be seen as having been at work in this regard. When the sect was founded, it attracted a cross section of crafts and was faced with the task of organizing these in such a way as to maximize their contribution to the community. The freedom to organize created an immediate competitive advantage for the sect because most guilds had adopted restrictive regulations in regard to the technology of the craft, securing of raw materials, hiring of labour, and marketing of goods. Since Hutterites were not hampered by some of these regulations, they could reorganize the various crafts so that a succession of craftsmen would transform the raw material into a finished product all in one place. The tanner, for example, would prepare the hides which later would be used as raw material by the harness maker, glove maker, and others who needed leather as one of the basic materials. This semi-industrial mode of production needed a bureaucracy in the form of a planning staff and supervisory personnel, all of which were supplied by the emerging authority of the *Guetergemeinschaft*. Detailed regulations for the various crafts appeared thirty years after the founding of the sect and increased in frequency and complexity over the next hundred years (Peter and Peter 1980). Hutterites were the first community in central Europe to create a semi-industrial mode of production under one roof and make it work.

The necessity for organizing crafts in the most efficient way can be related further to the fact that Hutterites were competitors of the guilds; but unlike the guilds they had no political power to secure markets and supplies of raw materials. Hutterite products were banned from local markets during much of the sixteenth and seventeenth centuries. As an outcast religious minority their only recourse was to produce better products cheaper.

The second process of concern here is one that was initiated by the Hutterites' need for a place to stay — a place where they were physically tolerated and protected. The cities with their elaborate religious and sociopolitical structures were, of course, quite hostile to Hutterites and offered no such protection. Any territorial authority willing to afford refuge to Hutterites had to be one which might realize from their presence benefits sufficient to outweigh the dangers which protection of this sect created for the protector (Klassen 1964: 106-13).

Such territorial authority was found among the members of the lower nobility in Moravia. Within the confines of their own estates, Moravian aristocrats were able to grant a degree of protection to these religious dissidents. But what status were they to be given on these estates, and what benefits would they bestow on their protectors? Were they to be serfs, tenured peasants, or employees of noble households, and how would any of these positions relate to the Hutterite doctrine of separation from the world? None of the aforementioned classes had much chance of remaining separated from the world.

After some initial experimentation, Hutterites adopted the practice of entering into contractual relations with the nobility who offered them toleration. In a *Hausbrief*, or house contract very similar to present-day union contracts, the aristocrat and the Hutterites spelled out in detail the obligations, privileges, and benefits of each (Hruby 1935: 1-20). The idea was not entirely new since Jewish groups for centuries had attempted to do the same. There was, however, a difference. The economic benefits Jews had to offer were financial, because no other occupations were open to them. Hutterites could offer professional skills, organizational talents, and honest, efficient management. As many insightful Jewish leaders recognized throughout the mediaeval period, their financial services were of marginal value in exchange for toleration when the benefits from expropriating their financial sources became greater than those that originated from their toleration. The benefits derived from the professional skills and organizational talents of Hutterites similarly attained marginal utility either when these talents became redundant in the larger society or when that society's political powers were exercised by those who could afford to be unconcerned about such benefits.

Hutterites, therefore, came under pressure to maximize the benefits to their protectors for tolerating their presence. This was achieved by various means. The Hutterites offered a detached, skilled, objective, and honest personnel for the local aristocrat. This working force was reliable and loyal to the employer as long as the socioreligious privileges of the sect were respected. They further offered products which in quality, design, and workmanship could not easily be duplicated. An outstanding example is their manufacture of majolica or faience pottery which, before the introduction of porcelain, was a preferred luxury item of the nobility. But there were other products such as coaches, all kinds of glassware, kitchenware, iron and steel products, etcetera, which served the same function (Klassen 1964: 83-97). They insisted on contractual exchange relations laid down in documentary form, and resorted to withdrawal of services if the contracts were not honoured (Zieglschmid 1947: 113).

In all cases where Hutterites settled during their 450 years of travel through Eastern Europe and North America, the survival of the group was in the last resort dependent on the value of those benefits which the group could bestow on its host through official or nonofficial contractual economic relations. This is true even in regard to the last country that received Hutterite settlements: Canada. When they applied for admission to Canada in 1899 they were regarded as "a most desirable class of settlers to locate upon vacant Dominion Lands in Manitoba and the North West Territories," and in return were granted immunity from military service, freedom of religion and worship, voluntarism as to taking the oath and accepting public office, noninterference in communal living, and freedom to maintain independent schools (Zieglschmid 1947: 631-32) (see Chapter 13). In order to maintain contractual relations within the host societies, the sect was forced to develop its economic potential in such a way that the probability of exchange relations taking place and remaining over time was maximized. That result was achieved through an extraordinary degree of economic rationality applied to the productive aims of their economic enterprise.

There was another factor that contributed greatly to the development of the economic rationality of Hutterites. A sect that aspired to be separated from the world was, of course, compelled to take care of its own material and social needs. Under no circumstances could it allow the outside world to interfere in internal matters in even a helping capacity. Hutterites in past centuries refused therefore even to be enumerated for census purposes. They never volunteered to have their internal conflicts settled by outside authorities or courts but attempted to avoid such intervention as much as possible.

Each male Hutterite pledges in his marriage vow that if he should leave the community he will not resort to worldly authorities to force his wife and children to leave also. While this pledge is mainly directed toward saving the souls of the innocent, it is also an attempt to prevent interference by outsiders. A major part of Hutterite socialization centres around inculcating in children a sense of what can appropriately be revealed to outsiders and what must be kept secret under all circumstances. Independence and separation from the world, however, were only possible under conditions of economic self–reliance and self-sufficiency. The latter by no means imply the absence of an economic interrelationship with non-Hutterites. But it clearly refers to a degree of economic viability which allows the sect to take effective action (migration, maintenance of isolation, or political lobbying) in case the interference from outside becomes intolerable. Hutterites always knew, and know today, that to be independent requires economic strength.

In summary, one can say that, contrary to Weber's assertion, the economic rationality of Hutterites cannot be traced to the working of individual psychological sanctions. The cooperative nature of the Hutterite ethic, its anticapital, antimarket emphasis, was carried over from the prefeudal period of peasant organizations and guilds and incorporated in the communal structure of the sect. Under the influence of being a dissident religious minority in need of protection, Hutterites tried to bestow economic benefits on their protectors in exchange for toleration. To enhance the probability of protection and independence, Hutterites were forced to rationalize their productive economic activities, while at the same time regulating consumption in accord with the egalitarian nature of the community of goods.

We are now in a position to draw a number of conclusions. Beginning with the "ideal" interests of Hutterite culture we started our inquiry with Weber's thesis that protestant asceticism, as a psychological sanction, gave a direction to practical conduct and held the individual to it. The uncertainty of salvation for the Calvinist and Baptist individual led to a psychotherapeutical form of introspection, the result of which was not only a critical self-evaluation but the rationalization of daily life in accordance with the characteristics of the elect. Our data suggest that the Anabaptist did not come from the same stratum of society as the Calvinists and Baptists, and that their ideal as well as their material interests differed also. Their aim was to recapture cooperative and common rights which had existed in the past but which had been usurped by feudalism, city states, the territorial prince, the Church and, by no means least, the emerging forces of the market and the flow of capital.

The particular Hutterite response to realize these ideal interests was the establishment of communal structures characterized by the mental state of *Gelassenheit* (psychological sanction) and the behavioural system of the *Guetergemeinschaft* (practical conduct). Acting in unison, these two elements gave the Hutterite individual the assurance of salvation. *Gelassenheit* and *Guetergemeinschaft* plus certainty of salvation, however, proved to be an unstable system. A hundred years after its inception the internal order of the Hutterite *Guetergemeinschaft* began to deteriorate and had disappeared completely after a century and a half. It was reinstated after another eighty years, collapsed a second time in less than sixty years, and was imposed a third time after a lapse of five decades.

How can these fluctuations be explained in light of our discussion? The effects of *Gelassenheit* and *Guetergemeinschaft* at first of course were self-control and ascetic behaviour, but to the extent that the institutions also produced certainty of salvation they lost their motivating quality. There are longstanding difficulties in understanding the term "psychological sanction." Whether Weber meant it to be understood as *Antrieb* (which means to propel, to drive forward, and not impulse as Reinhard Bendix claims (1962: 63-64), or sanction (as Parsons translates it), or whether it was intended as *Triebkraft* (driving force) or any of the other terms that Weber or his translators have used, there is little doubt that Weber saw it as an active motivating entity. Certainty of salvation over time must have had the effect of putting this active entity to rest, while uncertainty of salvation, as among the Calvinists, kept it alive. Without the active driving force of *Gelassenheit*, the *Guetergemeinschaft* lost its dynamic aspects and slipped into traditionalism. The loss of *Gelassenheit* in turn freed Hutterites from conscious ascetic self-controls and this loss made the deterioration of the *Guetergemeinschaft* possible.

Around the turn of the sixteenth century, only seventy years after the founding of the sect, Hutterite believers already had to be admonished not to come to the most holy of sacraments, the Lord's supper, in a drunken stupor, and the managers of the households at the same time were reminded that it was quite wrong to introduce females other than their wives into their beds (Peter and Peter 1980: 58, 17). In fact, the emergence of community ordinances, beginning with the School Ordinance of 1516, and their proliferation and extension to every aspect of life, bears vivid testimony to the fact that the conscientious motivation of *Gelassenheit* disappeared rapidly and had to be replaced by rules and regulations. Ascetic behaviour and ultimately those self-controls which were supposed to hold the sect members to the behavioural demands and restrictions of the *Guetergemeinschaft* also vanished.

Our findings suggest that the Hutterite form of Protestantism is characterized by a dynamic interrelationship between psychological sanctions (*Gelassenheit*), daily conduct (*Guetergemeinschaft*), and the certainty of salvation. However, this interrelationship is unstable because the psychological sanctions of *Gelassenheit* cannot be retained under conditions of certainty of salvation, and erosion of the sanctions initiates the decline of the *Guetergemeinschaft*. The opposite process takes place when the *Guetergemeinschaft* is absent. The state of grace of the individual is then uncertain and, believing that salvation can be obtained only in the *Guetergemeinschaft*, Hutterites are prone to reconstitute the old institution.

The economic rationality of the sect in terms of its organization of production, on the other hand, is correlated with the minority status of the group and the necessity of bestowing economic benefit on the protecting host in exchange for toleration. The Hutterite mode of production in essence is a political tool employed to ensure group survival.

Our inquiry gives powerful support to Weber's thesis regarding the effectiveness of religious sanctions in rationalizing the daily conduct of the believer. But religious rationalization takes place only under certain conditions (for example, the uncertainty of salvation) and can transform into traditionalization when certainty of salvation is obtained.

There is another important conclusion that can be drawn. Different social strata that were attracted toward Protestantism started the process of sect formation with different initial material and ideal interests. As quoted in the previous chapter, Weber does not deny the influences which these economic and political factors might have on the formulation of a religious ethic but claims that it receives its stamp primarily from its annunciation and its promise (Gerth and Mills 1958). But the very form which this annunciation and the promise takes also obtained the stamp of preceeding economic and political influences as we have shown. "Elective affinity" not only channels the subsequent development of a sect, but also influences its initial religious formulations. The argument, therefore, moves somewhat in the direction of Marx without embracing the exclusiveness of economic factors which he assumed.

This chapter cannot be concluded without adding a postscript to our findings. The present phase of the Hutterite *Guetergemeinschaft* has already lasted a century, and the system does not seem to display the signs of deterioration which were visible at similar periods during its first and second phases. One can argue, therefore, that the alternation of the phases described earlier is doubtful. We do not suggest that our observations on Hutterites present a circular movement in history. There are the intervening variables of a constantly changing wider society by which Hutterites are affected and to which they must adapt. The Hutterite *Guetergemeinschaft* today shows a high degree of asceticism without the presence of *Gelassenheit*. How is this possible?

In place of the relgious sanctions there has emerged a driving force which one may call the "self-discipline of exaggerated growth." Hutterites for the last century have had one of the highest birth rates in the world — 4.12 percent per year (Chapter 9). The population of the sect grew in a hundred years from 440 individuals to approximately 28,000, all by natural reproduction. This enormous population increase not only had to be accommodated but kept at a high level of technological production. Hutterites have scored a lonely first among the world's populations in maintaining one of the highest birth rates and at the same time modernizing and expanding economically so as to remain competitive among the most advanced forms of agriculture under capitalistic conditions. Such a performance was possible only by imposing the strictest forms of asceticism on the population. Yet the purposes for which these restrictions were imposed were eminently legitimate. The Hutterite community today, because of inbreeding, is a closely knit kinship group. Growth and expansion for the sake of kith and kin provides a form of motivation capable of drawing every member into communal activities. Although many Hutterites today are at a loss when confronted with the term *Gelassenheit*, there is nevertheless a willingness to work, plan, and participate in the *Guetergemeinschaft* which baffles those who see individual gain as the motivating force of all activities. Hutterites today have a type of spirit which the socialist countries are striving for but which has eluded them so far — the motivation to work enthusiastically in a communal enterprise. The key to this type of motivation is to be found in a number of characteristics which are present within Hutterite society, but which cannot be maintained in socialist countries: explosive growth, small, self–determining kinship groups of fewer than 140 individuals; legitimate institutions and legitimate procedures to transfer power; economic goals which directly benefit the kinship group; all contained within a competitive host environment.

For Hutterites the necessary economic rationality of exaggerated growth as we have seen it in this century emerged just at the time when the economic exchange for toleration by the host society diminished. This might be an accident. Most likely, however, the sect is engaged in a search for strenuous legitimate economic goals for the simple reason that the maintenance of the group's cohesion is more easily obtained with than without these goals. This leads to the conclusion that even where Weber's religious psychological sanctions leading to economic rationality are absent altogether, given conducive circumstance, others can take their place.

THREE

The Contemporary Dynamics of Religious Defection

Defections from Hutterite colonies have always occurred, but never in numbers large enough to seriously threaten the integrity or continuity of their established order. Moreover, of those who defected the vast majority eventually returned to become conforming members of the community. More recently, however, a form of defection has emerged which is usually permanent, and which represents not merely a dissatisfaction with an ascetic (and perhaps difficult) lifestyle, but a conscious repudiation of central Hutterite religious tenets. Individuals, and in some cases groups, are abandoning their colonies as a direct result of their conversion to evangelical, revivalistic Protestantism. Although the absolute number of such defections is still relatively small, the loss of members to a different and competing religious philosophy is disturbing to Hutterite leaders.[1]

Previous studies of Hutterite defection have focussed either on the attraction of an open, consumer-oriented host society as a primary motivating factor, or on the internal state of "disorganization" that develops in some colonies. Attempts have been made to correlate these defections with family background, conflict within the colony, and psychological dissatisfaction of individuals (Mackie 1975). Hostetler (1974: 273-76) has detected a greater tendency to defection among members of communities that have become moribund, or where there is a declining economy, as well as markedly differential status between family groups. Clark (1974) also shows that defections occur in dynastically-led communities, especially by those members whose families are not participants in the leadership.

Whilst such social factors as blatant and permanent discrimination of families and individuals in colony life patterns undoubtedly create a reservoir of potential defectors, the mere existence of forms of deprivation does not explain why defections actually occur. Defection, it must be remembered, is a painful and costly experiment. It means not only the severance of religious ties with the community, but also forsaking one's kin and foregoing the primary relations of the social community and the network of sentiments by which the kinship ties and the community are held together. To be a *Weggeloofener* (runaway) carries one of the most negative connotations in Hutterite culture and comes close to the notion of having joined the forces of the devil. But, in addition, there are strong counteracting forces toward defection, mainly in the form of the commitment to Hutterite values that socialization instills, and secondly on account of the very real practical barriers to easy movement from Hutterite colony to host society (Boldt 1976, 1978). These barriers have been shown to consist essentially of adjusting problems that defectors face as they attempt to make their own way in a new and highly competitive environment. Locating acceptable employment and housing, managing their own financial affairs, replacing the primary group ties of family and friends, and so on, can all pose formidable problems to newly transplanted Hutterites, and also account in large measure for their very high rate of return to the colony. These barriers, however, do not apply equally to all potential defectors; the very young, the elderly, the infirm, females, and married couples with children are all more likely to be deterred than young, single, and able-bodied men in search of adventure. It is this latter category that has traditionally contributed the large bulk of defectors.

However, for unbaptized young males who leave for certain periods of time, easy forgiveness is available, because they are regarded as lacking the knowledge of God. It is an entirely different story when baptized and married males and females leave, possibly with their children. These people are part of the religious and social community. They are committed and have made a pledge through baptism. The community has a claim to their children in the sense of being responsible for their souls. Even if an adult carelessly forsakes the spiritual security of the Hutterite community and accepts the consequences of this act for himself, he has no right to impose the same dire consequences on his children who, after all, are the children of the religious community as well. This suggests that the new phenomenon of defection for religious reasons differs markedly from the more conventional (nonreligious) form. The primary cause for such defection must be sought in certain stresses and strains imposed on Hutterite religious doctrines in contemporary society. The original, 450-year-old collectivistic orientation that characterized Hutterite religion has in large part become archaic in western society, which advocates an individualistic relationship to the Deity. It is this contrast that gives rise to the dynamics of successful proselytization among Hutterites, and ultimately to defection.

This contrast between the traditional Hutterite religion and modern Protestantism is most salient in the different perceptions of the means by which salvation may be obtained. In the previous chapters we have outlined the dynamic relationship between *Gelassenheit, Guetergemeinschaft*, and salvation. Even if the old concept of *Gelassenheit* has now been replaced by the dynamics of group salvation it still is not attainable on an individual basis, but only through participation in the *Guetergemeinschaft*. Individuals with personal anxieties and doubts concerning their state of grace are encouraged to bring these to the colony's spiritual leader (the "preacher") rather than approach God directly through prayer. The preacher, in turn, will typically deal with such matters by inquiring into the state of the individual's participation in the *Guetergemeinschaft*. If this participation is deemed adequate according to established standards, then the individual is reassured that his responsibilities have been met, that salvation is certain, and that the doubts are simply the work of the devil, which must be resisted.

The individual is expected to accept this advice implicitly, just as the preacher himself does not question the Biblical interpretations of the Hutterian founding fathers. To do so would be regarded as an expression of individualism in direct contradiction to the dictates of the *Guetergemeinschaft*. The individual who seeks guidance in the ritualized religious services certainly experiences an affirmation and acquiescence to the values and demands of the group but often finds no meaningful answers to personal problems and concerns.[2]

All this stands in stark contrast to the approach of evangelical Protestantism, which is now attracting Hutterite converts. The idea of Christ as *personal* saviour is of course central to the "born again" theology of the evangelical movement. The deity is now presented as eminently approachable for even relatively trivial personal matters. Blameless conduct is an ideal that sinful mortals can strive toward but are never expected to achieve. What really matters is the individual's "heart and mind" in contrast to the importance of behaviour among Hutterites — and these can exist in a state of grace despite behavioural failings. "Good works" and passive conformity to community expectations are insufficient to assure salvation. The individual must make a very personal and conscious commitment to Christ, a commitment which will change his/her life quite apart from (and perhaps despite) others. At the same time the psychological rewards (exhilaration, joy, relief from guilt) that derive from such a commitment promise to be more immediate, tangible, and personal. Finally, the message of revivalism is typically delivered by "preachers" who are articulate and impressive from their own sense of conviction. Coupled with the skillful use of musical and other props, as well as involvement rites such as "the laying on of hands," "speaking in tongues," etcetera, all of which are quite foreign to Hutterite religious experience, the contrast is complete. The attainment of salvation in these evangelical sects is assured through a psychological act, rather than by a behavioural one as is the case among Hutterites. It is also obtained on an individual basis, rather than being a group-based phenomenon, as is the case in Hutterite theology.

Such a contrasting theology and approach, it seems reasonable to assume, would be more likely to repel than attract Hutterites, and until recently this was indeed the case. The Hutterites looked upon evangelical Protestantism with dismay and even contempt, regarding its excessive fervour as debasing the sanctity of the deity. Officially that is still their position, but increasingly rank-and-file Hutterites are dissenting from this position and finding in evangelical Protestantism a desirable alternative. The reasons are several.[3]

There has occurred in Hutterite society a process of individualization and "privatization" that is now seriously eroding the traditional collectivist orientation. The Hutterite's migration to North America in the 1870s, and their gradual acceptance of agricultural technology, has in the long term forced them to abandon a division of labour designed to enhance cooperative effort, in favour of increasing specialization. Individuals now increasingly acquire complex, specialized skills which are then performed on an individual basis, often in isolation from others. This, in turn, has contributed to the development of individual pride and possessiveness. The uniformity in dress, household furnishings, etcetera, that once characterized Hutterite colonies has begun to give way to greater differentiation and competition. The family unit, once thoroughly subordinate to the community as a whole, is beginning to assert itself as a competing source of individual support. Members are now less deterred from engaging in activities that the colony would consider unacceptable if they know that their families will stand by them; and the colony, for its part, is less likely to take punitive action in these circumstances. The result is that more and more of the rules and regulations that were previously imposed on (and unquestioningly accepted by) individuals are now increasingly regarded as open to interpretation and negotiation (Boldt 1978).[4]

This applies to religious beliefs and practices as well. Some Hutterites are no longer content passively to listen to the preacher monotonically recite three–hundred–year–old sermons, without any opportunity for clarification and discussion. Members have recently been observed taking their notebooks to church services where they record the ideas expressed in the sermon for subsequent discussion with others. Such critical inquiry inevitably raises questions which, if not satisfactorily dealt with by the preacher, can lead to serious ongoing doubts and misgivings concerning the adequacy of fundamental religious tenets. Preachers, unfortunately, may find themselves ill-equipped to deal with such matters, even though they carry a heavy responsibility to do so, given that individuals are reluctant to approach the deity directly. Although Hutterite preachers have never been formally trained, they traditionally underwent a process of self-education through reading and reflection, such that they were legitimately perceived as learned men, well versed in all aspects of Hutterite theology. Currently, however, Hutterite preachers are perceived more as secular business leaders than spiritual shepherds. This change is again related to the technological/economic forces which have forced Hutterites to adopt an aggressive business stance in order to remain competitive and financially viable. The Hutterites know from experience that weak leadership can mean economic ruin, and it appears that their selection of preachers is now guided more by such secular considerations than by an assessment of pastoral or theological talent. Consequently rank–and–file Hutterites are forced to rely on their own or outside resources to help them resolve religious questions and issues, making them susceptible targets for outsiders in search of converts.

Once having located these potential converts, evangelists are then able to take advantage of both the relative austerity and tedium of Hutterite religious practice as well as its failure to provide more immediate, personal rewards. Additionally, they are able to offer converts the support of a network of others who have already been converted. This is a critical point, because Hutterites who do convert will almost certainly be forced to leave the colony. But defection, as has already been noted, is beset with difficulties that must be overcome if the individual is to make a successful adjustment to life outside the colony. These difficulties, however, can be significantly ameliorated if the defector has sufficient contacts and support on the outside, which is usually the case with the religious defector. The newly converted Hutterite, forced to leave his community, is immediately received into another community comprised of already converted followers of the evangelist. This new community can offer assistance in locating employment and housing, it can offset the loss of emotional support that derives from kith and kin, and it can provide enthusiastic spiritual support. It is precisely this point that accounts for the greater proportion of females and married couples with children among the ranks of religious defectors. The barriers that favour single able-bodied males in conventional defection are largely removed for the religious defector, creating a certain equality of opportunity that does not ordinarily exist.

Students of Hutterite society have always been impressed by the group's ability to maintain itself in the midst of a fast-paced twentieth century urban industrial society. Indeed, the Hutterites could be described as the pre-eminent example of successful ethnic boundary maintenance in North America today. Contact with the larger society has been carefully managed and controlled, allowing interchanges that enhance their ability to survive (e.g., in the economic/technological sphere), while forbidding potentially corrupting cultural influences such as radio and television. The distinction has not always been easy to maintain, and the Hutterites have changed a great deal since their arrival in North America. But overall they have clearly succeeded thus far in maintaining sufficient distance between themselves and the world, to avoid their assimilation into mainstream society. Given this demonstrated ability to fend off the world, how is it that the Hutterites are now losing members to outside religious influence?

We have already made reference to the individualization that has occurred in Hutterite society, and the consequent loosening of constraints that previously bound individuals to the collectivity. As was noted, this has had the effect of making members more susceptible to, and attracted by, evangelical Protestantism. But it has also made Hutterites more *accessible* to the message of the evangelists. The newly "liberated" Hutterite not only is beginning critically to examine his own religion, he also is less constrained in exploring alternatives. The once total ban on radio and television, for example, is gradually acquiring the status of "a strong suggestion";[5] books, magazines, and newspapers, which used to be in short supply and available for the most part only to the leadership, are now visible in quantity in most colonies; visits to nearby towns and cities, often for what would once have been considered frivolous reasons, are commonplace. The effect of this increased exposure to outside influences on rank-and-file Hutterites has been marked. They are now much more aware of, and better informed about, events in the larger society and indeed the world. The name of Billy Graham, for example, would probably have meant nothing to most Hutterites even a few short years ago; today most adult Hutterites have not only heard of him, many have also either seen him on T.V. or heard him preach on radio — either clandestinely in the colony, or at a non-Hutterite neighbour's house.

Most Hutterite conversions (and subsequent defections) to evangelical Protestantism, however, have come about as the result of personal contact, either with bona fide travelling evangelists, or simply with non-Hutterite converts during colony visits. Visitors to Hutterite colonies have always been accorded a friendly (if somewhat chary) welcome, even though they represent another source of potentially damaging outside influence. The reason for this is, at least in part, simply their basically friendly nature and adherence to the "golden rule." But there is also another factor that contributes to the Hutterites' hospitable attitude toward visiting outsiders which warrants some elaboration, namely, their own missionary zeal, or rather, the lack of it.

During the first half century of their existence Hutterites were active and successful missionaries.

> They carried out Christian mission according to the command of the Lord: 'As my Father has sent me, so I send you,' and also: 'I have chosen and established you that you go out and bear fruit.' Therefore each year servants of the Gospel and their helpers were sent out into the lands where there was a call. They visited those who desired to live better lives, and who sought and inquired after the truth. These they led out of their land by day and by night according to their desire, heedless of constable and hangman, so that many gave their lives for the cause. Thus they gathered God's people in a manner befitting good shepherds. (Zieglschmid 1943: 433 as translated by L. Gross)

Although motivated by Biblical injunction, missionary activity and the attendant martyrdom also served to strengthen communal life: "It was during the thirty-eight years of the golden period (1554-1592) that missionary passion was most ardent and the Hutterite Bruderhofs maintained their strongest internal discipline" (Hostetler 1974: 59).

Toward the end of the sixteenth century a number of factors began to intervene to make missionary activity more difficult. As the urgency of the issues underlying the Reformation faded, so did the appeal of the Hutterite message. Moreover, Hutterite migration to non-German speaking areas meant that missionaries had to travel long distances to reach their audience. By the middle of the seventeenth century missionary work had already declined substantially, and it subsequently virtually disappeared. Since their arrival in North America in 1874 the Hutterites have never attempted to win converts through active proselytizing, preferring to "bear witness" passively, by example: "I do mission work and preach daily with my humble way and walk of life. And if it should seem peculiar to someone, and he inquires about it, then I will preach" (Gross 1965: 193).

Hutterites today often feel and express some dismay over this lack of missionary effort, partly because it represents an abandonment of original ideals, but also because they recognize that the coexistence of "internal discipline" and "missionary passion" during the "golden period" of their history was not merely coincidental. They understand that the legitimacy and relevance of Hutterite beliefs and practices can more easily be maintained if others acknowledge their worth; that it is difficult to maintain the belief that "the Hutterite way" is superior while being ignored by the rest of the world. In other words, they recognize the importance of demonstrating to themselves and their fellow members that there are at least some outsiders who find in the Hutterites an attractive and desirable alternative. To a certain extent this can be accomplished by opening their colonies to visitors, who are usually duly impressed by the advanced agricultural technology and well-kept buildings and grounds. The Hutterites will typically claim that these achievements are possible only because of their religious beliefs, and in this indirect way gain spiritual reinforcement. But they prefer a more direct acknowledgement and usually subject visitors to a lecture on the evils of the world and the need to "see the light" as the Hutterites have. Outsiders who do respond positively and express a sincere interest in joining are encouraged and helped to do so. There have been very few such converts — less than a dozen in the last ten years — and even fewer have succeded on a permanent basis. Nevertheless, the Hutterites take great pride and satisfaction in these converts as living evidence of the fact that they have something which others desire. The need to proselytize, therefore, can be seen as being of deeper religious and psychological significance. It is an attempt to demonstrate to themselves and to others the relevance and the legitimacy of the Hutterite faith. It is this sense of significance which is the basis for persisting with proselytizing or missionary activities in spite of its overwhelming failure rate.

Hutterite society, therefore, is open to individuals who show some interest in their religious convictions and are willing to participate in their economy. and cultural activities. The 1960s and early 1970s with the accompanying social unrest and disorientation led to a number of outside individuals joining the Hutterite colonies for various periods of time.[6] It would seem that those few recruits who have stayed more than a few months in Hutterite colonies, as well perhaps as the more transient visitors who rejected, or were rejected by, the Hutterites, often display markedly abnormal psychological and social characteristics, which leads one to speculate that the main drive for their turning to the Hutterites stems from their maladjustment to the wider society from which they originate, rather than from any genuine interest in the Hutterite religion and way of life.

It is this category of persons, who come to a Hutterite colony and remain for a time, acquiring the confidence of some of the members among whom they interact, who seem most prone to depart eventually in the company of Hutterite defectors, thus contributing a serious tendency towards disruption and even fission within a community. This process is facilitated by the fact that the ultimately disaffected recruits acquire some of the values and vocabulary of the Hutterite community, and therefore present a plausible and even seductive rationale for their own departure and for the defection of one or more persons who were Hutterites by birth. Since, as we have seen, they are frequently drifters from one religious faith to another, they have often acquired some knowledge of other religious beliefs and organizations that enables them to elicit positive reactions from individual Hutterites, thus facilitating the process of disenchantment and even alienation from their own community by these Hutterites who then leave the sect, often not without disruption among the members who remain.[7] In this connection it is significant that those Hutterite groups within the three main divisions of the sect, the so-called *Leut*, which most have the tendency to attract such adherents from outside, however briefly, are also the groups which provide the greatest number of defectors from the Hutterite faith.

It is probably impossible for an outsider fully to acquire and internalize the significant characteristics of Hutterite identity, since these rest upon a cultural underlay that is at once based on kinship as well as being linguistic, social, and religious. The intending recruit is not merely confronted with a social group that still uses an archaic and highly particular variety of the German language, but he also seeks to join a community which is closely bound by kin-ties that unite not merely through marriages, but also by descent.

It may often be the religious ideas of the sect which attract the outsider to the community, but in everyday life the religious features are subordinated to those other cultural characteristics, which are the basis on which judgements are made by Hutterites on their fellows. A great proportion of Hutterite activities rests on the collectivist assumptions that are the basis of their religious philosophy; the newcomer, who has rejected any collectivist obligations that might have been present in his earlier life outside the sect, and has made an individual choice to join a new community, is unlikely to adapt to a social unit whose life is based on collective obligations. Their presence in a colony is an inherent contradiction of the Hutterite rule to subordinate and suppress individual desires, and therein lies the root of their ultimate dissatisfaction with the sect, and their subsequent departure.

The ongoing dilemma of the Hutterites is that their religious beliefs, as well as their psychological make-up, predispose them towards proselytizing. As we have seen, this activity is virtually doomed to failure, and in the process of seeking to effect such recruitment, there is a high probability of internal disruption among the people remaining "within the fold." We are left with the ironical conclusion that it is the Hutterites' own (largely unsuccessful) attempts to win converts that contributes to the loss of their members through conversion to evangelical Protestantism.

We have described a form of Hutterite defection which is not amenable to the type of explanation normally offered to explain conventional (nonreligious) defection. The motivation for religious defection is different, the defectors themselves do not conform to the usual profile, and the outcome is more permanent. Our analysis has shown that different notions of how salvation can be achieved have led to a subtle, but not insignificant, subversion of the Hutterite collectivist ideal by the individualistic conception of the personal saviour as advocated by fundamentalist sects. Hutterite religion is highly traditionalized, and eschews any appeal to the senses that might attract the religious mind. The service lacks any appeal through images, pictures, or music, so that for the outsider the immediate impression is one of dullness. The service is centred around the reading of printed sermons, thus lacking any spontaneity. There is no updating of the sermons, or indeed of Hutterite theology in general, so that the listener receives a highly traditionalized message, the content of which is already quite familiar. The religious service, therefore, provides no new inspiration, and this characterizes the sect as a whole, which supports no ongoing religious scholarship which might update their doctrine, and which might seek to bring it closer to that of the world within which the Hutterites live.

It may be argued that the Hutterites have not participated in the evolution which has been characteristic of other religious groups within the Christian tradition during the past three hundred years, so that it has remained, so to speak, a theological backwater outside the mainstream which, we believe, has been flowing in the direction of a more personalized conception of God. Thus movement elsewhere has been in favour of religious practice which caters for the psychological needs of the individual, who is increasingly attracted by sensory characteristics such as novel ritual and display. There is an increasing acceptance of God as the provider for the individual, who must approach Him by a personal act of faith. The believer is induced to undertake this act of faith by all sorts of appeal at the individual level. In contrast, the Hutterites have retained a God who does not approach the individual directly, and whom the individual can reach only through community action. The activities of the individual are not left to be determined by private judgement through a personal conscience, but rather are the subject of communal consensus achieved through community norms and sanctioning.

We have further shown that Hutterites have a strong social and psychological need to ascertain from their surrounding social environment signs of righteousness and religious worth. The martyr in the past, and groups that have converted to them in the past and present, gave them this indispensable feeling of divine selection. However, after such individuals (or even groups) have been converted to the Hutterite religious ideal, there rapidly emerges a discrepancy between the collectivist ideal of the Hutterites as opposed to the individualistic mode of thought of the outside world, that much more probably characterizes the incomer or incomers. This will be at its most salient in the differential view of salvation, which is the focal issue on which conversion to a religious sect is likely to be based. The reaction of the convert will tend towards strong sentiments of disillusionment, particularly concerning this religious issue, and will lead him to become a proselytizer among the Hutterites themselves, presenting them with this contrary view of the way to salvation. In this manner doubt and insecurity are sown among members of the colony, so that in the end when the incomer leaves, or is asked to leave, other Hutterites have become unsettled and their departure in turn has become likely. Although the incomer is an important ingredient in the situation leading to such defection, the Hutterites themselves will often have been made aware of the different view of salvation from their contacts with the outside world, and will often have already recognized the increasingly archaic nature of the Hutterite ideal, existing as it does in a modern world whose philosophical foundations are based upon individual initiative and personal effort. But the continuous contact with such ideas, through the new convert living within the colony, will lend greater emphasis to the discrepancy, and facilitate the defection of members from the colony.

The trend toward greater individual autonomy and decision-making will be difficult to halt, and unless the sect can devise workable strategies to cope with this development, the result could be a damaging loss of members. This result would be even more likely if defecting Hutterites should ever gain the right to demand their share of colony assets. So far the courts have disallowed such claims, forcing defectors to abandon their "investment" and rely on their own and sympathetic others' resources. However, there will no doubt be further challenges to the court's ruling which, if successful, could greatly exacerbate the situation unless the Hutterites can manage to reduce the number of potential defectors by recognizing and reducing the differential between their own theological position and that of the outside world from which they can no longer completely shield themselves.

PART II

Social Relations and Social Structures

FOUR

Family and Community Relations

Hutterite communities have a four-level male authority structure. The upper level is made up of the executive council consisting of six elders: two preachers, the manager, the field manager, the German school teacher, and one elder without portfolio. The second level of this hierarchy consists of department managers like the cattle boss, head mechanic, chicken boss, etc. Depending on the size of the community, the number of such managers ranges from eight to sixteen. The next level consists of young baptized male members. (Baptism is administered when adolescents reach the age of twenty years.) Unbaptized male adolescents under the age of twenty form a shifting labour force of helpers having, like females, no official voice in the community.

The number of Hutterites living in a single community is seldom less than sixty and equally seldom exceeds 140. Under the existing division of labour and given the specific age structure of the population, sixty members seems to be the minimum to keep a community functioning while 140 members designates the functional upper limit. Beyond this point competition for positions becomes so intense that it threatens the unity of the community. The community usually branches out to alleviate such disruptive pressures.

The approximately 28,000 Hutterites living in communal groups in North America today are the descendants of only eighteen families who escaped religious persecution by migrating from Hungary to Russia in 1760. Four of the original family names have since died out.

Kinship is patrilineal and patrilocal. One result of patrilineal descent and patrilocal residence is the lifelong association of Hutterite males in the same community, or of its branch. Females, in contrast, usually marry outside their community of birth. Hutterites have maintained the extended family. Three, sometimes four generations live in the same community although the members of an extended family might not necessarily live under the same roof. Due to the high degree of intermarriage, a community might have only one family name but nevertheless can consist of eight to fourteen extended families all related to each other to various degrees. A few communities have as many as seven family names. Under such conditions the functioning of the community can become rather difficult. The male authority structure can split into family factions which tend to form power blocks. Strife, dissent, and dissatisfaction by families which are excluded from participation in status positions are often the result.

The total Hutterite population is divided into three groups each having its own bishop and its own preachers' convention and differing from each other in some customs. Although these three groups have common roots, the years between 1840 and 1874 caused some differentiation in wealth and exposure to Mennonite influence, and finally each of these groups went through an experience of great integration when they migrated from Russia to the United States of America. Since 1879 when this migration was completed, these groups have remained endogamous. The existence of only fourteen family names and the enormous population increase from a few hundred to 28,000 (in 1985) has, of course, led to a high degree of intermarriage. Hutterites, however, have managed to maintain rules of incest which includes the first cousin in both directions.

Hutterite children spend the first three years of their lives entirely with their families. On a child's third birthday the mother brings the child to the community kindergarten. From this date on, the child will spend the time between seven or eight o'clock in the morning until about three or four o'clock in the afternoon in the kindergarten. At the age of six, the child will join the "big school" which is under the supervision of the German school teacher, although a teacher appointed by the local School Board will teach the normal provincial or state curriculum. The role of the German teacher is that of moral educator, supervisor, and religious teacher. At the age of fifteen the child will leave school and will join the labour force of young men or women. The socializing functions during the first fifteen years of a child's life therefore are divided between the family and various authorities of the community. A more detailed investigation may show the boundaries of such divided responsibilities.

The little school or kindergarten usually consists of a two-room structure located somewhere at the fringes of the community. It is operated by one or two women who are appointed as kindergarten nurses. The nurses do not have any special qualifications regarding the education of children besides being mothers themselves. Many nurses regard their duties like any other work duty in the community. There is little overt affection for the children, although the physical care is usually excellent. Nurses do not feel that they should try to cater to the individual personalities of the children, rather they attempt to fit individual personalities to community norms. They give children the opportunity to play but they do not join in the play. Toys were not allowed in the communities but this restriction is rapidly disappearing.

The rooms of the kindergarten hut contain benches, tables, a stove, and sleeping benches covered with mattresses. Besides eating, sleeping, and playing, the children are taught simple Bible sentences, songs, and prayers. Like adults, the children have a seating arrangement at the table according to sex and age. A child will start at the lower end of its sex structure and by age moves up until it reaches the upper end. From an early age the child therefore learns to see itself in relation to others. Up to its third birthday the child lives in the context of its own extended family, cared for by its mother or a close relative. Little children are considered cute and innocent, and some relatives are usually around to handle and carry the children. The sudden change occurs when the third birthday comes and the child is handed over to the kindergarten nurses. In most cases a younger child has already been born into the family with the result that much of the attention of the relatives has shifted to the new child. Consequently the joining of the kindergarten marks the loss of a great deal of parental attention. The three-year-old child ceases to be the centre of adult affection and is forced into the peer groups of three- to six-year-old children whose influence will become greater as age increases.

Correspondingly, the three-year-old, for the first time, is exposed to the discipline, the rules and regulations, and the authority of the community. Peter Rideman, the great Hutterite organizer, wrote ([1542] 1950: 98) on education: "'Provoke not your children to wrath, but bring them up in the nurture and admonition of the Lord.' For this reason is our education of children such that we permit them not to carry out their headstrong will and carnal practice." Children are seen as having a natural inclination to do what serves their carnal nature. To be loud, individualistic, aggressive, or hostile are characteristics which must be checked. This is effectively done by an ascetic, austere environment, and rigid discipline.

As a result of such socialization the three-year-old undergoes a drastic transformation from the affective and relatively permissive environment of his family to the rigid collective discipline of the kindergarten. The child becomes aware of the community authority and realizes the necessity to conform to the norms and regulations which flow from this authority.

Connections with persons outside the community are often used to frighten children. In the presence of a stranger, children are sometimes teased by telling them that the stranger might take them away. The invariable result is the violent embrace of the nearest relative who can provide security for the child.

The loss of some of the affective ties of the family, however, is replaced by the gain which the peer group provides. The child who joins the kindergarten enters into an existing group of youngsters whose example of discipline, norms, and customs is made attractive through the reward of companionship which the group provides. It is in the peer group of the three- to six-year-olds that the basic nature of the many community relations is taught. The differentiation of sex and age, the increase in expectations as age increases, plus the clear definition of one's own role in the community are part of this mechanism. The kindergarten provides an early blueprint of the community authority, its rules and regulations, customs and norms. Temper tantrums and "only child attitudes" among Hutterite children are largely unknown. The children are expected to show respect, be submissive, willing to obey orders, and to be unobtrusive in the presence of adults.

If these are the ideals of the socialization process the actual practice might differ widely from one colony to the next. A few colonies have discontinued the "little school" usually under the pretext that they had too few children to maintain it. Such an argument obviously has validity only for very small colonies. But even if these colonies grow larger they may fail to reinstitute this form of socialization. As a result children continue to live in their families up to the age of six. This changes the role of women drastically because family child care will become a major occupation leaving less time for women to participate in communal work. Within an extensive work load of child socialization at home, women tend to minimize the time spent in community endeavours in order to catch up with duties in the home. There is therefore a devaluation of community patterns in favour of family patterns. At the same time those women that are left to care for their young children within the family setting resort to individualistic means that help them to cope. Where there were few or no toys a few decades ago some households are now virtually littered with toys which are regarded as individual possessions, at least by the family that acquired them. Under such circumstances children become more demanding and quarrelsome. Lacking the stern discipline of the "little school" children become more family–oriented and the family becomes more child-oriented. Hutterite mothers are usually very indulgent and have neither the experience nor the self-assertion to enforce regulations which formerly were adhered to community–wide. Children who were sent to bed at a certain time might now sit up with their parents late into the night creating the spectacle of constantly promising but actually refusing to go to bed. Such uncertainties in obeying parents are a new but increasing phenomenon among Hutterites. They are by no means confined to the very young but reach into late adolescence, and they can increasingly be observed in colonies which in one way or another deviate in social structure, economy, or population size from the norm. It is therefore by no means rare to see Hutterite children being aggressive, loud, boisterous, and sometimes even cruel in their playing. Hutterite culture to a large extent has preserved aspects of a Middle European peasant culture whose mannerisms, mental frameworks, and choice of words do not necessarily conform to the pious Christianity which their religion radiates. That some colonies allow even very small children to witness the killing of animals must be seen in this light. The death convulsions of a gopher caught in a trap might be viewed with interest and elicit little or no empathy for the animal. While some Hutterites are very concerned with such responses of children, others find little if anything wrong with it.

For the first six years the language of the child consists, in most communities, of the Tyrolean-German dialect which the Hutterites have preserved for more than 450 years. The conceptual possibilities of this dialect are limited to the primary, direct, and concrete concerns of the community, excluding abstractions of a higher order. Through the memorization of Biblical quotations children are introduced to a second form of German which constitutes the language of the religious literature of Hutterites. This language consists of linguistic remnants carried over from religious writings that are 300 or 400 years old, mixed with the modern language of Luther's Bible translation and integrated with some grammatical aspects of the above–mentioned dialect. Most Hutterites feel uneasy about the use of this type of German. While they pronounce the words perfectly, according to Hutterite usage their conceptual abilities in relation to these words are rather limited. They therefore prefer either their dialect or, in an increasing manner, English as the predominant way of communication. These difficulties in conceptualizing their religious language have their origins in the forms of teaching which start in the little school and continue in later educational processes. Children are typically trained to memorize Bible quotations by "heart" without being required to understand the meaning of these quotes. There is the old saying among Hutterites that: "Children do not need to understand as long as they obey." This rather cynical remark stands in complete contrast to the early educational philosophy of the sect, which emphasized "understanding" as a precondition to the acquisition of faith: the former being under the control of man, the latter being a gift of God to those that had made the effort to understand "Him and His Word." The ritualistic nature of Hutterite church services and educational practices downplays the conceptualization of the Biblical content. This is already visible in the practices of the little school where the "intelligent and the good child" is the one that memorizes Biblical quotes easily. Demands to elaborate on the understanding of these quotes are rarely made during childhood and adolescent years and are largely absent during adulthood as well. Children and adults therefore have difficulty in deriving moral and religious concepts from general principles and consequently are not used to engaging in mental activities that require the manipulation of higher abstractions. Instead the child requires a Biblical imagery consisting of persons and events which carry concrete and simple moral messages. To use events in relation to King David, Solomon, or the People of Israel is very common among Hutterites. The American Space Program was seen as analogous to the Biblical event of building the Tower of Babel, and thereby obtained satisfactory meaning. The pictorial and concrete moral aspects of the Biblical imagery can be compared to the mentality of totem and myth in primitive societies. But the Biblical myth which carries Hutterite morality refers to specific events and messages. Its generalizability therefore is limited, its flexibility is low, and its applicability confined to concrete aspects of the Hutterite community. Those young Hutterites who quickly learn to operate, repair, and purposively use the most modern agricultural equipment find themselves in a situation where their mental processes seem to proceed on two increasingly divergent tracks. On the one hand they use modern rational logic in performing their economic tasks, while on the other hand they cannot employ this reasoning within the religious moral framework of their community, but have to fall back on an awkward system of socioreligious myths. They therefore often complain of being uneducated, unable to think, and incapable of analyzing what they feel to be right or wrong in their communities.

Managing communities on the legitimacy, the authority, and logic of these myths is much easier than trying to do so on rational grounds. The Hutterite leadership unconsciously realizes this fact, and on the whole tries to maintain those social structures that maintain these myths. Foremost among these are the formal features of Hutterite life, such as dress regulations, adherence to social and religious ritual, and suppression of deviant behaviour in those areas where deviance could mean trying to assess norms and folkways in modern rational terms. Consequently, the socialization processes for the "little school" (three- to six-year olds) as well as for the *"grosse Schule"* (six- to fifteen-year olds) are all roughly identical and convey the same messages. Stratification according to age and sex; status differentiation, authority patterns and responses of compliance. These messages therefore achieve the formation of a personality which indeed is well integrated with the community patterns at the age of early adulthood.

Beginning with its sixth birthday, a Hutterite child joins a new peer group consisting of children from six to fifteen years of age. The joining of this group is of great importance to a child because it presents a clear and definite promotion from a restricted "little child status" to a more respected participation in the *grosse Schule*. The formal structure of this peer group again follows the adult model of age and sex differentiation made visible in the organization of a separate dining group which the child joins. The appointed German teacher and his wife officially become the supervisors of these children throughout the day. The girls of this group are responsible for cleaning the dining room, doing the dishes, and also setting the table. There is some corporal punishment for children up to the age of fifteen, mostly applied by the German school teacher. As the age of children increases, shame, instead of corporal punishment, becomes the more common form of punishment.

The main features of the socialization process among Hutterites is the attempt to restrict the possible variety of personality structures to those that can with a reasonable amount of effort be integrated into the community. This goal is achieved by concentrating on the formal aspects of socioreligious ritual, on role and status definitions, authority and the acquisition of a religious imagery or mythology which functions to legitimize community patterns on the one hand, and thereby prevents disruptive critical mental processes on the other hand.

The rigid structures of roles and status in Hutterite communities unexpectedly are also a source of competitive and disruptive behaviour. The problem of dominance and/or submission produces a situation where individuals are usually subordinate to some and superordinate to others in the community. Despite the consistency in these patterns there are, nevertheless, enough roles and different levels of status that are close enough to each other to cause competition and rivalry. The main criteria of role differentiation, age and sex, create a vast gap as far as sex roles are concerned, but when it comes to age, role differentiations are often hard to make. A boy who might be two months older than another boy has no chance to rest on these laurels because the community is not really prepared to regard this small age difference as significant. As a result there is fierce competition for status among individuals in role clusters.

Hutterite peer group behaviour, therefore, is competitive and often aggressive. Where aggressive behaviour occurs, it is most often directed toward things rather than toward persons. When persons are the object of aggressive behaviour, such behaviour is usually indirect rather than direct.

One mechanism by which the community attempts to alleviate competitive behaviour is the almost automatic rise in the status structure and the division of labour by age. At least for the men it is possible to organize realistic role and status expectations at a relatively early age and see these expectations fulfilled. The enormous population increase, until recently 4.12 percent per annum, forces the communities to branch out about every seventeen years. With the establishment of a daughter community, a whole new set of roles and statuses is created which serves to satisfy the expectations of a new generation which has just reached the age when individuals expect social advancement. The culture therefore raises expectations in order to keep individuals motivated, and then proceeds to fulfill these expectations by handing out the rewards at the right time for appropriately displayed behaviour. The strength of the Hutterite community and the effectiveness of its socialization process is largely due to this mechanism.

While this mechanism of motivation and successive rewards works most effectively for males, females are largely left out of the system. The Hutterite community makes little attempt to support female motivation, nor is the female division of labour as satisfying and rewarding as the male counterpart. The much higher proportion of depressive mental disorders among females might be due to this lack of supportive motivational structures (Eaton and Weil 1953: 31-37).

The socialization of Hutterites through the exclusive involvement in primary relations of long duration inhibits the ability to form secondary relations. The "generalized other" of Hutterites in reference to the world outside the Hutterite community remains relatively undeveloped. The tendency is to perceive and to judge the world in primary not in secondary terms. This primary world of Hutterites consists of concrete particulars in the form of persons and well-defined situations.

The Hutterite individual who leaves the community encounters great difficulty in adapting to secondary relations. His primary perception of the world quickly comes in conflict with the secondary nature of human relations outside his community. He experiences a void of meaning and value which stands in marked contrast to the meaningful relations in his community. Many young individuals who left their communities were subject to these experiences. Facing a world which for them consisted only of secondary relations, for by leaving the community they cut themselves off from their primary group, they usually returned after a short time of experimentation in the world outside.

Hutterites leave school at the age of fifteen and join a peer group which in part carries adult status while in other aspects it is still set aside from adults. The membership of this peer group consists of fifteen-year-olds up to baptism. The halfway status towards adulthood is characterized by the full participation of the members of this group in the labour process, while on the other hand these adolescents attend Sunday school together with all children from the age of six. The males belonging to this group do most of the heavy manual work and actually take great pride in doing so. They learn a number of trades and usually structure their vocational aspirations in the community during these adolescent years.

The females have their own organization of labour and receive their place in the rotating workload of cooking and baking for the whole community. Both males and females join the adult dining room and take their respective place according to sex and age. In church the adolescents are allowed to sit on benches like adults while those under fifteen years of age have to use their school desks. (Hutterites usually do not have a church building but use the schoolroom for their services.) All corporal punishment stops when a youngster reaches the age of fifteen. Hutterites have labelled the age of adolescence "the foolish years." In general the communities are prepared to expect and to accept deviancy from adolescents without getting too excited about it. This tolerance is based on the expectation that young people will outgrow this foolishness and that fighting it would create more problems than tolerating it. Quite a number of young male Hutterites leave their communities for various periods of time. Most of them, however, return after having given the world a try. No blame is attached to such defection after the return of the juvenile, if his future behaviour is satisfactory.

Most of the youthful deviancy takes place within limits of adult toleration. The most common are drinking, smoking, possessing a transistor radio or some musical instrument, and meeting with girls without adult supervision. Premarital pregnancies were extremely rare. During the last five years, however, as many as eighty premarital pregnancies a year were reported for one of the three Leut. There was also one reported case of brother-sister incest.

The founding fathers of the Hutterite faith insisted that marriage must take place in three steps. There is first the marriage between God and the soul, then the marriage of the spirit with the body, and finally the marriage of bodies, which is the last and lowest grade.

The spiritual aspects of marriage were given enormous precedence over the carnal aspects, the marriage of one body to another. Hutterites felt that the customary courtship patterns of the early sixteenth century had nothing to do with the spiritual aspects of marriage but catered exclusively to the carnal desires of men and women. They therefore proceeded to ban all courtship within the sect. Instead they invented a matching procedure whereby once or twice a year the marriageable males and females were assembled. The preacher would give each male the choice of any one of three females which he selected as suitable. If the male chose not to accept any of the three females offered to him he had to wait for the next matching ritual. As impersonal as this may sound, Hutterites nevertheless took great care not to offend young people or to force marriages between incompatible individuals. Elaborate instructions were issued to insure that hurt feelings were alleviated and as little damage as possible was done to the self-image of individuals.

This matching ritual prevailed among Hutterites until 1830. The sect at this time was in a state of disorganization and a young girl who was to be married to an older man refused. In the ensuing uproar Hutterites finally changed their customs and allowed individuals to find their own marriage partners.

Today informal dating and courtship begin at the average age of sixteen to eighteen. No Hutterite is allowed to marry, however, unless baptized, and since most individuals receive baptism between the ages of nineteen to twenty-two there is a period of three to five years during which informal dating and courtship take place. Dating patterns take different forms depending on the liberal or orthodox orientation of the community. In communities where the traditional order is more strictly maintained, girls and boys might go for a walk in groups during summer evenings or on Sunday afternoons. Young Hutterites from these communities are not expected to enter into any serious relations until they are baptized. When a baptized female does not seem to be able to find a boyfriend some formal meetings will be arranged. According to the choice of the community elders and the parents, the female will be sent to another community where there is a chance to meet some marriageable males.

Most relations between young Hutterites, however, are established at social occasions like weddings, funerals, or the illness of relatives, when the young people have the opportunity to visit other communities. During these visits, which usually last several days or even weeks, the visiting individual must fit into the social organization of the host community. Consequently the young girl or boy comes in close contact with his peer group in the host community. This group consists, as a rule, of youngsters of his or her own age and sex and serves as a communication link between the sexes. Since the members of any of the peer groups have intimate cross connections to other peer groups through brothers or sisters, any affection that might develop between individuals travels from the original source to brothers and sisters of his or her own peer group, and from these to the individual to whom the affection is directed. Similarly, feedback is flowing in the other direction carrying encouragement or discouragement as the case may be. Through this procedure a number of people keep informed about the romantic affairs of boys and girls.

In communities where acculturation has taken a foothold, dating patterns tend to approach customs prevalent in the larger society. Terms like "going steady" or "going with him" are used. The dating patterns in these communities seem to include a greater frequency of dating and there is the tendency to escape the observation of the community. Since this depends upon some means of transportation, young boys try to gain access to a light truck with which to pick up a girl. Girls might sneak out of the community without the knowledge of their parents and meet the boys just outside. Such deviant behaviour is strongly disapproved. On the other hand Hutterite adults very often take an understanding and forgiving attitude toward the antics of their youngsters.

The attempt to "go steady" or to establish a relatively stable relationship is usually made quickly. One step in testing the other's intentions is made through the exchange of photographs. The boy usually suggests exchanging photographs with a girl and when the girl consents some tacit understanding about romantic relations is established. On the other hand refusal to exchange photos is a sign of discouragement. The taking of photographs, by the way, is strongly disapproved of by Hutterites. The customary rule, however, hardly prevents any adolescent or adult from having some pictures of himself and his friends. The relationship thus established is maintained through the exchange of letters and occasional visits.

The state of marriage among Hutterites is a normative pattern of behaviour strongly encouraged by the group. Young adults having received baptism between the ages of nineteen and twenty-two are expected to get married as soon as possible. Although there is no official punishment for bachelors and spinsters, some customs clearly have such an informal effect. Married Hutterite males grow beards as a sign of full manhood. The beardless unmarried male is visibly set aside from full male status. With advancing age this classification becomes very painful for the individual, particularly when he realizes that the middle and upper levels of the authority structure are closed to him.

Unmarried females are not visibly set aside through dress patterns, and due to their noninvolvement in the official power structure the sanctions that do exist for not getting married are relatively mild. They usually take the form of feeling sorry for a woman not having a husband and children. Unmarried women on the other hand might be valued as good workers. The lack of an immediate family enables women to concentrate on work patterns in the community and thereby achieve recognition which might serve as a substitute for husband and children. In recent years more and more Hutterite women could be found either postponing marriage or not marrying altogether. Many of these women are said to be "too choosy" which seems to indicate that the personal considerations of these women take precedence over community prescriptions. Such individual choices by women seem to indicate a trend toward greater female self-assertiveness totally absent only a few decades ago. Some women are said to be "too smart" to find a husband. What is meant by this remark is that certain females show too much independence, self-assertion, and intelligence, characteristics which lower the probability of finding a husband who would or could cope with such a woman.

Engagement and marriage take place within one week. They form the highlights of a ceremony which begins with the engagement in the community of the bride and then shifts to the community of the groom where the wedding takes place. Several weeks or even months before a wedding date is set the romantic relations between bride and groom form part of the gossip in their respective families and communities. Objections or consent of the families and communities involved are informally worked out so that when the formal procedures begin no serious objections exist.

Since the community prepares the wedding, the time is usually set for the convenience of the community. A convenient time is the early summer after seeding time, or late fall when the harvest has been brought in. A boy, however, has the right to ask for the preparations of a wedding at any time and the community will go along with it. Such insistence is, however, rather rare. The formal wedding procedure begins on the Sunday before the actual wedding takes place. Before the Sunday sermon the boy meets with his preacher and asks his help to get married. By this time the preacher usually has known about these intentions for a long time and has given his approval informally. Therefore the permission is in most cases quickly granted. After the Sunday sermon the elders of the community remain in the church and consider the request of the boy. The boy has to appear before them and usually receives a lecture on proper behaviour. He is urged to report his sins and change his behavior. Considerable emphasis is placed on the notion of entering marriage with a clean conscience. On the next day father and son travel to the community of the girl. The father approaches the parents of the girl and suggests that the children might get married. At this stage the informal consent given by all parties involved is so well established that the parents of the girl can hardly refuse or change their minds. In instances however where this was the case, lifelong animosities and hostilities resulted.

After the formal consent of the girl's parents is given, the preacher and the elders in the girl's community will be informed and on the next day the girl and boy will be "put together" in church. This ceremony is a remnant of the original matching process given up around 1830. Today this ceremony expresses the formal blessing of the church. There are two days of celebration in the community of the boy. These so-called chivarees are quite informal. Relatives and friends from other colonies are invited and join in a fun-filled atmosphere which encourages participants, mostly boys, to make various contributions. For Hutterites these chivarees are highlights of social interaction. The intimate atmosphere, the opportunity to participate, the laughter, and the fun-filled time is very appealing to them.

On Sunday morning at nine the wedding sermon begins. The preacher has a choice of several wedding sermons, but all are lectures on social control, dwelling on the duties of the wife, her submissive role, her manner of speech, and her actions in the community. The husband is reminded to be kind, generous and understanding, helpful and protective to his wife. During the sermon the groom sits among his peers on the men's side of the church and the bride's place is on the women's side. After the sermon there is a lengthy prayer followed by the wedding ceremony. The preacher steps forward from his desk and the groom and bride leave their seats and move forward to meet the preacher. There follows a lengthy exchange of questions and answers until the preacher finally declares the couple married.

In the early afternoon the people of the community assemble in the common dining hall. The two preachers take their seats at the head table and men and women arrange their seating according to sex. The bride and groom, holding hands, sit together with the preachers at the head table. The first preacher begins to sing a traditional Hutterite song. He usually chants a line or two and the community repeats these lines. At around four o'clock the preachers leave the hall and the community follows. When the evening sermon begins at around half past five the wedding is over and the community falls back into its weekly routine.

Within the next three months the newly-wed wife has the right to go back to her community for a visit which might last from one to three weeks. It is the duty of her husband's community to take care of the transportation and to fulfill her wishes as to the time of her stay. It seems that this custom is designed to ease the woman's mental strain, caused by the sudden loss of primary group support which she received in her home community.

The wedding establishes the married couple as a fundamental unit of the community. In regard to material resources the couple will be furnished with proper housing and furniture equal to the standard of other married couples. A washday and washing time will be allocated if automated washing facilities have not yet made this unnecessary. The distribution of material for clothing and the distribution of wine, wool, feathers and honey on a family basis demonstrate to the young couple that they are recognized by the community.

At the same time husband and wife acquire new responsibilities. The wife assumes the responsibility to sew and knit for her husband and herself. She has to keep her room clean and she has to fit into the existing female labour organization with its own norms and status hierarchy. She will also receive her "placing" in the church and the common dining hall according to age, demonstrating visibly to anyone her ranking in the female hierarchy.

In practice, however, this placing goes far beyond the visible limits. The young wife, being a newcomer to her husband's community, has to learn the whole role and status composition of all adults in the community and must try to adapt to these role networks. The ultimate outcome of her own role and status position is of course largely determined by her sex and age and the status of her husband and the family she married into. There is nevertheless a degree of voluntarism that allows for role achievements within a limited range of possibilities.

The new expectations, obligations, and restraints placed on the couple, and particularly on the wife, usually have profound psychological consequences to both. Husband and wife, who up to this time perceived themselves as adolescents enjoying a degree of *Narrenfreiheit* (the liberty of the jester), suddenly come under rigid and detailed obligations and expectations of great intensity. The primary group characteristics of the community have such an overpowering effect that the young couple usually does its best to conform to the existing norms.

For the husband of course the changes are less dramatic than for his wife. Due to the fact that he remains in his community of birth he has already established for himself a place in the hierarchy and therefore is not subject to the uncertainties and insecurities which his wife experiences. Nevertheless he is expected to disassociate himself from the peer group of unmarried adolescents and must join the peer group of young married men. His position in the occupational hierarchy takes a more responsible form. Any appointment to a higher position in the division of labour depends largely on his ability and willingness to accept these prescriptions. The alternatives to such conformity are very limited and usually very painful. Ridicule, shame, and disgrace are heaped upon those married men who refuse to conform.

The husband-wife relationship is structured mainly through their involvement in other communal structures. Economic activities keep husband and wife separated during most of the daytime hours. The meals are taken in the communal dining hall where husband and wife again sit among their respective sex groups. The general ascetic orientations of Hutterite culture forbids the display of individual affection among adults. Consequently, married life is almost exclusively confined to a few private hours in the couple's bedroom, but even here watchful eyes are never too far away. Whenever possible young couples are allocated a bedroom opposite the bedroom of the husband's parents. The arrangement of rooms is such that the parents and the young couple share a living room. The close physical proximity and the shared facilities between the old and the young couples automatically create a degree of supervision of the young by the old. After a year this arrangement is usually altered and the young couple might receive a bedroom somewhere else in the community.

The general attitude of female inferiority prevalent in Hutterite culture forces the husband to take up an attitude of superiority towards his wife. This attitude often prevents the young husband from establishing close affectional ties with his wife. The overtly affectionate husband is often called a "woman's man." There is hardly an expression which is more derogatory than calling a badly managed community a *Weiberregiment* (woman's operation).

This does not mean that husband and wife have nothing in common at all. But the point is that the social setting in a Hutterite community offers and enforces alternatives to close husband-wife relationships which may be of equal or greater importance, at least to the husband. It is the husband who in one way or another is an active participant in the important authority structure. He must be prepared to look at his wife in a double role. As a member of the authority structure he must be prepared to look at her as a member of the female organization equal to any other member. He cannot grant or allow for any favours or special treatment. This often brings him into conflict with the role of a husband who is obliged to support his wife.

Hutterite marriage problems are usually well hidden behind the quiet suffering of many women. Patterns of self-denial are part of the culture and personal incompatibilities, in the absence of divorce, are often silently endured. One Hutterite woman interviewed made the surprising statement that, in her opinion, seventy-five percent of Hutterite marriages were profoundly unhappy ones. This figure might be unreliable and of course depends heavily on a definition of what is a happy marriage in Hutterite terms. There can be no question, however, that under the serene surface of many colonies intense husband-wife tensions are simmering. The attitudes of Hutterites towards women is largely determined by the eighteenth century peasant society from which the present membership was recruited. Although changes as the result of being immersed in a twentieth century North American society are taking place, the role of women in a marriage is still largely one of submission. The predominant personality traits of many Hutterite women are those of resignation, self–denial, and withdrawal.

A distinction must be made between the attitudes toward the wife and those directed toward her as "mother." The concept of mother carries very positive connotations and these find acknowledgment among children and relatives. Even the husband is likely to make a distinction in his response to "wife" or "mother." Disagreements between husband and wife are likely to arise in response to colony affairs. The close interpersonal relations make for enhanced sensitivities. Status and status acknowledgments are taken very seriously. The hierarchical structure on the other hand makes it very difficult to change role and status positions because these would necessitate face to face confrontations. Hutterites, however, try to avoid these confrontations as much as possible because of their painfulness for all involved. As a result disagreements cannot easily be resolved and the conflict shifts to underground communication networks. Husbands and wives invariably get involved in such communication networks and since the husband must take different positions relative to his own involvement in the male hierarchy there is the potential of disagreement between husband and wife. On the psychological level, lack of understanding on the part of the husband; failing to give consideration and help regarding the concerns of the wife; failing to support her in colony affairs; and what is regarded as excessive drinking on the part of the husband seems to play a causal role in marriage problems. The unquestioned sexual availability of wives seems to be taken for granted by Hutterite husbands. There are indications that some wives try to inject a certain selectivity into the process. Women are known to refuse "to be nice" to their husbands when disagreements prevail, or when they try to exert pressure on their husbands. Female respondents feel that on the whole sexual activities do provide a very important bond between husbands and wives, sometimes the only bond that is left. In view of the fact that alternative sexual outlets are not available such an observation does not seem to be unreasonable.

The individual Hutterite family has no economic basis. It depends entirely on the redistribution of goods produced in the community. Allocation of work, and with it the allocation of roles and statuses, are likewise functions of the group. The lack of an economic basis for the family negates the role of the husband as breadwinner. His status does not derive from the material rewards he can produce for his family, but is derived from his participation in the authority structure of the community. He does not however participate in the community authority structure as an individual but as a member of the group of male relatives of his extended family. He supports and receives support from his father, his brothers, uncles, cousins, etc. Since all role and status positions with the exception of preacher are decided on by all baptized male members, the voting block of male relatives is of utmost importance to any married Hutterite over the age of twenty-five who expects to make some advances in the occupational hierarchy. This group, therefore, is the principal group of orientation.

An effective check on the formal powers of males often comes through the use of gossip. It can safely be assumed that any gossip in a Hutterite community will finally reach the person or persons toward whom it is directed. Such public opinion is almost impossible to disregard or ignore. A simmering state of conflict might be the result of such disregard, poisoning the whole social atmosphere.

Wives play an important part in the manipulation of these checks. Although their influence is mainly passive, such as preventing unpopular decisions being implemented, it is nevertheless real and effective. Hutterite wives seem to have a sense of loyalty and devotion toward their husbands rather than love in the sense of its romantic connotation, although romantic thought is slowly infiltrating Hutterite culture, mainly through adolescents who pick it up from Canadian and American cultural traits.

Marriage is thus largely a duty comparable to other duties such as work and going to church. This duty is performed under the eyes and supervision of the whole community, which takes great interest in its progression and controls it through its responses.

Conversely the marriage partners do not feel that marriage is only an affair of husband and wife, but accept and look to the community for guidance and direction. The result is that, while the romantic links between husband and wife are relatively weak, while husbands at least get a great deal of satisfaction from participating in other social structures, and while the wife is at times frustrated and rebuffed, marriage nevertheless is extremely durable. There are few cases of separation, usually only occurring when one marriage partner has left the community, and no divorces. (There were five broken marriages between 1875 and 1950.) Hutterite marriage patterns present a case where very strong community relations reinforce and hold together relatively weak romantic husband-wife relations. But most of all there are no alternatives to marriage for a Hutterite who wants to remain one.

The branching of communities every fifteen to twenty years ensures that, as they grow older, Hutterites come to occupy high status positions in the social hierarchy of their communities. As individuals pass their prime a gradual withdrawal from active participation in the community and family sets in. According to the customs women retire from all organized economic activities at the age of forty-five. However many continue on a voluntary basis.

Men, with the exception of the preacher who is elected for life, stay in their respective positions as long as they feel up to the demands made on them. As age increases they might retire to less demanding positions. The aged are respected in Hutterite communities and their advice is valued. The last years of a Hutterite are usually spent by being part of a son's or grandson's family. While the community takes excellent care of the aged in terms of health services, food, housing, and clothing, the family of immediate relatives provides the close emotional and personal ties so greatly satisfying to Hutterites. Death is regarded as natural and usually comes without fear.

FIVE

Childhood and Adolescent Socialization

The main characteristic of the Hutterite socialization process, distinguishing it from similar processes found in other Western societies, lies in the communal orientation of the group. To keep this way of life credible, attractive, and dynamic and to prevent comparisons with outside lifestyles constitutes the major socializing task of Hutterites.

It should be remembered, that Hutterites have chosen a mode of existence which continuously demands separation from their respective host society. "Separation from the World" originally was a conscious religious choice designed to separate the believer from the unbeliever and to protect that person from the contagious influence of a sinful world. The "chosen people," the "community of saints," were to stand out in a world of sin and spiritual corruption by being radically and visibly different.

Such sentiments, of course, are frequently found in social movements, particularly during their vigorous early stages. A critical stage however is reached when the social movement becomes institutionalized. The creation of permanent and enduring institutions on the part of the social movement requires the establishment of mutually agreeable relations with the host society. In the face of such requirements the initial anti-societal sentiments of the movement must be modified and replaced by a sense of coexistence and cooperation, however limited. The contracts established in this way make it more difficult for the movement to remain truly "separate" from its host. The more intense these contacts are, the longer they last and the greater the number of social contacts, the more difficult it is for the movement to remain separate. Separation in the sociological sense here refers to the ability of a sociocultural group to be predominantly socially and culturally self-determinate, despite relations of interdependence with outside sociocultural forces.

What distinguishes the Hutterite group from all other groups which are either religiously or communally similar, is their ability to maintain this separation and self-determination in an institutionalized form, even after the religious justification for separation has lost much of its original fervour.

The argument has been made that social isolation is the major force that insures a degree of self-determinate development for Hutterites. Social isolation here is seen as a cause, while in reality it is an effect. The maintenance of social isolation in itself is problematic for Hutterites, and far from being a cause of their self-determination it is, rather, the active ongoing dynamic toward self-determination which produces social isolation. There is no question that social isolation *facilitates* self-determination; it signifies conditions under which self-determination is more probable than under any other conditions but it is not the cause of it.

Hutterites have not withdrawn from contacts with the wider society; rather, they present to their membership an active, living, and viable lifestyle which stands in contrast to the values and institutions of their host society. This alternative must continuously be of such a nature that it can insulate itself against the encroachment of contemporary ideological and behavioural norms of the wider society, and as such can command the loyalty and allegiance of its members.

On these accounts Hutterites seem to succeed splendidly.

To state the fact that they do succeed is not to say that they succeed easily. To appreciate the nature of this task and the way in which the task is translated into processes of socialization one must be aware of some fundamental conditions.

The viability of the Hutterite lifestyle consists of maintaining a religious world view in the face of a modern scientifically coloured, individualistically oriented, secular, materialistic ideology.

This religious world view among Hutterites, as elsewhere, serves three basic social and psychological functions. In the first instance religion serves as a systematic symbolic universe which assigns meaning to the religious group and to the world in which it exists. It explains the origin of spiritual and material things and human life, and as such is able to make definitive statements about the meaning of the world, of life, and human existence.

To the extent that any systematic view of the above nature includes a definition of man and his place in the world, the second basic function of religion consists of making definitive statements in regard to the imperatives of human behaviour. Laws and norms, cults, rituals, taboos, and folkways constitute systematically selected and ethically consistent forms of behaviour which are perpetuated in processes of socialization, suggestion, education, example, and tradition.

The third basic function is of a psychological nature. It is designed to overcome the helplessness of man in the face of existential problems of being and nonbeing, and of anxieties derived from failure, suffering, accidents, and death. These existential anxieties are not very susceptible to rational scientific manipulation. Their alleviation seems to require some sort of supernatural legitimacy, something science, as a man-made imperfect, incomplete, and fragmented body of knowledge, is unable to provide. Religion, in contrast, organizes man's life energies, his drives, and basic needs into meaning, outlook, hope and optimism designed to overcome, or at least endure despair, failure, suffering, and death.

The Hutterite socializing task is to maintain the unity of these three religious functions in spite of the challenge of science to the first and the challenge of individualism (and materialism) to the second. Depending on the outcome of these two challenges, the third function will follow suit. Whether an individual consults his priest or his psychiatrist when plagued by existential anxieties depends into which ideological system he is integrated.

The particular Hutterite attempt to preserve the unity of these three religious functions is problematic due to two apparently contradictory orientations in Hutterite culture. As is the case in most religious sectarian movements, the Hutterite challenge toward the conformities of the times turned conservatively inward, as the larger society turned indifferent or became tolerant of nonconformism. Religious indifference or toleration relieved the sect from the necessity of developing and maintaining an intellectual elite whose task was the continuous reformulation of the sect's position in the struggle with contemporary ideologies. Religious persecution was eminently suited to do this, yet religiously mindless persecution, due to the ravages of war, oriented the group toward physical survival. By the middle of the seventeenth century Hutterite religious scholarship had come to a standstill. With the exception of a flurry of revival activities during the middle of the eighteenth century this is still the case today. As a result the Hutterite religious world view is not only extremely conservative but in many respects archaic. Moreover it has no culturally accepted and legitimized mechanism to update it.

The difficulties of maintaining an archaic world view are compounded in a fast changing modern world due to progressive Hutterite attitudes toward the production of goods. The economic sentiments of the sect were, and still are, essentially anticapitalistic. The concept of supply and demand as market regulating forces drew nothing but scathing condemnations from Hutterites. An entirely different attitude however prevailed in regard to the mode of production (see Chapter 2). Today the noncapitalistic Hutterite community, nevertheless, is a most efficient capitalistic enterprise in terms of its production and marketing.

It follows that a main part of the socializing task in Hutterite culture today is designed to overcome the contradictory influence between an archaic religious world view which denies to science any valid explanatory or causal function, and yet allows for technological orientations and encourages creativity in the field of productive technologies.

How is such a personality constructed, and what are the processes by which it is obtained?

Hutterites require a basic personality structure that is prepared to practice science for economic purposes, yet at the same time refuses to accept it as an explanatory system regarding the nature of man and the world he lives in. Such a personality structure, in addition, should not contain any individualistic aspects from which the validity of Hutterite behavioural norms and traditions might be judged.

Only a preliminary answer to these problems is possible at this time. The key elements in the construction of the Hutterite personality is the isomorphism between their view of the nature of human nature and their view of the real world. Both of these views are dualistic, postulating opposing forces which are in constant struggle with each other.

As we have seen, the Hutterite view of the nature of human nature contains the opposites of the spirit versus the flesh. The first is directed toward God, the latter to sin. The first leads to eternal life, the latter to eternal death.

The Hutterite view of the real world contains the opposites of the community of believers as opposed to the world of the unbelievers. The first consists of the Hutterite community, the second consists of the rest of the world. The community of believers incorporates the spirit of God; it constitutes a "forecourt of heaven" *Vorhof des Himmels*, the assurance of life. The bad, the ungodly, the flesh, the morally depraved inhabit the world where people are awaiting eternal death.

The consequences of this view is that the world and its contemporary manifestations are delegitimized. The causal and explanatory forces of this world are manifestly wrong. War, genocide, crime, poverty, human arrogance, and ignorance are evident everywhere in the world and are the demonstrations of its wrongfulness.

The Hutterite individual is trained to be deeply suspicious of the motives and attitudes of those raised in the image of the world. Since the final outcome of the world — eternal death — is known to him, he can have no desire to participate in it. While the delegitimation of the world is caused by its own refusal to accept the true meaning of God's spirit, Hutterites see no reason to reject the technological processes of the world as long as these processes are used in the spirit of God: that is to say for the good of the community and the spirit it stands for. Hutterites might become wealthy but they are not to use wealth for enjoyment. They might be skillful, but they are not allowed to develop false pride or arrogance because of it.

The physical world with all its attractions, successes, and failures really cannot touch the truly spiritual man. Earthly existence demands that he works and produces for himself and for others. But worldly attractions, successes, and failures in the end are of no consequence to him spiritually. The term *Gelassenheit* denotes a feeling of self-surrender to God's guidance: the forsaking of all concerns for personal property or pride. It defines a feeling of freedom from the anxieties and pains of the world by rendering the affairs of the world meaningless and trivial. But the extraordinary capacity of Hutterites to denigrate the predominant secular ideologies would be of relatively little consequence were it not backed up by an outstanding effective communal-behavioural system. It is of the greatest importance to realize that Hutterites have remained a small-group society despite their numerical growth during the last one hundred years. There are good psychological and educational reasons for not letting a community grow beyond a membership that allows for primary relations. There is a direct relationship between the opportunities to experience secular societal relations and the display of behavior incorporating such relations. Hutterites always grow up in a primary group and never experience any socialization into a secondary group, that might bring to bear different points of view in the individual's personality development.

There is furthermore the extraordinary consistency between the primary behavioural expressions in the community and the basic religious tenets. The communal validation of religious beliefs is behaviourally visible; it is direct and forms the basic life experience of Hutterite children. Lifelong primary interaction congruent with religious views elicits extremely strong habitual forms of behaviour on the part of Hutterite members.

When Hutterites purposefully were sent to educational institutions to become doctors or teachers, and when these members expressed opinions contrary to accepted Hutterite views, or violated behavioural norms, they were expelled. The same fate awaits any member who seriously dares to act in a similar way.

The possibility of expelling members is an effective mechanism to maintain Hutterite conservatism. The existence of a number of expelled ex–Hutterite groups in western Canada testifies to the determination of the sect to get rid of internal dissenters.

To understand Hutterite socialization, therefore, is to understand first the dynamics by which the sect keeps itself apart from the rest of society. In the second instance it requires an understanding of the effects which a primary group has on individuals when this group engages in a behavioural system fully integrated, validated, and legitimized with its religious beliefs.

Indeed the system is so well integrated that mothers having had twins, or having had two children within a very short space of time, occasionally give one of the children to a sister or another relative to care for. This arrangement might last for a number of years, until the mother feels able to carry the burden of an additional child. The exchange of these children is totally unproblematic, mainly due to the fact that the environments are very similar.

In addition, Hutterites tend to blend the personalities the child is exposed to, by having a relative accompany the child which changes its environment. The foster mother, for example, who has raised the child for two or three years, accompanies the child when it goes back to its biological family for up to six weeks.

Hutterite culture is an adult not a child–oriented culture. While there are many children to be found in every community due to the high birth rate of the sect, children are subordinate to adult activities, values, and expectations. The imposition of the community values and expectations begins at the third birthday of the child when it enters the "little school." Children are seen as lovable creatures, saved by God due to their innocence and ignorance; yet they carry in themselves the germ of Adam's sin, which if allowed to develop, will push them into carnal desires. As will be shown later in this chapter, the Hutterite ideal of man is that kind of man who knows about God, knows about his own carnal nature, is able to suppress his carnal nature, has acquired faith and consequently is able to live according to the will of God.

Since adult Hutterites are supposed to have reached this stage, children by necessity are being looked at, not as inferior, but as incomplete persons. They are seen as needing the help and assistance of adults in reaching the full stage of spiritual maturity. Therefore, there can be no question of adults assigning great value and importance to children's games and play other than keeping them busy. Nor do they regard these as means of developing child personalities.

It follows that personalities are seen to develop through the knowledge of God, the suppression of man's carnal nature, and the acquisition of faith.

The socialization process is therefore structured in accord with these convictions. For the "little school" this means that the kindergarten nurses teach the word of God to the young by having them learn and recite Bible quotations, songs, moral tenets, and other religious material until they know them by "heart." Other elements of socialization which are seen as important are discipline, modesty, respect for elders, sensitivity towards others, pacifism, sense of duty, and obediency.

Despite these stern principles Hutterites do not maintain a socialization environment that is extremely demanding. The primary group environment, the family and the peer group act as social modifiers through which the above–mentioned demands are reduced to endurable human levels.

A sympathetic understanding for human failings accompanies the demand for self-discipline. Patience, forgiving, and forgetting are as much a part of the process as is corporal punishment and exposure to communal shame. The peer group in particular is the place where individuality is allowed to develop within the limitations of sex and age role prescriptions. Competitions and rivalries are by no means absent in such groups.

The family influences the socialization process of the school through the role which it maintains in the community. While Hutterites pride themselves in saying that the communal socialization process recognizes no family ties, these nevertheless reassert themselves in very subtle ways.

It may be the small amount of extra care or attention which a child receives in a higher status family which might make a large difference in its performance in the socialization process. It might be an attitude of greater expectations for social mobility which influences a child from a higher status family; but there is also the recognition of individual talent, intelligence, and adaptability independent of family background which is capable of propelling one child further than another.

With its sixth birthday, the Hutterite child enters its next stage of development by joining the group of six- to fifteen-year-olds. This group is usually referred to as the "large school" since it falls within the years during which the requirements of public education are satisfied. By special arrangement with provincial governments Hutterites maintain public schools in their communities. While the building is publicly owned, the school grounds are made available by the community. The teachers are appointed by the local board and teach the provincial or state curriculum, but restrictions regarding the use of radios, television, and other devices are usually entered into between the school board and the community.

This group of adolescents incorporates the same age and sex division as outlined earlier. It is significant to note that the responsibility for socialization now passes from female into male hands. The rotating kindergarten nurses are replaced by the German school teacher who is a member of the council of elders, and therefore one of the six persons responsible for the administration of the community. This move brings the socialization process much closer to the central interest of the community. As a result, the discipline and the general demands are much stricter. The children have to care for their own dining room. They set the table, wash the dishes and dispense the food with the aid of the teacher's wife. Table manners are enforced, by the strap if necessary. Permission for any unusual activity must be obtained from the teacher whose jurisdiction is not confined to the school hours but extends to the waking hours of the children.

German school is held once a day for about one hour. The memorization of religious texts continues, to which is added the writing and reading in the German Gothic script. Since all of the Hutterite religious literature is handwritten, the ability to read and write this type of German is essential for the understanding of Hutterite religion.

Hutterites do not like to interfere with the appointed school teacher who conducts public school. If there are no objections on their part as to a "too worldly" exposure of their children, they like to leave the public teachers alone, oft times developing respectful, if not friendly, relations with them.

The Hutterite child who enters public school at the age of six is most likely unable to speak an adequate English, therefore losing a year or two before normal progress can resume. Since the child, however, is taken out of school at the earliest permissible age, usually when the child reaches his or her fifteenth birthday, few Hutterite children attain the ninth grade.

Hutterite parents tend to be rather indifferent about the grade their children reach in school. The one-room school environment makes the attainment of grades somewhat academic in the first place, and since the Hutterite child is not required to enter the public job market, the certification of any educational attainment is superfluous.

While still in school, usually at the age of twelve years, Hutterite children slowly begin to participate in the communal work patterns. Females begin to help their female relatives in their rotating tasks, while male children begin to attach themselves to some older male relative who happens to be one of the many bosses. These work patterns intensify particularly during the school holidays.

On a child's fifteenth birthday, the child is taken out of school. At the same time the child leaves the children's dining room and takes his or her place in the adult dining room. This event is of greatest significance since it demonstrates the attainment of an adult status. Where children are not allowed to leave school at such an age, they are known to have developed temporary emotional disorders. A number of Hutterite communities were fined and one or two Hutterite parents even went to jail because they insisted on taking their children out of school. The fifteenth birthday marks the day of social promotion from child to semi-adult status. A person still required to attend school has this promotion nullified, throwing it into an ambiguous in-between position which, in the highly status conscious Hutterite community, is very painful to endure.

At the same time the Hutterite adolescent enters his respective division of labour. Young females and young males form a group of unspecialized labourers who can quickly be moved from one work pattern to another. Much of the hard manual labour that is left in the communities is done by these young males. The females participate in the typical work reserved for women, e.g., cooking, baking, gardening, canning, dish-washing, sewing, cleaning, washing, and child supervision. Some of these activities are conducted within and supervised by the family, like cleaning, washing, and sewing. Most others are communal activities organized and supervised by the females of the community.

The status of adolescents over fifteen years and up to baptism is something of an apprenticeship for adult roles. While they are allowed to dine with the adults, and are part of the adult age and sex division, as unbaptised members they nevertheless have not achieved full religio-spiritual status. Certain privileges which are gradually bestowed on them, like the issuing of a hope chest for girls, the inclusion in the distribution circle of wine, honey, and wool, slowly draws the adolescent closer and closer into the adult environment. This is particularly true in the economic field where adolescents might develop special interests and skills which are needed and valued in the community.

A young boy, for example, may specialize in the wiring of electric motors. Although this is not a necessarily crucial skill for the community nor a full time occupation, it is a handy skill to have should the occasion arise. Young girls might corner certain occupations for themselves like cleaning eggs or even copying religious books, should their handwriting be good enough to be entrusted with such a job.

On the other hand, Hutterites call these adolescent years "the foolish years." They expect and, in fact, experience a lot of difficulties with their adolescents who find the world beyond the confines of the community too tempting.

If an adolescent defects and returns, he is faced either with making a whole-hearted commitment to the community becoming a full and loyal member, or existing on the social fringes, living a shadow existence being neither a full member of the community nor a nonmember. The latter alternative is extremely painful. The sight of an alcoholic, having been excommunicated from the community years ago yet begging the preacher to be reinstated, is indeed a tragic spectacle. Needless to say, no one will be reinstated unless he has convinced his fellow members through his behaviour, not through his verbalizations, that he deserves it.

While, as we have seen, the unmarried state for both sexes is frowned upon, there is no discrimination toward men or women who happen to be widowed nor is there any discrimination toward a childless couple. Children are expected to be born at the appropriate time after marriage and women who do not seem to be able to produce children are subject to sympathetic understanding when it is assumed that her childlessness is not due to birth control.

Baptism is a highly ritualized procedure. The applicant has to memorize a long list of questions and answers designed to test his religious knowledge. The elders who are requested by the applicant to help him in getting baptized, also subject him to rigorous questionings regarding his former and future life, his personal weaknesses, past failings, and future good intentions.

In accordance with the Hutterite world view, the applicant has to demonstrate that he has gone through the cycle of seeking and obtaining the spirit of God, followed by adherence to the narrow path of righteousness for the future. Baptism is the final stage of the conversion experience which begins when the child learns that it is endowed with a carnal nature and ends with the secure knowledge of being saved by God for all eternity.

Childhood and adolescent socialization among Hutterites follows a *Bildungsideal*, an image of what Hutterites consider to be a fully developed and mature person of the Hutterite faith. The formulation of such a *Bildungsideal* is extremely difficult, if not impossible, in complex societies, due to ideological and social diversities. The ideological and sociocultural homogeneity of Hutterites, and the relatively uniform demands which the Hutterite *Gemeinschaft* makes on the individual in contrast, tend to favour the formulation and the maintenance of a *Bildungsideal* as a guide for processes of education and socialization. This is not to say that the Hutterite *Bildungsideal* is a simple matter. On the contrary, the concept contains a number of historical, sociocultural, religious, and moral elements whose relation to each other have greatly changed from the founding days of the Hutterite sect to the present.

An exploration of the Hutterite *Bildungsideal* must begin with the principal religious doctrines of the sect, and at the same time must attempt to account for the changes in the sociocultural perceptions of these doctrines that have occurred during the last 450 years. Socialization of their children was for Hutterites only second in importance to the religious education of adults which, after all, aimed at the attainment of the goal of salvation. The literature on child socialization and education therefore goes back to the early sixteenth century when the sect was still in the social movement stage (Friedmann and Mais 1965: 172). Two radically new religious concepts, those of adult baptism, and the communal upbringing of children, were among the religious cornerstones of the sect and drew the attention and the inventiveness of the Brethren toward forms of child socialization different from anything practiced in Europe at the time.

Children were removed from their parents shortly after birth and reared as communal wards. Parent-children relationships were discouraged in favour of adult-children relations thereby de-emphasizing kinship ties in favour of communal ties. The practice of adult baptism was based on the assumption that only a fully matured person could understand the teachings of God and experience the gift of faith, which would draw it toward God as symbolized by the act of baptism.

These religious convictions not only put the community in place of the family as the main socializing agent, but also altered the child's societal role. While child baptism among Catholics and Protestants continued to constitute the child's entry into the civil and spiritual community, independent of the child's wishes, Hutterites emphasized voluntarism on the part of the individual capable of making a choice. As a result, Hutterite teachings were seen as being destructive not only of civil society but of the religious communities as well. In response to such accusations the sect devoted great care to develop and to justify a system of socialization and education sufficiently sophisticated to refute their critics and persecutors.

A shorthand version of the Hutterite world view is contained in the Codex Braitmichel written in 1566 and containing a collection of treatises by various Anabaptist writers of the previous forty years (Friedmann and Mais 1965: 136; cf. Friedmann,

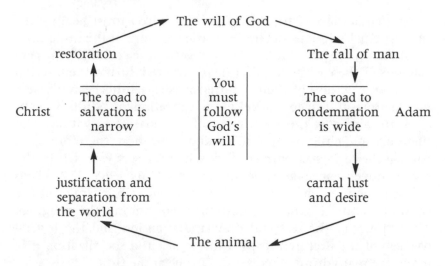

1961: 296). It is this world view which gives rise to the Hutterite *Bildungsideal* and assigns meaning to Hutterite institutions.

Reading clockwise from the top, the above diagram pictures man as going through a process of separation from God caused by the fall of Adam and resulting in man having the status of an animal. Through a process of separation from the (animal) world and justification through Christ can man be restored to the will of God again. It is the fate of every individual to go through this cycle during his lifetime. Burdened with original sin, man has the tendency to cater to carnal lust and animal desires. Only through the separation from the world, which is hopelessly lost to the carnal practices of man, and through the sacrifice of Christ, can man be restored to act again according to the will of God. Hutterite social institutions are designed to help man in his efforts to suppress the animal desires in himself and attain restoration to the will of God.

The community of goods, for example, is designed to suppress man's most dangerous desire — the lust for private property and power. The community of faith, that is the Hutterite religious community, is designed to bring about the restoration of man through communal teachings and mutual assistance in the acquisition of religious knowledge and faith. As the members of a community are obliged to help each other and to "watch over each other," so are the adults of every community obliged to aid all of their children in reaching the goal of eternal life.

There are a number of elements contained in the world view which highlight the understanding of Hutterite socialization processes. The will of God is seen as the supreme authority for everything that is good and desirable. God is the source of power (faith) and goodness (grace). A Hutterite therefore perceives these qualities as being situated outside himself but obtainable by himself through appropriate behaviour facilitated through the acquisition of knowledge (the knowledge of God and His will).

This perception of power sources outside the individual requires an orientation toward a greater authority which is possible only through a proportioned lessening of human self–assertiveness. Approved self–assertiveness on the other hand must operate through God, not through the individual. This raises the crucial question: "When and under what circumstances can the individual be certain that whenever he attempts to assert himself it takes the form required by God?" The immediate response to this question is individual uncertainty and this uncertainty acts as a factor of individual conformity under social conditions when much of the authority which is assumed to originate with God for all practical purposes now resides in the authority of the community.

The second important element is a definition of man's carnal nature. The carnality of man is perceived as a universal trait of mankind. While man can rise to come near the divine level of God, most likely (as for the world) he is bound to stay on the carnal level and therefore suffers eternal death.

For the purposes of socialization, Hutterites teach their children and expect to find in them, elements of their carnal nature. But at the same time they also expect them to acquire the means to suppress these carnal elements. Consequently there is no such thing in socialization as the simple acquisition of goodness for an individual who is neither born good nor bad. Hutterites must learn first that their nature is bad, followed by the suppression of badness and the final acquisition of goodness.

In the process of going through this cycle, Hutterites have no sacraments save baptism to assist them. While they retain in their teachings the sinful nature of man as found among the

Catholics, they eliminated the sacrament of absolution as the major instrument to alleviate the uncertainty of salvation. Hutterite preachers do not forgive sins but "wish" that sins might be forgiven. In every instance, God is seen as the deciding authority and the preacher does not presume to act in His name or exercise His powers.

The Hutterite individual therefore is very much alone with his doubts and uncertainties. His preacher is only a teacher who is believed to have some gifts for teaching, but does not act in the name of God. He possesses no divine power. The only support, albeit a powerful one, comes from his fellow man; that is his religious community, which for all practical purposes is also his social and economic community. In his association with the members of his community, the Hutterite individual finds the power source greater than his own, which helps him to deal with his carnal nature and assists him on the narrow path to salvation.

This association with his fellow man, although it has a rational religious explanation, reaches into the deeper layers of the individual's emotional equipment. Very powerful, probably biologically based feelings of primary group affiliation, are being activated and directed by it. The Hutterite community is seen as life leading to immortality. The outside world is characterized by decaying lust leading to death. The individual's participation in the community of the true believers, therefore, is capable of removing the individual's doubt about his eternal status and replaces it with certainties of salvation. The Hutterite community, through baptism, is also the vehicle which essentially provides an institutionalized conversion experience to the individual. From the depth of his carnal damnation the individual acquires in the community the certainty of his salvation.

This institutionalization of a conversion experience is of course correlated with the ritualization and traditionalization of the entire socioreligious system. The extremely high spiritual and intellectual level on which the founding generations of Hutterites operated has settled now on the common denominator of a people having variable psychological abilities, and disabilities. Because the sect cannot leave any of its members behind as long as this person is able to function in the group, conversion must be obtainable. As a result this conversion experience has become intellectually nondemanding. Its emphasis has shifted from a rational level toward an understanding on the emotional level which by its very nature often defies rational assessment or conscious verbalization. Bypassing the intellectual potentials of the individual the Hutterite *Bildungsideal* is communicated on the emotional level and addresses itself to the emotional capacities of the individual. Human emotions are lodged in the Limbic system of the brain which is much older than the neocortex which is the seat of language and rationality. The Limbic system can learn but its learning is nonverbal, slower, and much less flexible than the neocortex. On the other hand its power of retention is much higher than rational learning. Inquiries which formerly reflected the rational spiritual concerns of the early Hutterites are now transmitted through feelings, rituals, attitudes, and behaviour. The primary setting of the Hutterite community and the lifelong association of its members is superbly equipped to engage in this process of communication. In a real sense the community is the vehicle of this communication process and the manifestation of its validity.

The hierarchical structure of the Hutterite community is powerfully reinforced by religious images. Sex differentiation is justified by the allegory of Adam's fall. Eve listened to the serpent and gave Adam the fruit to eat and therefore was instrumental in *perceiving* evil while Adam himself was innocently duped. Women are seen therefore as being in greater need for spiritual guidance. Their exclusion from religious offices and decision-making bodies is justified in this way.

In this fashion the very structure of the community embodies many religious sentiments. It renders them concrete, visible, and teachable in behavioural and emotional terms. This process of socialization, of course, neglects intellectual activities that deal with verbal and rational abstractions. Yet the practical resilience of Hutterites and their self-image as a successful group is enough to overcome negative intellectual self–evaluations.

Several years ago a number of Hutterite preachers visited a large western Canadian university. After having been shown around and being duly impressed by the facilities from medicine to agriculture, one would have expected them to be at least ambiguous towards their objections to higher education. On the contrary, while praising the work done at the university, they unashamedly asserted that they knew all the things that were done at the university. Their knowledge came in a different way they claimed, but was equally valid and originating from a better authority, namely God. There was more in this assertion than a simple defence against an overwhelming amount of scientific knowledge. In a very self-confident manner these preachers compared their society with the outside world and felt they came out on top. Indeed, from the Hutterite point of view, the world daily gives so many examples of its follies, false pride, vanity, and immorality that it becomes unnecessary to point out that the Hutterite way of life is immeasurably better.

The young Hutterite therefore is presented with a world view that does not allow him to compare himself with the rest of the world in unfavourable terms. If he does not laugh at the world, after all, there are many things in this world which are rather good, he nevertheless is convinced that his own culture and community is incomparably better than the strife and crime-ridden society in which his own community forms an oasis of peace.

Self-confidence and self-esteem about the validity of his own culture sustains the Hutterite personality in the face of the complex demonstrations of an industrial society. That he must engage in intellectual limitations to maintain the validity of his culture can be favourable compared to those dreadful conditions, created when man's mind is allowed to develop freely.

The Hutterite *Bildungsideal* as outlined above therefore incorporates the three functions mentioned initially. It defines a symbolic universe from which meaning can be abstracted. It makes definitive statements about the imperatives of human behaviour and it outlines the means by which the helplessness of man in the face of existential problems can be overcome. In all three of these functions the Hutterite community plays the crucial role. Without the community these functions simply cannot exist. The existence of the Hutterite community and the socialization process that prepares the individual for his participation in it are two sides of the same coin.

Yet this complementary relationship between the Hutterite community and its socialization process increasingly has come under strains and stresses. When Hutterite women complain that many if not most married women are unhappy, one might suspect that either the socialization of women toward a submissive unobtrusive role performance, or the institutionalized structure of marriage, or both, might have come under pressure. When Hutterite youths strenuously complain about the lack of education they receive and when they decry their inabilities to put into words what they perceive to be wrong in their communities, another window opens showing the difficulties of maintaining such complementary relations between community life and the socialization process. Archaic means of social control like shunning or enforcement of rules and regulations which have been applied for centuries have already lost much of their effectiveness. In the first instance they cannot be applied in the same way as in the past, and, secondly, the social context of the modern colony has modified its severity and its impact. The young Hutterite who once defected from the colony and who jokingly remarks that he better stay in the colony for a while because he gets tired of asking for forgiveness, certainly differs greatly from the individual of the past who saw the doors of hell opening to him when expelled from the community. Rational thought patterns mainly confined to economic activities cannot be kept forever separate from the socioreligious world of the community.

More and more social problems arising in the institutional world of Hutterites are looked at and assessed in rational terms. Women talk about the educational ideas of a child psychologist they had seen on television. Marriage problems are often subtly treated by the family doctor or a psychiatrist, and this treatment is tolerated by the preacher who might already have lost the knowledge of how such cases ought to be treated by traditional means. Or if he is one of the older preachers, he might have seen that the effectiveness of the old answers has greatly diminished. The black-and-white image of the world outside the Hutterite community is slowly fading away. Personal contacts with outsiders teach Hutterites that good and bad people can be found everywhere. The Hutterites' claim toward moral superiority slowly recedes with the realization that people inside and outside the Hutterite community are very much alike. While they allow for the possibility, that what makes the Hutterite community work is the religious spirit of the people living in it, they are realistic enough to see also that the communal organization of labour has a lot to do with it. There are many Hutterite colonies that are in economic difficulties and being able to assess these difficulties in rational terms, they face the realization that even people who do have the spirit nevertheless can get into economic straitjackets.

All this is to say that, as effective as the Hutterite process of socialization has been in the past, one cannot assume that it will go on unchanged into the future. Changes in the socialization process do not spell the doom of this subculture. Hutterites are constantly adjusting to new conditions. Sometimes the price they have to pay is higher than at other times. As a whole the system is able and willing to pay a price for its survival and it is this fact that greatly enhances its resilience in the fast changing world of the twentieth century.

SIX

Problems in the Family, Community, and Culture

Hutterite institutions and patterns of behaviour have become the focus of considerable sociological attention in recent years. The question, how an institutionally complete *Gemeinschaft*-culture can be maintained and kept distinct in the middle of an industrialized, fast-changing society generated interest among sociologists and anthropologists alike. But very little attention so far has been paid to Hutterite individuals filling these institutions and roles on a day to day behavioural basis. Could it be true that Hutterites in fact form a "community of Saints," as they like to call themselves, living a serene, carefree, and conflict-free life as suggested by the ideal patterns of the culture? The absence of data on crime and social problems among Hutterites seems to suggest an idyllic, if not perfect, society. Yet there is some evidence that conflict and competition, strains and stresses, are neither absent nor particularly rare among Hutterites; they seem to be exceptionally well–managed and kept out of view of outsiders.

A cultural group like the Hutterites, which over the centuries maintained a process of dissimilarity from its ethnic base as well as from its respective host society, is compelled to achieve this goal through degrees of cultural self-determination and social independence. The latter are by no means total because Hutterites

103

require a host society as a basis for their own existence, and the adaptive responses to the social and cultural environment of the host, determine, to a large extent, the degrees of cultural self-determination and social independence, that are possible.

Cultural self-determination and social independence above all require economic strength and the ability to solve one's own internal problems, whether they be economic, religious, or social. To the extent that the group must resort to outside assistance to solve its own inherent strains and stresses, such assistance endangers the legitimacy of its own institutions and consequently endangers its existence as a distinct ethnic group. The apparent absence of problems among Hutterites might be nothing more than the effect of a problem-solving mechanism hidden from the view of outsiders. In fact Hutterites have institutionalized their determination to solve their own internal problems. This went so far as to enter into contractual relations with their respective feudal hosts during the sixteenth and seventeenth centuries, stipulating clearly the boundaries beyond which Hutterites would not tolerate any interference into their internal affairs. Today societal laws, social services, and welfare measures are carefully scrutinized as to their actual and potential consequences in impeding the sociocultural independence of the group. Hutterites have found, for example, that universal hospital coverage is no threat to their cultural fabric, but old age pensions and children's allowances are. The latter are social services bypassing the Hutterite community and providing economic assistance to group members. Not only are these members partially freed from their total dependency on the resources of the group, but the institutionalized access to the resources of the group is being disturbed, leading to disunity and discontent of members not receiving such benefits.

The Hutterites' resistance to outside interference above all compelled them to build a wall of secrecy around their internal affairs. There is nothing intentionally sinister or deceptive about such secrecy, although through the centuries it has often been interpreted in a conspiratorial fashion and has given rise to a great many prejudices against them. Secrecy about one's internal affairs is an attempt to limit the flow of information to the outsider and thereby limits his means of interference. It is a simple but essential mechanism of group survival, particularly if the outside world is either very hostile or uncomfortably paternalistic.

It is from this point of view that certain data on social problems among Hutterites cannot be taken at face value but must be very carefully investigated as to their actual significance. The virtual absence of divorce among Hutterites might not readily be interpreted to mean that the Hutterite family is unusually stable and free from difficulties. It might mean that the group chooses not to have marriage counselors and courts interfere in its own social problems. Hutterite preachers have the legal power to marry their people, but they cannot divorce them. It is, therefore, perceivable that the stability of the Hutterite family is at least in part due to the refusal of the group to have its internal social problems referred to outsiders for solutions.

Statistical data, therefore, are not reliable indicators regarding the nature or the frequency of social problems among Hutterites, nor are they a reflection of the true nature of interaction among the members of the group. Survey research in most cases does not penetrate the wall of secrecy and, if it does is extremely difficult to interpret. Participant observation, case studies, and individual biographies are only of value if they are obtained from inside the wall of secrecy, that is to say, under conditions of trust. This condition puts the observer under the moral constraint not to abuse his information.

The following is an attempt to look behind the wall of secrecy and to map out some problems which Hutterites encounter in their families and communities. It is based on a combination of participant observation and individual biography. We will start with an autobiographical sketch written by a Hutterite woman at the age of twenty-two, describing her childhood and adolescent relations, the school, community work patterns, social control, and family relations.[1]

To better comprehend the background, it must be noted that the Hutterite woman who wrote this autobiography went through a profound personal crisis at the time of writing. There were three interrelated processes which preoccupied her state of mind. For at least three years she had refused to receive baptism and thereby postponed her marriage, since marriage customarily is expected soon after baptism. Secondly, she was romantically linked to a young ex-Hutterite to whom she could not get married unless he rejoined his community and became properly baptized. Moreover, the exchange of letters and the occasional meetings which she had with this young man had to be kept secret from the rest of the community and her family, placing her under considerable mental strain. Thirdly, she became involved in the fundamentalist religious orientation which this ex-Hutterite had acquired, going so far as to enroll in a correspondence Bible course. This fundamentalist orientation served her as the major vehicle of criticism toward Hutterite life and religion.

The combined results of these processes were that the woman on occasions considered leaving the community, despite the fact that her father happened to be the preacher. However, she could not bring herself to take the initiative, but began to focus on outsiders, who she hoped could provide her with a solution. One of her uncles, who had defected from a Hutterite community twenty-five years earlier and lived in California, became the focus of her desire "to be taken away." Of course the uncle never took this initiative.

It was this experience of confusion and dissatisfaction that made her see things and say things which otherwise might never have occurred to her. What to the reader might appear as rather mild statements of criticism here and there are rather remarkable statements of a vigorous young mind bewildered by the disagreeable choices that were lying ahead of her.

As it happened, the woman eventually left her family and community in the middle of the night and joined a group of ex-Hutterites nearby who maintained a quasi-Hutterite group life. She could not endure to face her parents and her community with her decision beforehand, knowing very well that if she tried, she would not be able to go through with it — not because of any coercion, but because of the moral strains and pains which such a decision would impose on everyone.

A few months later she and her boyfriend got married, and for the next few years they participated in the life patterns of the group mentioned. The unrelenting pains of having separated herself from her family and community nevertheless caught up with her. Her husband found himself in a similar position.

Eventually both rejoined the Hutterite community of the husband in a reconciliation ceremony, followed by baptism and marriage according to the Hutterite ritual. They have been seemingly solid members of this community ever since, but entertain some resentments which they keep to themselves.

The Autobiography

I can remember the time when I was going to kindergarten. This was from three to six years of age. I guess my mother and dad took good care of me the first three years.

Each year, winter or summer, we had to get up and get dressed. By eight o'clock we were on our way to kindergarten school. There we had our breakfast, but first of all we thanked the Lord for our food. After breakfast, the mother who was looking after us for the day recited a number of songs and prayers, while we repeated them with her. When we were through with this ten or fifteen minute recital, we could go out and play together until ten o'clock, at which time our dinner was brought over from the kitchen. These were only simple meals, milk with potatoes or soup. On Sunday it was special, soup with duck and fruit. When the bell rang at 11:30 a.m., all the children had to take a nap, no questions asked. Most of the time we slept because the mother was watching over us. When we got up after an hour or so, we could play until lunch time, after this we had to recite a couple of songs, say our prayers, and then we could go home by 3:00 or 3:30 p.m.

So the days dragged by, every day the same. All the enjoyment we had was when we kids played together — whatever came to our mind, hide-and-seek, tag. We could go on the swing or see-saw when there was one. We climbed fences and often tore our skirts. Oh, many things happened. One time I remember two boys, another girl, and I planned on running away from school. Sure enough, when we were alone in the afternoon when the other kids were taking a nap, we sneaked through the fence and walked away. It did not take long and an older girl followed us to take us back, and then we got such a spanking, I don't think we ever dared to run away again.

From six to seven was a wasted year as far as I am concerned.

We joined the children from seven to fifteen years old and had to help with the dishes and sweep the dining room after each meal, but I did associate only with children my own age. Rules and regulations began and were expected to be followed. When fifteen years old, we had to join the women in all the work there was to do; whenever the bell rang we had to go.

Spring is the beginning of a busy time in the colony, although daily work is carried out through the winter months. Spring brings its extra work, with house cleaning, and many are quite anxious to spring clean all the community buildings, such as the kitchen, cooler, milking parlour, school house, and church house. When all the women and girls help, it takes only two to three hours and all is clean. The girls have to do the finishing touches, like cleaning windows, or if there is something to paint or varnish.

When the garden is ready and prepared for seeding, all the women and girls age fifteen to forty-five help in cutting potatoes. It takes about two days to cut enough potatoes, that is five tons. We help plant the onions and garlic, the rest of the vegetables are seeded by the gardener. Then hoeing begins, twice a week early in June until July, at which time some of the vegetables are picked for canning. As soon as the peas are ready, they are picked and put into jars, we can about fifty to sixty jars, depending on the harvest. The same with beets and cucumbers, but cucumbers are canned in three different ways. This is the time when the girls are together most of the time during the day. In the month of July we go swimming to cool off in the river from the hot kitchen, as the girls take turns in cooking the vegetables and put them in order on shelves in the cellar. During July and August we get into the fruit. Cherries and strawberries are picked in British Columbia; in the fall, apples and plums and pears are also picked there. The rest of the fruit, like apricots and peaches, is bought. Ever so often we girls enjoyed ourselves, we sang songs together a lot, and if we didn't, our women asked us to. I guess the work goes faster. Ducks and geese are butchered in the fall, but here the men folk helped, because it took all day to clean three hundred or so.

The girl who was cooking did not help with this work because she was preparing the meals, as the head cook told her.

The relatives helped to clean the kitchen after each meal. Since we were divided into three groups, the women took turns in washing dishes and tables, as we had so many.

Girls have to begin to cook and bake when they are seventeen years of age, but with fifteen we start milking. This is a hard job and I wish the men would milk, but it seems our men will not do this.

So this all takes care of the rules we are to follow. If we don't, we are talked to and asked why, or where we have been. Unless we are sick, we have to attend to the work. The person is excused of the work in times of emergency.

This way food and clothing is provided for all who work for the colony. Even furniture is given. At the age of fifteen we get a chest to store our clothes or whatever we please.

As for the women, they do not have much to say outside their business; they have to learn to be quiet.

In the colony much talk is going on, you can be talked of in one of the two ways. In a thoughtful way and a thoughtless way, and the girl gets to hear either one. If a girl does only things which please her, she is not favoured or liked by others. She becomes a hindrance instead of a help to other girls. This covers a great area, but I will not go into details. Unless the girl becomes mindful of others, nothing will change her and she is subject to be talked of because of carelessness, and the personality shows the character she has.

I think the older women think much of how they have lived in the colony and want to set an example to the younger ones, but most of all, they are concerned with the welfare of their own children. They are happy to see their children be subject to the colony rules and regulations without complaining, and they want them to remain in the colony because security is provided for them.

Some parents really see to it that their children receive proper training, and help them under discipline, while there are those who neglect the responsibility to instruct their children.

Since I was the only girl in our family with half a dozen boys, there was always a lot of work in our home. Responsibilities were put on me very early in life. I had to wash and polish floors in a number of rooms. At the age of ten I had my own room, and I arranged it the way I wanted to. I remember when I cleaned up and did not do it nicely, mother made me go back and do it all over again. I didn't like it at that time, but this is how I have been taught and now it cannot be otherwise. I want everything nice and in order. Now I have the nicest rooms of all the girls in the colony; this is what I have heard others say too.

I needed a girl's companionship. When I was eleven years old I became close friends with Sarah. She always was so nice to me and helped wherever she could. She was only ten months older than I and had seven sisters. She knew more about the facts of life and she passed it on to me. Some of the things frightened me at first, because I did not know about them. Our parents, who should tell us about this, did not tell us children. The change from girlhood to womanhood is unknown to us.

So Sarah helped me to be better prepared to meet these changes and I was glad I was not the only one who had to face this. We got to know each other quite well, for we were cleaning chicken eggs every evening for some years. Sarah is married now, nevertheless we are very happy to see each other; and if we have time, we enjoy to recall the past and talk about bygone days which were wonderful. We shared our joys and disappointments, which made double the joy and half the sorrow. We also had a lot of fun in cleaning three to six pails of eggs daily. On our birthdays we gave each other gifts, not much, but one time Sarah cross-stitched for me a pair of pillowcases with my initials on. I still have them and I still have the presents dad gave me and Sarah at Christmas time, for cleaning eggs. Often we had ice cream or a chocolate bar. In the summer evenings we would go for a walk. Sometimes boys followed us and we all walked home together.

I guess I was thirteen years old when I had my first date. And this same boy, who is here on the colony, is still after me; he wants me to be his wife. There is nothing more his mother and all the family would like better than this to happen, but ...

I remember I was still very young when my mother and dad had an argument. I didn't want to hear what they said; I thought to myself, "I am going to think twice before I will marry."

I cannot stand it when people argue and get angry, sometimes over nothing. I know it is in our nature, but we must learn to control our emotions. Our parents could teach us children by telling us we may quarrel as much as we like, if we hear mother and dad quarrel, but if mother and dad don't, then we children are not supposed to quarrel with each other.

Now I would not know how much love is received by either husband or wife. I think it is taken for granted, while others are quite happy when a woman gives birth to a child. As soon as the woman knows she is expecting a child, preparations are made for the little one with the help of the husband. Everyone thinks it is quite natural, I guess. Young parents receive gifts, help, and advice, and anyone may feel free to give it. Clothes and bedding is provided for the child and given by the boss in the colony. One woman is elected to cook extra and special meals for the mother for four weeks. Her work in the colony is carried out by others for the next thirteen weeks. After that she slowly begins to join in the work with the rest.

Husband and wife support each other in the colony. It all depends on the person, and at times the man does not receive the stand he could have, on account of his wife. Then again, in some cases it is quite the opposite, on account of his wife the man might get a job because of the help and influence given by his wife.

Sometimes the man will refuse the position or job he is appointed to, because he didn't like it or would not go for this particular job. I guess this causes disagreement between husband and wife, especially if he is careless and tries to get by without a job, and someone else is elected. Then I guess husband and wife are faced daily with decisions, and if there is no consideration or understanding, this can cause a quarrel between the two. But not all people have the same personalities; much depends on how you are taught.

As the parents are, this is how the children will be. They lose all respect even when the parents are around.

I could tell of incidents with my brothers and me. Once my brother and I had a long discussion; he can be understanding if he wants to, but he tried not to. I came to the point of speaking harshly to him and it ended in an argument, but at night before going to bed, I just waited for my brother to get home. It was not easy to apologize, but after this I was so happy, I had peace in my heart. Doing this helps me to be conscious of the fact that I must be careful, because there are so many who watch me.

I am sure if all of us in our family would obey this rule, we would have a happier home, but how do they burden and discourage dad by doing things he does not approve of. I am reminded of the verse: "Train a child in the way he should go, and when he is old, he will not depart from it." Proverbs 22:6.

If only dad would sit down and take the time and speak in love and explain the wasted time and money spent on liquor, smoking, going to shows, and the many other evil influences that have the tendency to lead wayward. I am so glad the colony objects to this; that is how I have been kept from youth until I was old enough to choose. More could be said about this, but this is sufficient for now. Anyway, I still have to see my first show. 1 Cor. 6:19-20.

I like to recall my school days, taught by our good teacher who was teaching at our colony for a long time. Much respect, praise, and honour was given to him. Not only by the many school children who were going through grades one to eight, but also by the inspector, for the best teaching in colonies and regular attendance by the children. Our daily record proved to be so.

These were eight wonderful years of much study and strict discipline, and all that goes with it. I am thankful for all this now and the way I was taught in school. I have learned many valuable lessons, because our teacher talked to us about the Bible story, which he read to us every morning. It was then that we began to read the Bible each day, and I still do so, not only out of habit, but to satisfy my longing and searching heart. What a help this has been and so many questions have been answered.

Our teacher strongly emphasized the wrong and right. He was very much against taking what is not ours — he called it stealing — or speaking untruths (lying), dishonesty, cheating, using bad language (swearing), bad habits, such as drinking, smoking, etc. If we were found out doing any of these while still going to school, we did not get by, we had to face the consequences. Our teacher not only taught the subjects in school, but also how to build an honest and upright character. How glad and thankful I am for having had a teacher like him who was strict and demanded obedience upon his word. In English periods we were not supposed to speak German, and in German not to speak English. We had enjoyable times as well. We had parties on special occasions — like on Valentine's Day, we kids sent each other cards. On the teacher's birthday we played a number of games, and each child gave him a present. Then we had lunch.

As soon as spring weather was here we played baseball, and most of the year round. We did have some excellent ball players, girls as well as boys. Picnic in June the last was always an exciting time for all, even for those older boys and girls who were already out of school. They came to join the ball games. We picked two teams and the one who had the most innings was the winner. We also had different games, like racing, jumping in a sack, threading needles while walking, walking with a potato on head. Everyone tried to be a winner in order to win a prize.

At Christmas time we had programs, and every child had to know their pieces well. We had to act when on stage, and not just stand. Some of the plays were a great success. Once we had to charge fifty cents a seat from the visitors who came from far and near. Still this did not stop them from coming, the school house was just packed, the children had to stand.

The teacher who came after our longtime teacher left and moved away also had a program he asked us to join, even those who were out of school. So there were six girls and four boys who took part in singing the Christmas carols. We could hardly believe our young people could perform such good singing.

In the winter time we were sleigh riding on the hill. Most every child had something to go down on, even if it was only a piece of tin. I had many rides with boys. In the evening when we were too loud with shouting, the German schoolteacher came and sent us home and we all had to go. When the ice was thick on the duckpond, the kids were on, the boys who had skates were skating.

In the summer time we went swimming in the river — we were more in the water than out on some days. As we grew older, we girls did not like to swim with the boys, as they were too rough. The teacher told the boys to leave when the girls came for a swim, or else look for another place. Sure enough, the boys found another place, a good place, where they could dive, and so we were left alone. Our teacher was careful, he did not want anything to happen which he did not approve of. He was responsible for us kids and rightly so. He felt it was his duty.

My dad was German schoolteacher at my time and he taught us in this same way. I guess he resembled his father very much. I do respect him for his rightness and honesty, which he leaves as an example for his children to follow.

The Analysis

The first part of the woman's autobiography is concerned with her childhood experiences in the kindergarten or "little school." There is an air of monotony in the narrative which is rather remarkable, in that a twenty-two-year-old is able to remember it with the intensity that flows from her account. It seems to reflect a lack of outside stimulation during this period of her childhood. It is rather interesting to inquire why a couple of youngsters at such an early age might be motivated to run away from the community, which after all constitutes the totality of the world known to them. While there might be any number of situational factors that might have triggered such behaviour in this particular case, some important contributory social conditions nevertheless seem worthwhile to be investigated.

When children run away from their family it is usually either the attraction of some idealized world beyond the boundaries of the family and community, or the repulsion of some experiences or relations within the family, or both. These young Hutterites had no conception of the world beyond the boundaries of their community, therefore no focus of attraction could be formed. If one assumes that they were repulsed by relations in their school, family, or community, one would have to find conditions leading to such feelings of repulsion in some patters of these institutions.

For the young Hutterite, entering the little school coincides with the partial withdrawal of parental affection and the affection of relatives. He is bound to lose at least part of his sense of security. The adjustment to a set of impersonal rules, to changing, nonaffectionate supervisors, combined with a lack of outside stimulation, might very well not only produce a feeling of monotony, but one of temporary rejection and dissatisfaction as well.

According to the testimony of the woman, corporal punishment seemed to be an effective treatment. Physical punishment at this age can only be responded to by total submission of the child. To the extent that this submission is achieved, it can possibly substitute for the missing emotional states previously induced by affection. Submission, it should be remembered, is a rather comfortable, if passive, emotional state, particularly if it is directed toward a powerful and admired figure, as fathers at this stage usually are.

Hutterites are consciously aware of the fact that love alone is insufficient as a mode of socialization for the type of personality which they envision. Physical punishment of children is seen as a means to suppress man's carnal nature, its animal desires and wants, until the time arrives when knowledge and reason can take over these functions. In this sense, their conception is not very different from Freud's "Id," "Ego" and "Superego" and George Herbert Mead's "I" and "Me" (Mead 1934). The Hutterites' belief in the other side to human nature, consisting of knowledge, reason, and faith, all of which are acquired in the social context through socialization and education, is strikingly similar to that of Freud and Mead. The necessity for physical punishment is based on the assumption that the carnal part of man's nature develops very quickly after birth, while the acquisition of reason, knowledge, and morality takes a very long time. Corporal punishment, therefore, is a temporary tool to suppress asocial behaviour until reason and morality are developed and act as a guide to conduct. While it is assumed that a child of fifteen has fully developed these means of self-control, and therefore corporal punishment ceases at this age, the changeover from the control of behaviour through corporal punishment to individual self-control is seen as proceeding throughout childhood, but at different speeds. Most important, Hutterites have clearly staked out the limitations of corporal punishment by not making any assumption that corporal punishment could teach anything. While it is effective in temporarily preventing unacceptable behaviour, a change in behaviour toward more acceptable forms can only be achieved through an increase in self-control, for which the appropriate means are education and socialization.

Education, aiming at the acquisition of knowledge and reason, is a very modern concept and became widespread in Western societies only after the Enlightenment. The rationality of the Enlightenment rejected religious and traditional legitimacies as the sole criteria of the validity of social and physical phenomena and substituted a new concept, that of human credibility. What is credible to the human mind on the basis of existential experiences became the main criteria in the construction of social institutions and human relations.

Hutterites were never touched by the spirit of the Enlightenment due to their geographic and social isolation at the time. Their understanding of what constitutes knowledge and reason is very different from those concepts generated by the Enlightenment. It is based on conceptions essentially going back to the Protestant Reformation two centuries before the Enlightenment. The religious tenets of Anabaptism adapted to and sanctified in the traditionally oriented communal lifestyle of the group provide the raw material of what constitutes knowledge and reason among Hutterites.

The woman's account of her experiences in school sheds some light on some of these fundamental differences and problems. The Hutterite school is a form of public school, in the sense that the teacher is appointed by the local School Board and teaches the provincial curriculum. The school is, however, located on community property, maintained by the community, and forms part of the communal set of interaction. The German school solely conducted by Hutterites themselves for about one hour every day is mainly concerned with the reading and writing of German, the memorization of Bible quotations, and singing. The teaching methods of the German school and its curriculum are highly ritualized, and the woman mentions this school only in passing, when at one time she refers to her father being the school teacher at the time.

In contrast the public school teacher referred to in her autobiography was a much respected Mennonite, who perfectly spoke and understood the Hutterite German dialect. What is so remarkable in her description of him is her emphasis on moral

definitions like lying, stealing, etc. She describes these definitions as if they were enormous moral discoveries never before
heard of in Hutterite communities. While Hutterites would
strenuously argue that lying and stealing, etcetera, are strictly
disapproved of and severely punished if engaged in, the conceptual context in which this Mennonite teacher approached such
definitions seems to have surprised the woman very much.

Indeed, Hutterite socialization is geared not so much to the
teaching of general moral principles from which conscious
moral decisions can be deduced, but to teach situationally appropriate norms containing specific aspects of behaviour and morality.

The Hutterite situational normative approach toward behaviour to a large extent lacks internal rational logic and consistency. Norms have developed historically, and while their
development certainly was guided by values, historical accidents
and precedents injected inconsistencies and illogicalities that
accumulatively defined normative behaviour and morality in
nonlogical specifics. The intense and lifelong primary interaction in Hutterite communities, of course, is the major vehicle by
which this process takes place.

What Hutterites call knowledge and reason therefore is, in
fact, codified in situational norms, and it is these situational
norms which not only apply to all behavioural situations in
their communities, but they also form the content of much of
their education and all of their socialization. These norms need
not be logically consistent, in the sense in which conduct deduced from generalized principles is understood to be consistent,
but yield to some social, religious, or traditional consistency
which might appear arbitrary if not properly understood by the
observer. An example might shed some light on this problem.
All Hutterites are required to attend their common dining hall
for their daily meals unless someone is temporarily excused because of illness or other legitimate reasons. The two preachers of
each community, however, are exempted from this common
norm on the basis of a historical precedent going back to the year
1537, when a disagreement over the eating facilities of preachers
was solved by allowing preachers to take their meals in their
own homes. While the logic of communal meals is powerfully

supported by religious principles (the Lord's supper, etcetera) and by the whole communal orientation of the group, this logic as a general principle of conduct nevertheless is being rendered useless by a historical precedent which justified a deviation from the norm for specific persons. Given the communal emphasis of Hutterites regarding the sharing of spiritual things and material goods between man and man, nothing can be more contradictory than excepting "the servants of the word" (the preachers) from participating in the communal meals of their flock. Yet this behaviour is strictly observed in all Hutterite communities.

Jewish Law, in comparison, which originated to a large extent as situational norms (The Commandments, etcetera) similar to those of Hutterites, was subsequently subjected to profound philosophical analyses to elicit its basic principles by generation after generation of scholars. The principles so abstracted not only established the universal character of Jewish Law, but also gave Jews of all ages the means of modifying their behaviour according to new situations, yet remaining within the principles of the Law.

In contrast, scholarship among Hutterites, which was profound during the sixteenth century, died out in the seventeenth century and has never been revived. Thus, with religious scholarship at a standstill for more than 300 years, social adaptation with the help of continuous religious reinterpretations is impossible. The absence of any creative religious activity facilitated the emergence of traditionalism among Hutterites, which was already well under way at the end of the sixteenth century. The issuing of community ordinances during the latter half of the sixteenth century, and the periodic renewal of these same ordinances time after time, testifies to a process of progressive traditionalization of the group.

But traditionalism is nonadaptive in a fast changing environment demanding flexible responses to changing conditions. Successive migrations and the industrial revolution rendered traditional Hutterite designs obsolete. It was at this point that Hutterites decided on the two-prong development of their culture. By this strategy they tried to maintain a traditional configuration wherever this was possible, and to modernize wherever such modernization contributed to the survival of the group as a whole. Modernization, of course, affected mostly the economic institution, and traditionalism was maintained predominantly in social relations and religious observances. The educational institution was caught somewhat in the middle, insofar as it became necessary to educate Hutterites for adequate roles in their traditional as well as in their modernized institutions.

There is, however, a basic incompatibility between traditionalism and modernization which poses a dire threat to the group. The manager of a Hutterite community, for example, handles a cash flow of more than a million dollars a year, which, if done adequately, as is most often the case, requires countless well-informed, hard-nosed decisions. To the extent that he is capable of complying he is also required to accept traditional rules that forbid him to possess a radio or T.V. and even forbid him to hang a picture on the wall of his bedroom. How is the credibility of these traditional rules maintained?

The woman's description of her family relations throws some light on this question. She feels that they could have had a happier home if only the sons had not discouraged and burdened their father with "wasted time and money spent on liquor, smoking, going to shows." Then she laments the fact that the family cannot sit down together "to speak in love" and discuss these matters. Hutterites are unable to justify their norms in other than religious and traditional terms. But these terms have lost much of their credibility because religious scholarship has failed to update them, and the modernizing influences which have found entry into the communities have rendered many of them obsolete.

Faced with the dilemma of not being able to justify their norms in modern, more credible terms, Hutterites have only one choice if they want to maintain their group life: to compartmentalize the contradictions and leave them unexamined. Much of the socialization process, therefore, is geared toward such compartmentalization of contradictory elements. The emphasis on behavioural norms and the de-emphasis on abstract principles and values produces a personality structure which is well-equipped to endure such compartmentalization without suffering too many anxieties.

As a result, the Hutterite personality structure differs markedly from those encountered in most parts of North American society. Hutterites emphasize appropriate *behaviour*, not so much appropriate motives, attitudes, intentions, or generalized values. They look for and judge a person by his or her *behaviour*, not so much by his or her attitudes. A silent prayer is no prayer at all; one must be able to hear the spoken word.

With only a slight exaggeration, one can say that a Hutterite is free to think what he pleases; as long as he *behaves* according to prescribed and appropriate norms, he is fully acceptable to his fellow men. Norms, as the embodiment of religious and traditional legitimacies, do not require the mental consensus of Hutterites as they require behavioural adherence.

George Herbert Mead's notion of the "generalized other" as a level of orientation from which to judge oneself and others seems relatively localized among Hutterites. The reference group is the community, and there is little beyond the group which a Hutterite can systematically build into his personality.

The scarcity of role models and role varieties not only perpetuates a relatively homogeneous personality structure within the communities, but of course limits the development of individual capacities and talents to the predominant model. In this sense Hutterites put intellectual restrictions onto themselves and their offspring. They recognize very clearly that intellectual variety among their members creates problems in communal decision-making and conduct detrimental to the cooperative functioning of the communities. "Being of one mind," the desired goal of the religious and economic community, is paid for by intellectual and educational limitations imposed on the Hutterite individual. Whether he suffers from such limitations or whether he enjoys them is dependent on the degree of objectivity, or lack of it, with which the individual can see himself as being distinct from the group.

The group's preoccupation with behavioural specifics of course enhances the forces of social control enormously. The detailed knowledge of each other's behavioural obligations injects an intensity into the process of social control which forced the woman to say after she apologized to her brother: "Doing this helps me to be conscious of the fact that I must be careful, because there are so many who watch me."

The forces of social control among Hutterites do not allow for any withdrawal or escape, save that of leaving the community. The individual has no other choice but to live with it, and to swim against the stream might be possible only for a limited period of time. While many Hutterites try it, it usually exceeds the powers of any individual if it is attempted for life. The social cohesion of the group rests on the simple fact that the group at all times is stronger than any individual. Once the individual has been socialized, it has the power to bend him to meet its own terms or to force him out. The latter decision is extremely painful and, as shown in this inquiry, hardly a solution for life.

SEVEN

Psychophysiological Typologies

The aim of this chapter is to present and analyse preliminary information relating to an unusual form of psychophysiological differentiation which Hutterites ascribe to inheritance, and which we have encountered during anthropological fieldwork among them. Our attention was drawn to the particular form of differentiation during fieldwork among one of the three main divisions of the Hutterites, the *Dariusleut*, although we have since confirmed that the phenomenon is present in the other two sections of the sect, the *Schmiedeleut* and *Lehrerleut*. In the course of conversations, conducted in the South German dialect used by Hutterites, which originated in the Tyrol and Carinthia but which has been augmented by loan words acquired during the successive wanderings of the sect through Eastern Europe and Russia, we encountered the term *Sabôt*, the use of which we have not been able so far to detect any written example. The term, the precise etymology of which remains obscure, is apparently not found in Russian, but there are some indications that it might be related to the archaic German word *Schabab* (from *schab ab*, "go away, pull away") defined by Luther as, among other things, a "person with whom one wishes to have nothing to do" (Zieglschmid 1943: 1008). The term is only used by Hutterites in relatively private circumstances when speaking among themselves, and usually is not employed in direct conversation with persons who are being differentiated by the ascription of characteristics associated with a particular *Sabôt*. After our discovery of the term we encountered some marked reluctance in identifying or explaining the word itself, as well as the underlying concepts associated with its use. The term has not been noted by other writers describing the Hutterites, and is, we believe, totally absent from the now substantial literature relating to this sect.

The term *Sabôt* denotes diverse groups of individuals who are designated by names such as *Tatela, Stuhna, Juba, Jana, Fritzen, Franzen, Benjaminita*, etcetera.[1] Again these names do not appear in written form, with the single exception of *Tatela*, a variant of which appears in an early list of Hutterite immigrants to North America derived from a list of passengers on a boat, and is included almost like a nickname of an individual male.

The *Sabôt* designates a group of individuals who bear common physical and psychological characteristics which are believed to be inherited. Among the physical traits are such features as height, complexion, growth of hair (especially the beard or baldness), habitual posture, body morphology, susceptibility to disease, facial features, and voice patterns. It should be noted that these characteristics are only noticed when several of them are present in the same individual, and are recognized in this combination. It must also be observed, however, that not all Hutterites will be perceived as bearing any recognizable combination of these features, and therefore such persons will not be labelled as belonging to any *Sabôt*.

At the same time as the *Sabôt* is defined in terms of common physical traits there is also an attribution of common personality characteristics. Thus different *Sabôt* will be said to be identified as outgoing, or outspoken, or aggressive. Some *Sabôt* will be seen to provide leaders, whilst others will comprise followers; some will be seen to be secretive, whilst others are said to be sly. However, the same personality characteristic that is defined negatively by nonmembers, will be construed positively by people who identify themselves as belonging to a *Sabôt*; thus a group known generally to the community as "sly" will describe themselves as "smart."

There is a strong indication that the verbal descriptions which Hutterites give relative to the psychological characteristics of any *Sabôt* are rather incomplete. Such terms as "secretive" and "sly," which are used to describe the psychological characteristics of a particular *Sabôt*, are only a shorthand version of a complex and holistic personality structure which is spontaneously recognized and understood. The basis of this understanding is found in the lifelong experience that a Hutterite individual has with people of a particular *Sabôt*. It would appear that Hutterite informants have some difficulty in describing the full personality structure of each *Sabôt*, which may in part be due to their unfamiliarity with different terms relating to human personality, but is, we believe, also due to some reluctance to breach the principle of group solidarity by discussing what may be perceived as negative characteristics with persons who are not members of the sect. In any case the result of this hesitance is that only a few adjectives can be elicited to cover the complexity that seems to be associated with each *Sabôt*. Some of the characteristics, such as the habitual posture of individuals of a given *Sabôt*, will have been perceived on a subconscious level, and will not have been generally discussed in conversations.

Hutterites who were asked how they would be able to recognize the particular *Sabôt* of a given member of the sect whom they had never met before, would respond that recognition would come as a spontaneous reaction to appearance, speech, voice-patterns, and mannerisms. It must be said that even to the relatively untrained eye of the investigators, not fully attuned to Hutterite cultural experience, there are nonetheless certain physical characteristics including the lower physiognomy, patterns of obesity, etcetera, which are strikingly similar between various members of the sect. This process of impressionistic recognition obtains some credibility by the fact that Hutterite informants also claim vehemently that certain individuals whom they encounter are not classifiable in this sense at all.

The origins of these perceived psychophysiological patterns in at least half the *Sabôt* we observed are traced by Hutterites to specific ancestors who showed these characteristics in a somewhat pure form, and seem to have been celebrated for them. Stuhna, for example, are traced to a female ancestor named Justina. The same is true with respect to the Tatela and the Fritzen. There is no suggestion that one must be a direct descendent of these specific individuals in order to display these characteristics and to be attributed to a particular *Sabôt*. However, these characteristics are popularly associated with a particular family name, which was also borne by the eponymous ancestor, and therefore an individual displaying these traits, and who is described as belonging to the *Sabôt* in question, will be descended either in the male or female line from some recent ancestor bearing that family name.

We should observe that since some of the *Sabôt* are to be found in all three *Leut*, which have not generally intermarried during the past century, it may be assumed that these *Sabôt* probably go back as a recognized grouping to well before 1870, and that the traits so distinguished were already identifiable at that time, even though the person from whom the *Sabôt* presently derives its name was not yet alive at the time of the separation into *Leut*.

One of the major functions of the concept of the *Sabôt* seems to be in the area of self-identification. Individual Hutterites identify themselves with the characteristics recognized in the group labelled by such names as Stuhna, Franzen, etcetera, and this identification is always positive. Even generally negative characteristics such as a susceptibility to illness meet a great degree of tolerance and do not incur any feeling of guilt, on the part of the person so afflicted. In this sense the *Sabôt* offers role-models for behaviour. This system of role-models seems to be superimposed on the existing set of qualities present in an individual who provides an example for emulation. Schludermann and Schludermann (1975) have shown that Hutterites are likely to model themselves on parents or on other individuals who possess certain characteristics or ideals. However any single individual who might be chosen as a model for emulation will necessarily only possess a number of the qualities which are highly valued in Hutterite society. The identification with a *Sabôt* offers an opportunity to add a combination of characteristics with which the individual might choose to identify.

The labelling of an individual as belonging to a particular *Sabôt* is by no means purely a matter of choice. Indeed in a father/son or mother/daughter relationship, where there is some resemblance between the generations, it is impossible for the individual to escape from the label borne by the parent whom he or she resembles. Other characteristics that may have been inherited will be ignored in this labelling process. It might also be stressed that some of the characteristics which might at first sight seem to be the occasion for stigma rather than esteem, such as small stature, are in fact often valued because they form part of Hutterite human tradition. In this way the *Sabôt* does not bestow on its members any permanent stigma of inferiority: it may however on occasion be used as a form of negative stereotyping by individuals in situations of conflict. Such negative stigmatization is, however, usually temporary; indeed, in Hutterite society one detects a general proscription against negative confrontation in face-to-face situations. This proscription is often defined in terms of religious obligation, but the same pattern of avoidance of face-to-face conflict is, of course, common to many small group situations, especially where a group is defined by the outside world as a minority, or may itself choose to define its separation as the religiously privileged Elect.

In spite of the above, the reference to the *Sabôt* may in fact be made by a member of the group, in conversation with one or more fellow members, and the descriptive terms used may be quite uncomplimentary. In this way the *Sabôt* serves as a means of expressing hostility, albeit in a covert form. At the level of the sect as a whole, the existence of the various *Sabôt* reduces the multitude of possible personality structures to a few that are well known. This permits the formation of stereotyped expectations. At the same time the rest of the community, being fully aware of these expectations or obligations, can treat a given member of a *Sabôt* with a considerable measure of predictability regarding his behaviour. In a traditionally oriented society, where there is a high degree of required conformity, such obligations and expectations are extremely important for the maintenance of order.

In spite of the sociocultural significance of the *Sabôt*, Hutterites ascribe the existence of such differentiation to inheritance. The method by which this ascription is obtained is necessarily impressionistic, and as such is subject to considerable doubt when it is put forward as a scientific tool. Hutterites are not unique in recognizing psychophysiological differences impressionistically. The ancient Greeks had a repertoire of thirty-six different character-structures which were employed in their drama, and which were depicted on stage in such a way that the audience would immediately recognize them from their appearance. It is also generally understood that much medical diagnosis proceeds from an initial impressionistic appraisal by the doctor, simply on the basis of the patient's appearance, and this is only later followed up by specific examinations of, perhaps, a part of the anatomy. Scholars of Greek drama and physicians alike have some difficulty in verbalizing the characteristics which they utilize. Exact quantified measurements tend to miss many characteristics which are readily available on an impressionistic basis. A particular form of the head, for example, which will be immediately recognized impressionistically, might not show up in a quantified formula.

The possibility that psychophysiological structures exist was scientifically treated among others by the German psychologist Kretschmer (1936) and by the American scholar Sheldon (1944). These theories have never found general acceptance in North American academic circles. It seems, however, that the phenomenon of the *Sabôt*, which Hutterites recognize in their highly inbred population, might justify re-examination of the possibility that psychophysiological structures indeed exist, and that these might be passed on through hereditary mechanisms. Such processes as the "founder's effect" in migratory populations, the reduction of variability through inbreeding, gene flow and gene drift, are well recognized in human populations (Weiss & Mann 1978: 343-50), although little is known about the precise application of these biological mechanisms to the unity of physique and temperament or character.

Since the Hutterites perceive these characteristics to be a consequence of inheritance, we will present some unique population parameters found among Hutterites which could possibly facilitate the emergence of such psychophysiological groupings. But we do not consider these parameters as proving the inheritability of these characteristics nor are we able to confirm from our present research that Hutterite perceptions are indeed grounded in an empirically verifiable reality — the data for such an investigation are not available to us at this time. We can, however, attest to the certitude with which Hutterites discuss the phenomenon, and we believe that it merits precise examination in the future.

The Hutterite population has shown unique characteristics: the 4.12 percent annual growth has been discussed on several occasions, but other important features such as the high degree of inbreeding and genetic drift, and the repeated incidence of the founder's effect have not attracted the attention of social scientists. Present-day Hutterites are differentiated by three endogamous divisions, the so-called *Leut* referred to above, whose origins go back to the migratory experience of the 1870s. They in fact derive from social experiments in Russia prior to emigration, during which a number of attempts were made by different groups to reinstitute the traditional patterns of the sharing of all worldly goods, the *Guetergemeinschaft*, which had been abandoned between 1818 and 1854. This gave rise to some degree of demographic differentiation which was continued in North America and survives to the present day. The process of relocation on this continent led to the formation of three different segments, which became the ancestral groups of the three *Leut*.

When the Hutterites arrived in North America they each bore one of eighteen surnames which had been transmitted patrilineally from individuals who had borne the same name at the time the sect had revived the practice of the communal sharing of property in 1760. Of these eighteen surnames, four have since died out in the male line. Only five of the surnames are common to all three *Leut*, and there is one surname unique to the *Dariusleut* and another confined to the *Lehrerleut*; yet two more are only to be found among the *Schmiedeleut*. Five new surnames have been added through conversions during the present century, but are so far borne by only an insignificant element of the present Hutterite population. A.P. Mange (1964: 104-33) reported that these eighteen family names were derived from only sixty-eight Hutterite individuals living in the second half of the eighteenth century. Many of these were already related to each other in numerous ways. Steinberg et al. (1967: 274) traced the remote ancestors of the present day Hutterites to ninety-two people of whom only twenty-nine could not be shown to be related to any other person in the group. The remaining sixty-three represented various constellations of relationships ranging from parent/child (three pairs) and siblings (seven pairs) through third cousins (one pair).

This restricted gene pool which was separated from the wider population in 1760 may be expected to show the phenomenon known as the "founder's effect," which designates the difference in gene frequencies between the migrating group and the parent group from which it has been derived. As Martin (1969) has shown the founder effect has recurred within the Hutterite population on several occasions over the past two centuries.

The psychological background of the founding ancestors of present day Hutterites is of particular interest, due to the presence of selective factors which seem to have led to certain psychological uniformities in this group. The ancestral group which Martin and Mange describe biologically consisted of a very few individuals belonging to the so-called "Old" Hutterites. This group existed since the early 1500s, and later migrated to Hungary and Transylvania; over the following two hundred years they had been largely assimilated into the native population of that region. The last remnants of these Old Hutterites were subjected to severe forms of persecution in the 1740s and 1750s, which resulted in the conversion to the Catholic faith of all but a few individuals, who were prepared to endure severe hardships while maintaining their religious faith. These individuals were joined by a group of inhabitants of Carinthia, who in 1750 had converted to the Lutheran faith, in a country which was almost exclusively Catholic. The Catholic authorities tried to subdue this Lutheran movement by first confiscating all their religious writings, and secondly by threatening forced migration to the eastern parts of the Austrian Empire. For a number of Lutherans these threats were sufficient inducement for them to return to Catholicism; the remainder stuck to their religious convictions.

When further threats proved to be ineffective, these Lutherans were arrested and their belongings confiscated. After a four months' delay in prison, where they were offered the opportunity to recant, they were finally shipped several hundred miles eastward to the Transylvanian city of Szaszvaros, where they were supposed to be resettled. Under orders of the Catholic authorities, the settlers were to take an oath of loyalty to the Austrian Crown. While most of the migrants eventually consented to this oath, a small group refused. They were punished by not receiving land and monies from the Crown, nor did they ever receive any compensation for their confiscated belongings in Carinthia. When this small group proved to be too troublesome for the authorities, due to its influence on other settlers, they were forcefully dispersed over the country. As we have seen, by accident, some of these Carinthians came in contact with some of the remaining Old Hutterites. Under the influence of the religious ideas of the Hutterites, these two groups combined, and in 1761 spontaneously reinstated the *Guetergemeinschaft* among themselves. When finally the persecution began to catch up with this group as well, they boldly packed their belongings onto wagons, and fled across the Transylvanian Alps to Rumania, from where they later migrated to Russia. About forty persons recruited from Hutterite settlements who earlier were converted to Catholicism joined the group in 1782. These two groups form the ancestral origin of all present day Hutterites.

It is clear that these individuals did possess extraordinary qualities of perseverance, of courage, of initiative, and even of obstinacy. Invoking the degree of punishment as they did, by remaining faithful to a religious ideology which they themselves had chosen, demanded strong personalities, willpower, and a sense of identity, which allowed them to pit themselves against overpowering adverse forces. The composition of these groups was established through successive self-selective processes where individuals refused to yield to the persecution imposed on them. As the Hutterite population diminished in size at each point in this historical process of persecution, the surviving remnants showed a high degree of uniformity in those psychological characteristics that were indispensable for defying the authorities. It is not too far-fetched to assume, therefore, that a physiological founder's effect incorporating these characteristics might very well be present in contemporary Hutterite society.

We have earlier mentioned that there are only fourteen surviving Hutterite surnames; these are by no means evenly distributed through the sect: indeed four or five of them seem to dominate in the list of members. The proliferation of some family names relative to others seems to indicate a considerable gene flow among Hutterites. "Gene flow" is the transfer of inheritable material from one group to another through matings that decrease differences between populations, making them more alike genetically. This effect among Hutterites has been intensively studied by a number of researchers (Mange 1964; Kurczynski 1969; Vana 1974; Weeks 1977). The data of Steinberg et al. (1967) offers considerable evidence to indicate the effects of gene flow among Hutterites. Thus an investigation into four colonies existing at the beginning of this century showed that each of these colonies is becoming more like its subsequently founded offspring colonies, than were the four original colonies relative to each other.

There are patterns of preferential intermarriage between colonies due to factors of social proximity, geographical distance, and economic success and failure (which give rise to a reluctance of women to marry spouses belonging to colonies where the living standards are perceived to be lower). Steinberg et al. (1967: 271-73) have calculated the coefficient of inbreeding[2] for a sample of *Schmiedeleut* and *Lehrerleut*. Six hundred and sixty *Schmiedeleut* and 618 *Lehrerleut* matings that met the criteria of having sufficiently complete genealogical records, and of having occurred in one of the colonies formed in the United States, provided the data for calculating the co-efficient, which for the *Schmiedeleut* sample turned out to be .0211, and that for the *Lehrerleut* was determined at .0255. The Roman Catholic population in the United States, for example, has an inbreeding co-efficient of .00001-.0001, whilst the Ramah Navajo have a similar co-efficient of .001-.01 (Reid 1973). The highly inbred population of the South Atlantic island of Tristan de Cunha prior to its evacuation in the 1960s showed a co-efficient of .048 (Weiss & Mann 1978: 349-50). There is no doubt that the Hutterite population shows a somewhat high co-efficient of inbreeding, but for the full biological significance of this phenomenon we refer the reader to Steinberg et al. (1967).

Finally we must remember that the population increase of Hutterites since their arrival in North America has been one of the highest in the world: 4.12 percent per annum (Eaton & Mayer, 1954). Only recently have there been indications that this enormous growth is declining (see Chapter 9). It must also be noted that the increase, at least between the years 1880 and 1964, proceeded in the form of a stable population growth, which is an unusual phenomenon for a natural population. At the same time this produces a broad population base within a few generations. From 440 persons in 1880, the population has increased to about 28,000 in 1985.

In this chapter we have suggested that the ancestral group of the present day Hutterite population possibly displayed a high degree of psychological uniformity, due to the selective processes that led to this group's appearance in history. At the same time Martin has shown, from the standpoint of biology, that there has been a repeated founder's effect, and that there are also present a high degree of inbreeding, gene flow, and genetic drift. Our discovery of the concept of the *Sabôt* coincides with unique population parameters. It therefore suggests a relationship, which, however, we are unable to verify at this moment. We put this proposition forward so that other scientists might examine it, and perhaps look for comparable material in other populations. What makes the Hutterites particularly suitable for further investigations into these problems is the isolation of the group through history, and the particular cultural practices which have precluded the intervention of such factors as differential nutrition, education, religion, socioeconomic status, varied health services, etcetera, variables which might impede the analysis of this phenomenon elsewhere. The testing of this hypothesis, if successful, would have considerable theoretical importance, particularly for students working in the area of personality and culture.

PART III

Demographic Dynamics

This section analyses the dynamics of Hutterite society through the application of a "demographic theory." Hutterites, having had one of the highest rates of natural increase in the world, channelled their investments derived from an up-to-date productive system into the financing of their enormous population increase while at the same time minimizing home consumption. In chapter 8, based on research that began in the 1960s, a model showing the particular Hutterite application to this "demographic theory" is developed. New data have been added that indicate to what extent this original model has been changed up to the mid-1980s. Chapter 9 documents a decline in Hutterite population growth since the mid-1960s and examines a number of structural and social variables which seem to have as yet unknown effects on the previously established dynamic equilibrium of Hutterite communities. In a postscript to chapter 9, additional data recently acquired documenting the nature and magnitude of the decline in population growth is presented. Current research is still ongoing and only a small portion has been finalized, so that a complete and comprehensive account of the Hutterite demographic situation in the 1980s was unavailable at this time. The material presented here does give an indication of the adaptive changes that Hutterites must make in the near future to maintain their internal cohesion.

EIGHT

A "Demographic" Theory of Hutterite Population Growth

The population growth of Hutterites was studied by Joseph Eaton and Albert Mayer in the 1950s as part of a larger study on cultural and psychiatric factors in the mental health of the Hutterites. They gathered their demographic data from two sources. First they consulted the United States census data of 1880 and checked the reliability of these data with numerous private documents and colony histories. They found that the data gathered by census enumerators in 1880 were extremely accurate. The combination of these data with Hutterite records made it possible to trace groups or persons, who should have been enumerated at one place, but turned out to have been counted elsewhere.

The second source of information was gathered during 1950 when the vital statistics of Hutterites were needed for this particular Mental Health study. Although a complete physical examination of all Hutterites living on the North American continent was not possible, Eaton and Mayer made examinations of eighty percent of the Hutterite population. Further they enumerated the remaining twenty percent of the population. Comparisons of the eighty percent sample with records based on a one hundred percent enumeration, however, showed that this eighty percent was representative of the whole population (Eaton and Mayer 1954).

A comparison of the 1880 and 1950 populations produced the statistical data in Table 8.1.

Eaton and Mayer supplied another set of figures which was used to compare the age distribution of women for the periods 1926-30, 1936-40, and 1946-50. Table 8.2 gave the age specific

Table 8.1 Comparison of 1880 and 1950 Age Distribution of Ethnic Hutterites as a Percentage of the Total Population

Age Distribution	Percent 1880	Percent 1950	Percent Between 1880 and 1950 Increase or Decrease
Under 15 years of age	47.85	51.25	−3.40
15 - 19	9.73	10.76	−1.03
20 - 24	8.80	7.90	.90
25 - 29	6.77	7.13	.36
30 - 34	6.32	5.47	.85
35 - 39	4.96	4.76	.20
40 - 44	3.83	3.37	.46
45 - 49	3.38	2.79	.59
50 - 54	1.12	2.15	−1.03
55 - 59	2.25	1.69	.56
60 - 64	2.03	1.01	1.02
65 and over	2.70	1.65	1.05

Table 8.2 Age Specific Distribution for Hutterite Women in 1926-30, 1936-40, and 1946-50 in Percent to the Total Population.

Age Group	Percent 1926-30	Percent 1936-40	Percent 1946-50
15 - 19	25.79	24.87	23.98
20 - 24	20.23	22.11	20.07
25 - 29	18.25	16.20	17.52
30 - 34	13.69	12.31	14.34
35 - 39	7.93	10.67	10.35
40 - 44	7.14	8.54	7.64
45 - 49	6.74	5.27	6.05

distribution of women as a percentage of the total population. Eaton and Mayer come to the following conclusion:

> The Hutterite population growth during the last seventy [1884-1954] years resembles the statistical model of a *stable* population. Such a population must be distinguished from a *stationary* population. The latter is neither growing nor decreasing. It remains, as the term indicates, stationary in size. A stable population may be growing or decreasing, but it has a constant net reproduction rate. The true birth and death rates are stable. The total number of persons can change, but the percentage distribution by age and sex does not. The statistical model of a stable population has never, to our knowledge, been found in nature. The Hutterites come very close to showing its characteristics ... This finding is more than a statistical curiosity. It indicates that it is meaningful to compare the rates of phenomena within the sect at different times, because the composition of the population base remains the same. Within the Hutterite population even crude rates can be a basis for comparison over time (1954: 43,44).

It is no surprise that Eaton and Mayer were unable to fit the "Pearl-Reed Logistic Curve" to the Hutterite patterns of growth. This curve which is characterized by a slow rate of growth at the beginning, a fast rate of growth in the middle, and a slow rate of growth at the end, simply did not fit the Hutterite pattern of growth at that time because there was no point of inflection on the upper end. Even in the early 1960s Hutterites were still in the fast rate of growth. Eaton and Mayer had this to say:

> Ultimately, it may well follow such a pattern [slower rate of growth], but our data contain no biological clue that would permit us to predict how long the fertility of this population will continue to remain high, when it will begin to decline, how fast it will decline and whether the decline will be continuous. We showed previously that the rate of growth was somewhat slower prior to

1910 than after that date. Higher mortality and disease rates during the early years probably can explain this phenomena rather than any change in fertility. There also is the suggestion of a slight diminution in the rate of growth in the latter half of the 1940-1950 period, accounted for by a drop in the age specific birth rate of women age thirty-five to thirty-nine .... If and when the decline comes we suspect that it will come despite a further improvement in health conditions of both mothers and children. It will be caused by a shift in Hutterite attitudes toward birth–control .... Some evidence is now available that a shift in outlook in favor of controlled parenthood is in the making (1954: 47).

It is interesting to note that Eaton and Mayer declared themselves unable to predict a decline of the Hutterite birth rate in terms of biological causes. They referred to changes in attitude regarding controlled parenthood as the only possible mechanism for changing growth in this population.

Attitudes toward various forms of parenthood are of course social in origin. Particularly a change in attitudes from the desirability of a large nuclear family to a somewhat smaller one takes place only in the social context of the group and it seems reasonable to assume that it must be correlated with a number of social factors which give rise to a change in such attitudes. The question may be asked: Is there a theoretical framework that enables us to understand the interrelationship of attitudes toward parenthood and the sociocultural conditions in which such attitudes are held?

Frank Lorimer while investigating the relationship between culture and fertility remarked (1958: 202):

A highly structured society will tend to enforce high fertility (a) if the objective conditions of its existence, such as wealth or resources, or opportunity for unlimited expansion through conquest, are favourable to high fertility, or (b) if its accepted religious or other cultural values prescribe high fertility.

Expanding on these conditions Lorimer states that three pre-requisites or a combination of them must be met if a society produces a high fertility rate. These are:

(a) *A stable intact society which is highly structured.* The term "social structure" in this context denotes the "implicit constitution" of a society, its interacting, customary modes of behaviour that define personal relations and provide an accepted basis for the co-ordination of interests and activities. It includes forms of political control, household and village arrangements, economic activities, religious institutions and obligations, as well as kinship and family patterns.

(b) *Objective conditions of existence favourable for expansion.* This term implies a tendency toward dominance in intersocietal competition for control of resources.

(c) *An accepted value system prescribing a high fertility rate.* The term "cultural values" is understood to refer to attitudes and interests which are, in part, engendered by a particular social structure and which in turn motivate and direct activities of individuals or groups who form a society.

If one applies Lorimer's prerequisites to the Hutterite data, one sees that indeed that society was characterized by a high rate of fertility. From 1927 to 1966, Hutterite colonies in Alberta multiplied from sixteen to sixty-five. This population increase coincided with a tremendous expansion in land holdings, and this in turn indicated that the sect was highly competitive in relation to the western Canadian farm population. This raises the important question: How were the sociocultural factors of a stable society, the objective conditions for expansion and value regarding a high fertility integrated in Hutterite society? The comparison of two structural studies might throw some light on the social–cultural dynamics operating in a Hutterite colony. The first case study is concerned with a colony which had just been founded in the 1960s, the second with a colony that was established fifteen to twenty years before. The phenomenon of "social dynamics" as used in this context should not be confused with social change. Although social change might be one of the consequences of dynamic processes the term "dynamics" refer to organizing forces expressing themselves in the elaboration, maintenance, or expansion of a social-cultural system. A man riding an exercise bicycle tranforms a tremendous amount of energy in his biological system while the actual change of his system (aging, for example) is relatively slow. Social systems likewise can be engaged in dynamic processes while the actual change of the system might hardly be noticeable. This distinction between "dynamics" and "social change" is important for the understanding of the Hutterite sociocultural system. It allows us to see this culture as one that expanded rapidly but remained structurally stable in spite of this expansion.

When a new colony is set up, it usually has around sixty to seventy people. In the colony established in the 1960s about half of the population consisted of children under the age of fifteen years. Another six people were between fifteen and nineteen years old and the rest, twenty-four people in all, were adults over the age of twenty years. Of these twenty–four people, about half were males. This new community therefore started with a labour force of twelve males over twenty years of age and three males between the ages of fifteen and nineteen. The female labour force had roughly the same proportions.

The internal organization of each colony demands the appointment of an executive council comprised of six elders (two preachers, the manager, the fieldboss, the German schoolteacher, and an elder at large), which forms the highest authority in the community. Until recent economic changes were introduced a second authority level consisted of various department heads like the cattle boss, a pig boss, sheep boss, chicken boss, the blacksmith, and so on. The number of these positions varied from a minimum of perhaps six to a maximum of fourteen. Not all of these positions had an equal status. Depending upon the size and importance of an operation, the position of cattle boss might have carried much higher status than that of the chicken boss. These jobs were held by persons who were at least in the age group twenty-five to thirty, and they had to be baptized members of the sect, as well as being married. A third and lowest level in the division of labour consisted of a group of helpers who were shifted around according to the demands of the agricultural operations to be performed under different weather conditions and seasons.

The middle and the upper levels in this structure provided advancement from the group of shifting labourers. The numbers of openings in these two levels, however, were restricted. They ranged from a minimum of twelve to a maximum of twenty.

With only fifteen males over the age of fifteen years, work and status positions in a "young" colony were plentiful while workers were scarce. To alleviate the situation a number of positions had to be held by one and the same person burdening this person with additional work. A young colony then was characterized by much work and a great many jobs and status positions for which there was little or no competition. The opportunity structure was wide open.

As the colony reached its "old stage" this trend reversed. Fifteen to twenty years after the colony had been established, the population reached about 130 persons. There were about thirty-five males in such an "old" colony between the ages of fifteen and seventy years. Sixteen males were over the age of thirty. These sixteen people in all probability occupied all the important role and status positions as outlined earlier. Some of them might have aspired to positions which were already filled. Another five persons were between the ages of twenty-five and thirty years. They expected to receive positions soon. However, since all appointments can be life appointments, unless the person proves to be incompetent or dishonest, the opportunities for these younger people were extremely limited. Within the next ten years eleven persons would have reached an age between thirty and forty without any hope of obtaining important positions in the colony hierarchy. The scarcity of jobs could produce fierce competition, which, when it happened, usually took place along family lines.

As Bruno Bettelheim observes in *The Challenge of Youth* (1961), the self-identity and even more the self-realization of the young man implies to a large degree an upwards mobility in the opportunity and authority structure of society. In the past, a predominantly agricultural society solved this problem through the replacement of the older generation by the younger. The crucial and natural criteria for such replacement of generations was physical strength. Physical strength, however, has lost its survival value among Hutterites as it has lost its survival value in all technologically advanced societies. The older generation in charge of the Hutterite authority structure is relatively young in relation to the real skills necessary to run an economically and socially successful community. Business acumen, complex agricultural know-how, and social skills to generate consensus are more likely found in Hutterites who are in their forties, fifties, and even sixties than among the young.

A closed opportunity structure can quickly generate dissatisfaction, frustration, and suspicion on the part of those younger men excluded from advancement in the economic and social hierarchy. For Hutterite communities which depended and still depend largely on informal social controls rather than formal ones, the existence of a dissatisfied, frustrated younger generation would have been disastrous. The motivation to participate in the community would be extremely problematic, particularly for those young boys who just needed to step outside their communities to find good agricultural work plus a lot of personal amenities the Hutterite community normally does not offer. Although a loss of membership could have provided some sort of a solution for a dissatisfied group of young men, such losses were religiously unacceptable for Hutterite communities. The problems of a closed opportunity structure could often become magnified by the manipulation of the few opportunities arising. Elders holding authority positions were often trying to push their sons up the ladder. Such nepotism is bound to lead to social resistance and conflict. In the colony described above life became troublesome and unpleasant. Work rules were hard to enforce because a fine division of labour led to a diffusion of responsibility. Factionalization and the formation of cliques followed in the path of nepotism. The acknowledgment of authority decreased as the age differences between leader and followers decreased also. The colony operation became unwieldy, and inefficient. Shortly before this general unrest reached a point where it became destructive to the group, the colony branched out. The "branching out" occurs on a voluntaristic and opportunistic basis. New land acquisitions were made, buildings were erected, and surplus machinery and livestock were accumulated. For some years both units were farmed as one. Manpower was allocated as necessary, moving back and forth between the old and new colony without any decision being made as to who would reside ultimately in which colony. Only after the total assets were split into two equal portions — which might include the "old" colony assuming a mortgage for the new one — did the two preachers put their names on two pieces of paper posted in a public place. The population of the colony would then sort itself out by signing up for one of the two divisions. This signing up usually took place in order of rank, so that those who were eligible for high status positions would sign up first, and the junior people in the colony followed. In addition care was taken that the proportions of young and old people would be constant in both new units. Only after this process of signing up had been completed, discussed, and found to be sound were lots drawn to determine which group would occupy which colony.

Thus we can see that the maintenance of social stability and the retention of an established value system in a Hutterite community depended on the avoidance of overpopulation in any one colony. The "dynamics" of Hutterite society consisted of managing an extremely high rate of natural increase (4.12 percent per year), while avoiding the overpopulation of individual communities. The "branching" process described above served that purpose. Structural stability, therefore, was maintained in spite of rapid population growth and therefore satisfied conditions (a) and (c) in Lorimer's theoretical framework. Condition (b) which relates to an environment favourable for expansion consisted of the area of agricultural changes that swept over the American and Canadian prairie regions during the last century. The technological changes in agriculture replaced small farms by larger ones and in the process provided opportunities for expansion for those that intended to stay on the land and had the financial resources to do so. Therefore all three of Lorimer's conditions applied during the period under investigation by Eaton.

But if, as we have asserted, a Hutterite community had to branch out to maintain social stability it also had to accept the responsibility to make the establishment of a new colony financially possible. Land was always available for expansion but at a price. The financing of new Hutterite communities generation after generation demanded a most efficient system of production in combination with severe restrictions on consumption.

Financing the branching of colonies was and still is difficult particularly when the population increase was so enormous that each community experienced a state of constant tension caused by the possible danger of not being able to accumulate enough capital to create a new community for the generation to come. There is much justification for assuming that the Hutterite sociocultural system might be actively seeking this state of tension because this state and the dynamics by which the tensions are resolved from one moment in time to another lends legitimacy to the system, provides goals to be reached, gives justification to the system of stratification (the social structure), provides motivation and inducement for the individual member, and finally draws Hutterites into an ascetic communal work ethic that has born the stamp of religious legitimacy and tradition for the last 470 years.

The irony is, that for this pacifistic, primary group being oriented toward co-operation and neighbourly love, life on earth or the vestibule of paradise, as they call it, does not consist of affluence, equilibrium, and tension reduction, but of the constant, intense, and continuous involvement in ever new tensions arising in barely manageable proportions. Hutterites, up until recently, had institutionalized the creation and maintenance of tensions within their dynamic configuration. These tensions put Hutterite society on a steady course and kept it there. A high rate of natural increase, therefore, was perfectly functional within the dynamic processes described here. Hutterites, in fact, thrived under population pressures. There is no other population in the whole world that was able to maintain as high a rate of natural increase as the Hutterites and at the same time accumulate the financial means to provide the next generation with the same assets and technological standards as the previous one.

Alfred Sauvy (1961: 89) provides a theoretical model that helps to understand the processes involved. He classified the investment needs of a society into four groups:
(a) to produce consumer goods (for home consumption)
(b) to keep up the maintenance of the productive equipment
(c) to aim at improving this equipment

(d) to aim at giving the supplementary inhabitants (from population growth) the necessary installations for a standard of living equal to the others.

A society has the choice to invest in (b) and (c) either to increase (a) or to increase (d). In most cases a balance between the two will be found. Among Hutterites, however, the items (b) and (c) were maximized not to increase (a) beyond the state of necessity as defined by the communal standard of living. Instead they were maximized in favour of (d), which of course supports Hutterite expansion. Alfred Sauvy calls this type of investment a "demographic" investment. Third World countries who often have a high rate of natural increase suffer greatly from their inability to provide an adequate standard of living for future generations. Huttterites, in contrast, have done so without being aware that they have accomplished what no other population was able to do during the last century. Industrial societies which of course improve the living conditions of future generations greatly, nevertheless grow at a much smaller rate.

For Hutterites pouring the accumulated wealth into the expansion of the group was important from two other points of view as well. First, it protected the communities against the temptation and dangers of wealth in general. Secondly, it provided a psychological environment which promoted an attitude of scarcity, even of poverty. Both of these attributes facilitate group unity and consensus. In earlier chapters we have seen that wealth that is allowed to be distributed in a communal society leads to the eventual disintegration of that society. The hierarchical organization of such a society inevitably leads to unequal access to the resources of the group and this unequal access cannot be legitimized. As a result the motivational level of the members drops quickly, leading to inefficiency and a run of all for the spoils. Under conditions of psychological scarcity or poverty access to the resources of the group is still unequal but this inequality is legitimized. Members who work harder for the group are entitled to more food or clothing. The elderly, the sick or children need special care and nobody can quarrel with such a mode of redistribution. The whole system of internal consumption therefore obtains the stamp of a time-honoured legitimacy which forms part of the Hutterite value system.

Hutterite expansion, as we have seen, demanded severe restrictions on home consumption (Item (a) in Alfred Sauvy's classification). Such restrictions in turn created a psychological environment of scarcity and scarcity provided a sociocultural milieu favourable for the redistribution of goods on the basis of the Hutterite value system. Group consensus and unity followed almost automatically.

The social scenario outlined above should not be confused with the possible interpretation that poor Hutterite colonies experience a high degree of unity and consensus. This is not the case. On the contrary poor colonies usually suffer from a great deal of internal disunity. There is a difference between a psychological milieu of scarcity as the result of working and saving toward the desired goal of expansion and the inability of poor colonies to do so. In the latter case it is the frustration of not being able to progress toward legitimate and necessary group goals that often is the source of frictions and social fragmentations.

The stability of the Hutterite population growth and the maintenance of the social structure as described here, characterized the history of the sect from the 1880s to the 1960s. As long as Hutterite growth patterns could be accommodated through expansion and as long as expansion could be financed to maintain the social structure and the value system, the society was engaged in highly dynamic activities but experienced little change in its basic social order. But the interrelationship of these factors is and always has been precarious. The alteration of any one factor, may it be the population growth, the external conditions for expansion, the ability to finance or the maintenance of the social structure could create a situation where the smooth functioning of this integrative system could collapse.

Prior to the 1960s there already were a number of colonies which were unable to accumulate enough financial means to branch out. Instead of relying on accumulated capital they resorted to financing part or most of the costs of branching through bank loans. The repayment of these loans was usually guaranteed by the new and the old colony. As a result of this, these colonies had to repay the loan first before they were able to save for the next expansion. While their population increase remained constant, the time available to accumulate capital for the next expansion became shorter. The repayment of loans retarded the saving powers of two colonies, these two had to put off their expansion for a longer period than was usually required to alleviate the population pressure. The social and financial problems of these colonies not only accumulated but they also multiplied. There were as many as twelve percent of the total number of colonies in Alberta in the 1960s which were in financial difficulties. Many, but not all of these, were in one way or another associated with the difficulties of expansion. Bad management, a relatively rare occurrence among Hutterites, and natural calamities are two other factors which can create difficult situations for the colonies.

Having financial difficulties does not necessarily mean that the colony is unable to overcome the crisis, at least for the time being. But there were colonies where the accumulation of social problems led to the breakdown of the central authority to be replaced by the antagonistic cooperation of several factions. Such a faction sometimes tries to settle somewhere else, usually with the less than wholehearted approval of the rest. During difficult economic times such as occurred in the early 1980s these factions found it impossible to sustain themselves economically. Since disagreements usually preceded such moves, financial aid from the parent colony was either insufficient or not forthcoming at all. Consequently, there are in the mid 1980s, a number of stranded Hutterite settlements which do not have the full status of a colony. These settlements are all in financial difficulties; they do not grow, nor are women willing to marry into them. On the other hand the members of these settlements are afraid to return to their parent colony for a number of individual and social reasons. Such stranded groups can be found particularly among the *Dariusleut* and they constitute a festering problem which so far has defied all attempts by the bishop to resolve it.

In 1983 the *Lehrerleut* had to bail out thirteen of their colonies who had borrowed extensively and were suffering from high interest rates. A levy imposed on the savings of all solvent colonies raised the necessary funds which will have to be repaid but without interest. This move originated with the *Lehrerleut* bishop now deceased. It is questionable whether the *Dariusleut* bishop has the authority and the initiative to perform a similar rescue mission for the many colonies that are in difficulties in the mid-eighties.

Another factor threatening the integrated dynamic system of Hutterite communities is technological change. Technological inventions directly influence the social structure and pose challenges to the value system. The chapters on contemporary changes outline some of these alterations in more detail. Looking at the influences of technology from a general point of view one notices that the colony membership declines with an increase in technology. One outstanding example is a colony that farms 22,000 acres of irrigated land having only a total membership of fifty–four. And there are no complaints of being overworked or short of manpower. A reduction in membership renders some social institutions ineffective. With fewer children the kindergarten might be abandoned. Church services due to lower attendance become more sporadic and the atmosphere in church loses its emotional impact on the individual. Technology promotes specialization. Combined with a greater geographic distribution of Hutterites the all-round farming system is being replaced with highly specialized and highly efficient operations whose justification is derived from the debit and credit columns of the bookkeeper. Inefficient operations which are discontinued alter the traditional social structure and those structures that remain must be redefined in the light of the ongoing changes.

As there are few role models, a great deal of experimentation occurs which allows the individual a degree of initiative and freedom in the restructuring of a role. An electronics specialist in the colony still is tied down to the specific community purposes that require his skills. But the acquisition of his skills, their detailed application, their constant updating, the requirements for journals and magazines, the securing of parts and materials open an area of behavioural freedom in which he alone is the expert and therefore the deciding force. He can make claims on time, resources, and transportation which the colony authority cannot deny. Such behavioural freedoms do not remain isolated but branch out into the mental and often behavioural exploration of the outside culture. As a result the system must accommodate new role models all the time which means that the traditional authority patterns have to change to make such accommodation possible.

Finally a decrease in the rate of population increase threatens the integration of the Hutterite system by removing or lessening the need for expansion. (See Chapter 9.) The evidence that the natural growth patterns of Hutterites are decreasing substantially is presently so overwhelming that one can take it as a fact. This decrease coincides with a tendency toward lowering the colony membership due to technological changes. It is therefore not clear at this time to what extent a decline in the growth patterns of the population will also lessen the need for expansion. A minimum colony size is for social reasons unavoidable and if the Hutterite population in future will grow at a rate at which it seems to be growing now the pressures for expansion will be much reduced relative to former times. There is good evidence that Hutterites have already reallocated some of their investments into increasing (a) the production of consumer goods for home consumption. Most colonies are in the process or already have rebuilt their housing facilities and upgraded the sanitary and housing standards comparable to those in Canada and the United States. Food consumption and the usage of dry goods have broadened and greatly increased the cash outlay which only a few decades ago was confined to buying sugar and coffee. At least those colonies which are no longer under the pressure to double their holdings every time the populations doubles (every seventeen to twenty years in the past) are now in a position to increase the consumption of consumer goods. As indicated earlier the consumption of more consumer goods threatens the principle of legitimate inequality which is part of the traditional value system. While one would be ill advised to underestimate the adaptive capabilities of Hutterites, after all their experience in this area goes back 470 years, it cannot be taken for granted that all colonies possess the quality of leadership and initiative to solve the emerging problems without major frictions.

The decrease in the growth rate of Hutterites seems to be due to a decrease in Hutterite fertility. (See postscript to Chapter 9.) Eaton expected that such a decrease would come about as a change in attitude toward parenthood. It is indeed very difficult to detect such attitudinal changes. Hutterite women as well as men are not prepared to make overt statements that lower the value of children or lament the burden of parenthood. An expression of active hostility or even indifference toward parenthood seems to run counter to accepted cultural values. Hutterites seem to have taken a more passive route, which allows them to lower their birth rate but requires no verbalized change toward children and parenthood. In this respect Hutterite women have taken advantage of an unexpected outsider — the family doctor. By the early 1970s the family doctor had emerged as an influential agent in the restructuring of the role of women. Medical practitioners treat Hutterite women according to prevalent standards which often means that surgical and other means of birth control are recommended if the health of the woman is in danger. With the one exception of abortion these recommendations are accepted even by the elders. One of the preachers recently commented on the declining size of the Hutterite family and said: "The number of children a Hutterite woman can have now is in the hands of her doctor. And there is nothing we can do about this." Health insurance and hospital insurance in turn have made access to medical services commonplace and independent from the colony's permission or financing. Health care, including birth control, therefore, is no longer a colony but a private affair and as such handled in ways very different from the former uniform model.

Summary

Proceeding from Eaton's observations regarding the natural increase of Hutterites during the period 1880–1950 we explored the dynamics of such an expanding society through the application of Lorimer's and Sauvy's models. The interrelationship of natural increase, colony expansion, maximization of production, minimization of consumption and allocation of accumulated wealth for a "demographic" investment that maintained structural stability and preserved the value system transmitted a vivid picture of the "dynamics" of Hutterite society. As indicated in Chapter 9 this dynamic constellation seems to have changed drastically beginning in the 1960s. While it is impossible at this time to say what the total effects of these changes will be, we selected some of the major variables and indicated the kind of changes that are likely to be produced if these variables in fact are being changed; as of course already is the case in regard to Hutterite growth patterns and increases in technology. It is often assumed that social change will spell the doom of Hutterite society. That certainly is a conclusion that is unfounded. Hutterites have the uncanny ability to translate changes into challenges to be mastered. The threats to the dynamics of the old integrative system as outlined in this chapter are just that, challenges to be mastered in a new dynamic system. Given that the active unit in Hutterite society is the colony, it can be assumed that not all colonies might be successful in mastering these challenges. But if history provides any lesson, most of the Hutterites will.

NINE

The Decline of Hutterite Population Growth

The preceding chapter, "A 'Demographic' Theory of Hutterite Population Growth" outlines a framework showing the dynamic interrelationship of population growth, expansion, structural maintenance, and capital accumulation in Hutterite society. The functioning of this model was first observed by the author in the mid 1960s. However, even at that time there were signs that the smooth progression of this dynamic model was in danger. In the latter part of the preceding chapter several of the variables making up the model were considered. It was indicated that as these variables changed from the 1960s to the mid 1980s Hutterite communities were forced to restructure the dynamic model which served them so well during the first half of the twentieth century. (Part 4 dealing with contemporary changes elaborates on this topic.) The underlying assumption of this original dynamic model, an assumption shared by Eaton, was that Hutterite population growth was the motor that kept the dynamics going. This is a reasonable assumption and it leads directly to the questions when and how will the growth patterns decline; what are the possible causes of such a decline; and what will happen if a decline does take place? It is impossible at this time to answer all of these questions, however, a number of partial answers can be provided. There is first the all important question: Has a decline in population growth occurred? This chapter and the postscript that follows attempt to give an affirmative answer to this question. There are also a number of observations and statistical indicators that seem to have some explanatory value as to how the decline occurred. These observations are offered here without claiming to have proven the case. Since 1966 when the outline of the dynamic model was originally published evidence began to accumulate indicating that the Hutterite growth rate experienced a decline beginning in 1965 and that the rate of decline has accelerated since. The point of inflection in the growth curve of the population which Eaton and Mayer were unable to detect during the period 1880-1950 seems to have occurred between 1965 and 1968. Data collected in the late 1970s suggest that the growth rate of Hutterites has declined from 4.12 percent per year to 2.91 percent a year — a decline of 1.2 percent.

Having made this assertion, it is most appropriate to add a word of caution. Hard data in the form of scientifically collected census data are not available. Hutterite communities are distributed over four Canadian provinces and five states in the northern United States. A total enumeration of the Hutterite population would be extremely time-consuming and costly and is beyond the resources of this author. What is available, however, is a series of Hutterite self-enumerations done in the 1960s and 1970s. As John Hostetler, working with self-enumerations, has pointed out, self-enumerations tend to underestimate up to one-third. At least that was the experience of Hostetler on the basis of a fertility study among the Amish. There are, however, significant differences between the enumeration procedures of Hutterites and of Amish. The organizational structure of the Hutterite community and the religious, social and economic powers of the preacher who keeps the community records stand in contrast to a dispersed congregation among the Amish, where preachers do not occupy the same central position as they do among Hutterites. Furthermore there is a long tradition of record keeping among Hutterites, going back to the beginnings of the sect four and a half centuries ago. Record keeping of births and deaths are among the most important religious duties of the preacher. There is therefore reason to believe that the margin of error among Hutterites is much smaller than among the Amish. Furthermore, if one assumes that the errors always go in the same direction, namely underestimation, and remain fairly constant as to their magnitudes, a comparison of Hutterite self-enumerations over time should give a fairly accurate picture in regard to the population *trend* even if the figures themselves are not entirely accurate. Our investigation is based on these assumptions.

If one starts with a total Hutterite population of 8,542 as found by Eaton and Mayer in 1950 and assumes a compound net increase of 4.1265 percent per year (Eaton and Mayer, 1954: 44-46) (the true rate of natural increase 1946–1950), the following predictions can be made in Table 9.1.

If one compares these predicted increases with the *actual* increase as found through Hutterite self-enumerations, the information in Table 9.2 can be presented.

The enumeration in 1964 showed an increase of 204 over the prediction and thereby indicated that up to that point the rate of natural increase was almost exactly what Eaton and Mayer had

Table 9.1 Population Estimates of Hutterites.

Year	Population based on true rate of natural increase (4.1265% per year)
1950	8,542
1964	15,045
1968	17,687
1977	25,451

Table 9.2 Population Estimates and Population Enumeration by Hutterites.

	1964	1968	1977
Predicted	15,045	17,687	25,451
Actual	15,249	16,931	21,828
Increase or decrease over predicted	+204	−756	−3,623

observed between 1946 and 1950. But four years later the Hutterite count falls below the expected and this decrease accelerates as time goes on. In 1977 there were 3,623 fewer Hutterites living than could be expected if the rate of natural increase had continued to be 4.1265 percent per year.

How reliable are these data? The 1964 count was published by John Hostetler in *Education and Marginality in the Communal Society of the Hutterites* (1965) and was based on reports of the colony heads to the Conference of the Hutterite Brethren Church. The date was January 1st, 1965. The 1968 count was undertaken by the Rev. Paul Gross of the Espanola Colony in Washington and was actually conducted in the summer of 1969 in response to a request by Robert Friedmann (1970: 100-113). The 1977 count was again undertaken by the Rev. Paul Gross and communicated to the author. It was subsequently published in the *1978 Mennonite World Handbook* (Kraybill 1978).

There exists another population count published by John Hostetler in *Hutterite Society* (1974) which shows a major inconsistency with the above figures. Hostetler lists 21,521 Hutterites for 1974, which is only 307 less than the enumeration of the Rev. Paul Gross for 1977, namely 21,828. However, John Hostetler has explained in private correspondence that his figures are estimates based on the predictions of Eaton and Mayer. For our purposes, therefore, we can ignore these figures.

Can the decline in population growth of Hutterites be verified by sources independent of the Rev. Paul Gross with whom the above figures originated? Fortunately such an independent source seems to be available in John Ryan's *The Agricultural Economy of Manitoba Hutterite Colonies* (1977). Being concerned with the Manitoba Hutterite population only, Ryan found that this population in 1970 was 4,666 and increased in five years up to the end of 1975 to 5,191 (1977: 261). This is a total increase of 11.25 percent or a compound rate of increase of 2.2 percent per year. In appendix B and C of his book Ryan presents a population count of Manitoba Hutterite colonies for July 1st, 1968 based on genealogy records of the Rev. Jacob Kleinsasser of Crystal Spring Colony and a population count for December 1970 based on Income Tax records provided by the accountant employed by the Manitoba Hutterite colonies (Ryan 1977: 278-82). According to these counts the Manitoba Hutterite population increased in two and a half years from 4,362 on July 1st, 1968, to 4,666 on December 31st, 1970. That amounts to a compound rate of 2.73 percent per year. It is significant to note the trend in the decrease of Hutterite population growth. During the two and a half years prior to 1970 the increase was still 2.73 percent per year, dropping during the five years following 1970 to 2.2 percent per year.

Given the sources of these enumerations and considering the painstaking work of Ryan, who presents his data detailed as to colonies and the number of families involved, there is every reason to believe that these data have a high probability of accuracy.

A further check on these data can be made in regard to family size. Eaton and Mayer had reported an average number of slightly more than ten children per completed Hutterite family. This author asked an accidental sample of Hutterite acquaintances in *Dariusleut* and *Lehrerleut* communities whether or not they could recall knowing a family with more than twelve children. Very few could report knowing a family with even ten children. None could recall knowing a family with more than twelve children. If ten children would still be the average, the results of this admittedly unscientific sampling could be expected to be very different. Due to intense intermarriage every adult Hutterite is fairly familiar with the family structure of an average of ten colonies; thus the frequency of knowing a family with twelve or more children should be fairly high. That none was found does not mean that none exists, but the absence of reports of twelve or more children nevertheless seems to indicate that an average number of ten children per completed Hutterite family is no longer tenable.

All respondents in this accidental sample, on the other hand, had no difficulties recalling one or more acquaintances who in their thirties and forties remained unmarried. Asked to state what in their opinion the average age of marriage among Hutterites is today, the answers ranged from twenty-five to thirty-two years. Given the fact that only twenty years ago very few unmarried Hutterites could be found and that the average age of marriage was between twenty and twenty-two years, all

Table 9.3 Hutterite Population Counts According to Kinship Groups.

	1964	1969	1977
Lehrerleut	4,338	5,161	6,312
Dariusleut	4,383	4,633	6,512
Schmiedeleut	6,528	7,137	9,004
Total	15,249	16,931	21,828

Table 9.4 Rate of Population Increase According to Kinship Groups.

	Rate of Increase 1964 to 1969	Rate of Increase 1969 to 1977	Rate of Increase 1964 to 1977
Lehrerleut	3.94	2.55	3.05
Dariusleut	1.24	4.35	3.22
Schmiedeleut	2.00	2.95	2.61

indications are that there is enough cumulative evidence to suggest a decline in the growth rate of the Hutterite population.

Fortunately, the data for 1964, 1969, and 1977 are broken down according to the three endogamous Hutterite kinship groups, *Lehrerleut*, *Dariusleut*, and *Schmiedeleut*. Comparing these different groups it is possible to check the data for internal consistency. We would expect that a comparison between these groups and a comparison over time within these groups would not show great fluctuations, but a steady trend. See Table 9.3.

If one calculates the rate of increase for each of these groups, the information in Table 9.4 can be presented.

The expectation that the variations between these groups for the time span 1964 to 1977 would not be very great seems to be affirmed by the data. The total rate of increase of the *Lehrerleut* and the *Dariusleut* groups that occupy the same territory in western Canada varies by only 0.17 percent. The *Schmiedeleut*, who are somewhat separated from the other groups due to their concentration in Manitoba and the Dakotas, vary from the former by an average of 0.52 percent, a reasonable variation.

If one compares the rates of increase in each kinship group for the two time periods covered, greater variations are encountered than could be expected. The variations of 1.24 and 4.35 for the *Dariusleut* seem to indicate that this group was underestimated in 1969, as indeed an increase of only 250 people for the time period is unrealistic. The rate of increase for the 1969 to 1977 period on the other hand, is much too high. This gives us reason to believe that the underestimation in 1969 was subsequently corrected by the 1977 count, which appears to be inflated.

Similarly the *Schmiedeleut* seemed to have been underenumerated in 1969, giving an unrealistically low rate of 2.0 for the time period 1964 to 1969. As a result the rate of increase for the period 1969 to 1977 appears inflated. The total increase of this group for 1964 to 1977 of 2.61 percent compares favourably with the Ryan data for Manitoba *Schmiedeleut* which showed an increase of 2.73 percent for 1969 to 1970 and 2.2 percent for the period 1969 to 1975.

If these considerations do give us some confidence that a trend toward a lower birth rate has indeed occurred among Hutterites, it might help even further to consider the magnitude of error that the Rev. Paul Gross must have been making in his enumerations, if the above figures were indeed wrong. Proceeding from his 1977 count he would have failed to enumerate 3,623 Hutterites or fourteen percent of the total population. Under the prevailing administrative circumstances in Hutterite colonies, this seems most unlikely.

Our conclusion that the Hutterite growth rate has dropped from 4.12 percent per year prior to 1965 to 2.91 percent per year in 1980 is not proven beyond any doubt. What can be accepted with a high degree of certainty is the inference that a drastic change in the constant growth of Hutterites has occurred. The point of inflection in the growth rate seems to have taken place after 1965 and the question is: What factors can possibly have contributed to this decline that so suddenly became apparent after this date?

As already indicated in the preceding chapter under the impact of modern technology Hutterite society has entered a phase where a major revamping of its social structure is under way. In the 1930s Hutterites made the important decision to incorporate modern technologies into their mode of production, realizing that technology was necessary to obtain the degree of efficiency which alone could safeguard the capital accumulation for expansion. Increasingly, efficiency and technology have made it necessary to restructure the division of labour in accord with these demands. The division of labour in turn is intimately intertwined with the social structure of Hutterite colonies. Under the impact of technological changes this social structure undergoes a transformation from a socially–oriented to a technologically-oriented structure. Such trades as shoemaker, breadcutter, tanner, furniture-maker, bookbinder, broom-maker, etcetera, were labour intensive occupations but low in efficiency and profitability. Their existence could not be justified by reference to their economic utility. However, the availability of an extensive pool of manpower under seasonal agricultural conditions required that a certain amount of nonutilitarian work should be available as a means for employment when weather and seasons made certain agricultural operations impossible. The old principle that "all men must be employed all the time" is one of the most important functional requirements of a Hutterite community. It should be supplemented by the equally important saying among Hutterites that "a woman's work is never done."

Social order among Hutterites is easier to enforce if all members of the community are employed in such a way that this employment reflects a degree of status and prestige satisfying to its performer. If such employment cannot be provided on the scale necessary to satisfy all members, dissatisfied factions will arise and social order becomes problematic. A technologically-oriented social structure does not have the easy interchangeability of roles which the traditional Hutterite social structure possessed. Nor do newly created roles contain the social relatedness of the old role prescriptions. The hog man who also doubled as shoemaker maintained countless relationships between himself and the rest of the colony membership. He not only raised hogs for sale, but designated the pigs to be slaughtered which drew the colony membership into a variety of activities. As a shoemaker he maintained intimate relations with every member who may have come to him for repairs, etcetera. The electronic specialist who might double as a colony electrician is mainly oriented toward objects and performs work which the rest of the membership does not understand. His work certainly is appreciated, but it lacks the social involvement of the older role prescriptions. There is, therefore, a qualitative difference between a socially-oriented and a technologically-oriented social structure. Role performances which are justified mainly by their technical utility lack the closeness and the intimacy which constitute the essentials of social relations among Hutterites.

The restructuring of the division of labour and the accompanying dangers of social dislocation of community members are increasing to the same degree that technological improvements are adopted by Hutterites who follow trends characteristic for the agricultural industry as a whole. Modern equipment today allows one person to do the work that was done by five persons only ten years ago. Under these conditions the pool of young adults over the age of fifteen, which formerly performed the manual labour in Hutterite communities, is no longer employable all the time. The mechanization of hog raising, egg production, and milk production, for example, have become one-man operations and no longer depend on the unskilled labour of a pool of young adults. Hutterites today no longer need a large group of young people doing the manual work in order to have an efficient and profitable operation. On the contrary, unemployable and idle young men are a source of social problems, undermining the social order of the community. Unable to find meaningful work in the communities, these young people tend to "moonlight" for outsiders thereby introducing social habits and attitudes into the communities which are disruptive of the traditional order.

The so-called "foolish years" of adolescence ranging from fifteen years of age to baptism, which are characterized by tolerated forms of juvenile deviancy, are extended beyond baptism. With fewer positions open to them, young adults can legitimately postpone the acceptance of the rigid conformity that is required with marriage. The saying: "I remained single and enjoyed every minute of it," designates a degree of individual freedom of those in their twenties who find various means to adopt a lifestyle at least partially removed from the supervision of the colony authority. Work performed by these young adults for non-Hutterite neighbours and friends generates money which in turn allows them to travel to nearby towns and join in activities offered there. Women in their twenties enjoy the company of their friends in the colony with whom they plan activities that provide some joy and entertainment. In this situation the idea of assuming the restricted and conforming role of a married woman is no longer so attractive.

The irritating and dysfunctional presence of too many young single men and women, of course, translates itself only very slowly into a drop in the rate of reproduction. The conscious realization that too many offspring cause social problems must work itself through a great number of social habits and attitudes until it becomes effective. Most Hutterites, however, agree with the statement that compared with only twenty years ago, young people today tend to marry four to five years later than they did previously. Such a tendency is very much related to the longer waiting period for individuals to move into higher positions in the division of labour. Since marriage designates full manhood, the growing of a beard, and the expectation of status advancement, a shrinking number of jobs that carry such status would postpone social advancement which in turn tends to discourage marriage. And the postponement of marriage for four or five years during the most fertile period of the twenties leads to a decline in the overall fertility rate.

It is interesting to note that the structural problems caused by an increasingly technologically-oriented social structure has led as well to a constant decrease in colony size. The constancy of this decrease seems to be indicative of a shrinking division of labour, although it must be kept in mind that various restrictions on Hutterite expansion, particularly during the 1940s and 1950s, might have kept the average colony size artificially high during these periods. See A.J.F. Zieglschmid's information regarding colony size up to 1947 in Table 9.5 (1947: 685-86).

The last of the figures in Table 9.5 certainly is indicative of problems which Hutterites encountered under the "Land Sales Prohibition Act" passed during the latter part of the war. By 1950, when expansion under the "Communal Properties Act" in Alberta was still restricted but nevertheless possible, the situation

Table 9.5 Average Population Size per Colony.

Year	Population	No. of Colonies	Population per Colony
1926	3,000	29	103.4
1944	estimate	57	108.7
1947	7,023	62	113.3

Table 9.6 Hutterite Population and Number of Colonies According to Year.

Year	Population	No. of Colonies	Population per Colony
1950	8,542	87	98
By 1964 Hosteler reports the following:			
1964	15,249	162	94
The 1969 enumeration by the Rev. Paul Gross showed the following:			
1969	16,931	182	90.3

Table 9.7 Total Hutterite Population Number of Colonies and Colony Size 1977.

Year	Population	No. of Colonies	Population per Colony
1977	21,828	247	88.37

outlined in Table 9.6 occurred. The 1977 enumeration by the Rev. Paul Gross can be found in Table 9.7.

While there is a decline in colony size in all three kinship groups, much of the decline is due to only one group. The average colony size of the *Dariusleut* by 1977 had declined to 76.61. Incidentally, this is also the group that has retained the highest rate of population increase among the three groups as previously shown. The implication that can be drawn from this is that population pressure in the three kinship groups is being handled

Table 9.8 Growth of Hutterite Colonies 1964 to 1977.

	1964	1977	% rate of annual increase
Total number of colonies	170	247	3.03

Sources: Hostetler 1964 and Gross 1977.

Table 9.9 Growth of Hutterite Colonies 1964-1977 According to Kinship Groups.

	1964	1977	% rate of annual increase
Dariusleut	57	85	3.25
Lehrerleut	43	64	3.23
Schmiedeleut	70	98	2.73

Sources: Hostetler 1964 and Gross 1977.

Table 9.10 Growth of Schmiedeleut Colonies 1964 - 1977 According to Country.

	1964	1977	% rate of annual increase
U.S. Schmiedeleut	28	37(1)*	2.25
Manitoba Schmiedeleut	42	60	2.89

* One colony branched out from Canada to U.S.
Sources: Hostetler 1964 and Gross 1977.

in slightly different ways. While the *Dariusleut* during the period 1950 to 1977 accommodated a population increase of 4,059 persons in fifty–six new colonies at an average colony size of 72.48, the *Schmiedeleut* accommodated a total increase of 5,522 people during the same time period in sixty–two new colonies at an average colony size of 89.06. The *Lehrerleut* finally maintained the highest average colony size of 91.59 which accommodated a population increase of 3,847 new members from 1950 to 1977.

These differences in the average colony size are in all likelihood due to different cultural traditions among these kinship groups, but could also be the result of differences in the dynamic conditions that either facilitated or retarded expansion.

To what extent the decline in Hutterite population growth has led to a lessening of their expansive drive is difficult to specify at this time, because the reduction in colony size counters such a trend. Although Ryan found an average annual increase in new colonies of 4.25 percent per year during 1960 to 1970 in Manitoba and even reported an increase to 4.5 percent per year for the period 1970 to 1975 (Ryan 1977: 260), the overall expansion of Hutterites seems to be declining with their declining population growth.

If these figures in Table 9.8 are broken down according to kinship groups the information in Table 9.9 emerges.

It is rather remarkable that the percentage rate of annual increase in the number of colonies for the *Dariusleut* and *Lehrerleut* is nearly identical, yet their population growth differed by 0.44 percent. The group with the lowest population growth, namely the *Schmiedeleut*, also has the lowest rate of annual increase in the number of colonies, while the *Dariusleut* have the highest rate of increase in the number of colonies as well as in population growth but have the lowest average colony size. The above figures, however, do not conform with Ryan's report (Ryan, 1977: 260). It must be remembered that Ryan investigated Manitoba *Schmiedeleut* only. If all *Schmiedeleut* colonies in Canada and the U.S. are considered, the information in Table 9.10 results.

The *Schmiedeleut* in the United States have the lowest rate of annual increase in the number of colonies. This is probably due to their being relatively new colonies which had not reached the stage of expansion, while the older Canadian colonies tended to expand which is reflected in the high rate of expansion reported by Ryan. A similar situation is found among the *Lehrerleut* of Montana. This group consisted of fourteen colonies in 1964 and increased to only sixteen in 1977.

Our theoretical perspective outlined in the previous chapter hypothesized a dynamic relationship between population growth, structural stability, opportunities for expansion and the ability to accumulate capital. The present chapter demonstrated that the motor that kept this dynamic relationship going — Hutterite population growth — has changed drastically during the last twenty years. Hutterites no longer experience the enormous pressures which one of the highest rates of natural increase imposed on them during former times. As a result the dynamic equilibrium which gave a peculiar character to Hutterite society must change. There are some indications regarding the direction in which such changes seem to proceed. Part 4 which deals with contemporary changes in Hutterite society indicates some of these. But there are certainly others not yet observed and there might be changes only visible in the near or distant future. The formal social structure, in contrast to the informal social structure, is highly resistant to social change. So is the value system at least in its verbalized and ideal form.

But as we have shown the necessity to change not only comes from a reduction in the growth rate but also from the ever increasing drive to make Hutterite colonies more efficient. This striving toward greater efficiency injects the characteristics of technology into a social system which owes its longevity to the skills by which intimate social relations were maintained. There is something very contradictory between the effects of technology and the social needs of Hutterite communities. To compete successfully in a capitalistic technological society and yet maintain a communal social system is indeed a most difficult if not impossible task, at least in the long run. Yet Hutterites have managed similar tasks before, if only barely.

In previous chapters we have shown that processes of social reconstruction were preceded by a shrinking membership toward a hard core of devoted adherents. Only after those parts that endangered the system through incompatible ideas and behaviours were pushed off and discarded could the social system of Hutterites find a new dynamic equilibrium. This process assumes that religious and communal values finally will triumph over economic and even kinship values. It also assumes that religious ideas are subjected to an intense scrutiny strong enough to command the loyalty, the suffering, and the devotion of those adherents that carry on the torch. A revival of religious fervour therefore is a prerequisite for social reconstruction. But we have also shown that Hutterite religion today is a ritualized institution devoid of scholarship and ideological leadership, although crises of decline, external dangers, and attacks on religious beliefs have produced ideological leaders more often than during times of creeping erosion of religious values. Given the existing political conditions in North America such attacks and dangers have a high improbability of occurrence. This leaves us with the conclusion that there is very little incentive for a revitalization of Hutterite religious and communal values but there is a continuous growth of economic and kinship values. The struggle between these two sets of values need not necessarily spell the doom of this culture but it forecasts a period of intense social upheavals over the next four or five decades that require all the social and psychological skills that Hutterites can muster to avoid their cultural assimilation.

Postscript

After parts of the preceding chapter were published in *Canadian Ethnic Studies,* no. 3 (1980), a lively debate regarding the causes and consequences of Hutterite population changes developed between Drs. Edward Boldt and Lance Roberts of the University of Manitoba and myself. (See *Canadian Ethnic Studies,* no. 3 (1980): 111-123.) Although there were differences of opinion between the three of us, we all agreed that more information in regard to the population dynamics of Hutterites was needed before verifiable conclusions could be drawn. Subsequently we joined forces to undertake the duplication of the Eaton tables for 1980 which thirty years earlier had started the world–wide interest in the population dynamics of Hutterites. Dr. Ian Whitaker of Simon Fraser University accompanied us part of the way. Since a total and controlled enumeration of all Hutterites was out of the question for financial reasons we approached Dr. Alice Martin and her associates at Northwestern University in Evanston, Illinois. Dr. Martin is the current custodian of a data bank which was started about thirty years ago by Drs. Arthur G. Steinberg and Herman Bleibtreu and which underwent accumulating improvements by several generations of researchers. These scientists from Northwestern University are geneticists and they are particularly interested in the inbreeding effects that take place in such an isolated gene pool as the Hutterites. The data bank they collected consists of the genealogical records of Hutterites going back 200 years.

Although this data bank was ideally suited for our purposes it had two drawbacks. The *Dariusleut* data were very incomplete and the *Lehrerleut* and *Schmiedeleut* data were only updated to the early 1970s. Supported by a grant from the Secretary of State our team undertook the updating of all records up to 1980 and in exchange was given access to the entire data bank for statistical purposes within the range of sociological inquiries. In addition we share ownership for the *Dariusleut* data. The task of updating was undertaken with the active support of Rev. Jacob Kleinsasser, Chrystal Spring Colony, Manitoba, the current President of the Hutterite Church. We expected to complete the updating of the entire data bank in a year. As it turned out it took five years. The checking and cleaning required almost full–time attendance of one person and the constant cooperation of the computer staff of Northwestern Memorial Hospital in Chicago whose cooperation and dedication were excellent.

In the spring of 1986 sets of data that duplicate the Eaton tables as much as possible finally became available to our team. We had of course used the occasion to break down the overall tables into a great many categories and as a result ended up with printout sheets half a foot high. We are now facing the task of validating the data through comparisons with data not collected through our own resources. Dr. Joseph Eaton, who still takes a great interest in Hutterite research, gracefully submitted to us all his fieldnotes and unpublished sources which will expedite our work enormously. Two or three years from now we expect to have a lengthy manuscript ready that documents the population dynamics of Hutterites for the last one hundred years with a high degree of completeness and accuracy.

In the preceding two chapters however, we were not concerned with the Hutterite population dynamics as a demographic problem but with the decline of population growth within the context of Lorimer's and Sauvy's models and their application to the Hutterite case. In this regard we took great pains to document that a decline in population growth indeed has taken place and we asserted that this decline was significant enough to warrant the prediction that the dynamic integration of the communities will undergo changes. The data that have become available to us this spring and which seem to satisfy our criteria of validity seem to confirm the first of these assertions. The first two tables presenting data on age specific birth rates and age specific nuptial birth rates are not identical with rates of natural increase or decrease because the mortality rate would have to be deducted. Yet we have reason to believe that the mortality rate among Hutterites has remained fairly constant. While the data refer only to *Dariusleut* women we are also confident that there are only minor deviations between the three *Leut*. These variations may be of significance for a detailed analysis between these groups for our present purposes however, we may take these data as representing a general trend among Hutterites. On the basis of the birth rate alone we are therefore justified in saying that a significant decline in Hutterite population growth has occurred. The tables do give us some clues as to the nature of this decline. Prior to 1970 all age groups show a very high birth rate. Suddenly the nuptial birth rate for 1970 shows a remarkable decline for women over thirty–five years of age which in 1980 drastically declines again. The age specific birth rate for 1980 shows the same tendency for the over thirty–five groups. Another remarkable decline can be observed in the twenty to twenty–four year group. The nuptial birth rate here declines not at all in 1970 but dips to one–third of the 1970 rate in 1980. If one compares the nuptial birth rate of the twenty to twenty–four year old woman with the birth rate for all women a drastic decline from 1960 on is shown reaching by 1980 about one–third of the rate of 1970. This seems to indicate that fewer *Dariusleut* women between twenty and twenty–four got married during this period. The third table showing the age specific marriage rates confirms this conclusion. Beginning already in 1950 the marriage rate of women in this age group declined to one–half by 1980. There are two conclusions we might draw from these tables. A marked decline in the birth rate of Hutterites has taken place among women thirty–five years and over and among women twenty to twenty–four years of age. The high birth rate for Hutterite women which formerly stretched over the whole fertility priod of women has effectively been shortened to ten

Table 9.11 Annual Age Specific Birth Rate per 1000 of Dariusleut Women for the Years 1920 - 1980.

Age	1920	1930	1940	1950	1960	1970	1980
20-24	223.2	169.5	189.9	170.0	97.1	147.7	52.0
25-29	160.0	285.7	403.0	413.0	377.6	305.1	178.8
30-34	269.3	388.9	280.7	315.8	363.6	285.7	127.1
35-39	217.4	160.0	333.3	257.6	228.3	192.9	96.0
40-44	200.0	240.0	121.2	160.7	213.3	142.9	23.3

Table 9.12 Annual Age Specific Nuptial Birth Rate per 1000 of Dariusleut Women for the Years 1920 - 1980.

Age	1920	1930	1940	1950	1960	1970	1980
20-24	391.3	270.3	312.5	377.8	326.9	466.7	180.0
25-29	250.0	387.1	519.2	558.8	551.0	457.6	257.1
30-34	444.4	451.6	372.1	369.2	455.7	370.4	161.3
35-39	416.7	250.0	448.3	320.8	295.8	241.1	118.9
40-44	238.1	352.9	142.9	204.5	242.4	175.0	28.4

Table 9.13 Age Specific Marriage Rates in Percent of Dariusleut Women for the Years 1920 - 1980.

Age	1920	1930	1940	1950	1960	1970	1980
20-24	62.2	62.7	60.8	45.0	29.7	31.6	28.9
25-29	64.0	73.8	77.6	73.9	68.5	66.7	69.5
30-34	66.7	86.1	75.4	85.5	79.8	77.1	78.8
35-39	52.2	64.0	74.4	80.3	77.2	80.0	80.0
40-44	84.0	68.0	84.8	78.6	88.0	81.6	82.0

years applying now to women from twenty–five to thirty–five years of age. The cause for the population decline of Hutterites must be sought among the twenty to twenty–four year old women who seem to postpone marriage and the thirty–five and over women who seem to be able to terminate their reproductive capacity in one way or another. But whatever the detailed causes may be a substantial decline in the population growth of Hutterites has occurred and must be dealt with when analysing this culture.

Contemporary Social Changes

PART IV

Contemporary
Social
Changes

TEN

Changing Attitudes and Practices Regarding the Acquisition of Property

The Hutterites are an interesting social laboratory, more especially since in recent years the colonies are coming under significant pressure from the surrounding North American society and culture. In this chapter we shall discuss changes in respect to the acquisition of personal property which we believe have crucial importance for understanding the process of social change among members of this sect.

The colonies, which often present an austere appearance in keeping with the religious teaching of the sect, are essentially agricultural collectives. It should be observed, however, that they conform to no single ethnographic description. Between the three major divisions within the sect — the *Dariusleut*, the *Schmiedeleut* and the *Lehrerleut* — there is demonstrated a range of cultural behaviour which makes it difficult to make meaningful generalizations. As other anthropologists have discovered, selected observations of a part of a society cannot form the basis of widesweeping generalizations without much imprecision in the final statements: this is certainly the case among the Hutterites who display a continuum of practices from the most severe and "traditional" on the one hand, to relatively "liberal" and emancipated on the other. Furthermore it is often difficult to capture the correct descriptive adjective, since the social reality consists of a moving boundary of principle, so that a characterization at one point in time may rapidly date. Yet to ignore this inherent dynamic is to neglect one of the most important elements in many contemporary Hutterite communities: their pragmatic adaptability to the changing social world in which they are located.

We might ask why Hutterite research in particular has often consisted of the presentation of a uniform model in the place of the actual diversity which is to be empirically observed. Perhaps the visible but deceptive uniformity in dress, in standards of housing, and even to some extent in the more superficial aspects of behaviour to outsiders, might lead an observer to assume that there is such a thing as a single Hutterite ideal type. Certainly the Hutterites themselves might welcome such a false assumption, since it could serve as a protective device in their relations with the outside world, as well perhaps as concealing temporarily, even from themselves, the degree to which in practice different Hutterite colonies have moved away from the severe code that characterized the foundation and early history of their sect. Moreover the presentation of this ideal type and its reinforcement is an effective way of eliciting the desired response from the outside world. It is, however, necessary to look beyond such an idealization to the dynamics that contemporary Hutterite life documents.

Keeping this diversity in mind, we shall discuss changes recently observed in *Dariusleut* colonies. Although the communities observed show many departures from the archetypal model in such matters as the restriction of community size, the adoption of an aggressive and highly sophisticated technology and marketing, and their utilization of a highly specialized economic base, additional observations show that the phenomena we analyse here are much more widespread in Hutterite society; indeed the process of acquisition of personal property by individual Hutterites is to be found in some degree in almost all colonies. Rather it is here suggested that in the most modernized colonies the process has evolved further.

From the spring of 1528 when Jakob Wiedemann and his followers inaugurated the *Guetergemeinschaft* (community of goods) (Zieglschmid, 1947: 18) onwards, sharing has characterized the sect, and became the foundation stone of their religious doctrine and practice. The "community of goods" bestows the security of salvation on the individual. All statements of Hutterite doctrine take this feature as axiomatic for the members. Thus when Peter Rideman, one of the earliest leaders, after Jakob Hutter,[1] compiled his *Rechenschaft unserer Religion, Lehr und Glaubens* (Account of our religion, doctrine and faith) about 1540 while he was imprisoned in Hesse, he wrote of this doctrinal feature as follows (we quote the somewhat lengthy passage in full so as to include the theological rationalizations):

Concerning community of goods

Now since all the saints have fellowship in holy things, that is in God, who also hath given to them all things in his Son Jesus Christ — which gift none should have for himself, but each for the other; as Christ also hath naught for himself, but hath everything for us, even so all the members of his body have naught for themselves, but for the whole body, for all the members. For his gifts are not sanctified and given to one member alone, or for one member's sake, but for the whole body with its members.

Now, since all God's gifts — not only spiritual, but also material things — are given to man, not that he should have them for himself or alone but with all his fellows, therefore the communion of saints itself must show itself not only in spiritual but also in temporal things; that as Paul saith, one might not have abundance and another suffer want, but that there may be equality. This he showeth from the law touching manna, in that he who gathered much had nothing over, whereas he who gathered little had no less, since each was given what he needed according to the measure.

Furthermore, one seeth in all things created, which testify to us still to-day, that God from the beginning ordained naught private for man, but all things to be common. But through wrong taking, since man took what he should not and forsook what he should take, he drew such things to himself and made them his

> property, and so grew and became hardened therein. Through such wrong taking and collecting of created things he hath been led so far from God that he hath even forgotten the Creator, and hath even raised up and honoured as God the created things which had been put under and made subject to him. And such is still the case if one steppeth out of God's order and forsaketh the same. (Rideman [1542] 1950: 88)

The "community of goods," it should be noted, did not provide for equal sharing of all the material possessions; rather it became a finely tuned rationale which secured an individual member's access to communal resources according to needs. Many of the earliest Hutterite *Ordnungen* (ordinances) acknowledged differences in such important matters as diet, by granting persons in occupations which involved much expenditure of physical energy a higher scale of rations. Other differences, such as those of age and sex, were also recognized in this way. In fact it might be asserted that the community of goods offered members of the sect unequal access to resources according to demonstrated needs, and these needs might be physical, emotional, or spiritual. In this respect the early Hutterite practice resembled some of the provision of the social programmes of the twentieth century.

Given Rideman's elaboration (as well as many others in Hutterite religious writing), how is it possible that the possession of private property seems to be increasing? We believe that this is facilitated by the more frequent occurrence of what might be termed "grey areas" (our terminology) in Hutterite conduct: that is to say an expansion in the number of situations where individual deviation on a minor scale is not formally subject to sanction, even though flagrant persistence in such deviance might ultimately elicit formal disapproval. In making this distinction it should perhaps be pointed out that Hutterite doctrine provides for the individual to come forward voluntarily, recognizing his wayward departure from the traditional code, and expressing repentance and requesting the elders for punishment and forgiveness. The onus to seek atonement must come from the offender, except in the most culpable offences when an intransigent person may be confronted with his misdeeds. Although originally

such requests for punishment were seen to originate in the conscience of the individual, today forces of social control most
likely push the individual towards making such a request. This
resort to social control, which is no longer directly tied to the
conscience as used to be the case, results in a more relaxed mode
of conduct, and the display of a degree of tolerance. It follows,
therefore, that minor deviations may occur, and even be remarked casually by other members of the community, but the
offending individual must take the first step towards repentance
and change. Although, therefore, gossip may be expressed
against the offender, a more decisive process of retribution will
not necessarily follow until the offence has been acknowledged
by the deviant member.

Since many of the minor deviations with respect to the acquisition of personal property may be essentially private, and perhaps known only to the offender and his family, such
behaviour may continue without eliciting any formal expression
of disapproval. We believe that a significant factor in this connection is the growing tendency for the dwelling to be a private
sphere. In earlier times there was essentially no private domain,
as Peter Rideman indicated when he wrote: "Therefore do we
watch over one another, telling each his faults, warning and re-
buking with all diligence" (Rideman [1542] 1950: 132).

Now, however, there is a degree of privacy, and this is associated firstly with the dwelling, and secondly with the kin-group,
who will be trusted to overlook minor deviance without attracting the attention of the whole community. This process, which
may be labelled "privatization," is one of the keys to the developing trend to acquire personal items. Another, and compounding,
feature of such deviance is to be found in the shifting nature of
the boundary between the permissible and the illegitimate. It is
our belief that in earlier times the division between "right" and
"wrong" in Hutterite society was perhaps more clear-cut, and in
any case the same standards were in force for many decades, so
that the present confusion among younger Hutterites, as among
other people in western society, was not present. Today the
boundary is continually changing, as deviant practice becomes
sufficiently widespread for new norms to prevail.

It might be argued that there is a basic Hutterite principle that precludes personal possessions, although this is no longer universal. Indeed in respect of property in the form of land, housing, and the means of production, this remains the rule. A colony is a corporation whose property belongs to all the members. There are no private pieces of land, and the houses themselves are owned by the colony as a whole. They are built collectively, still on a somewhat spartan model — although increasingly in some of the most modern colonies major concessions are made to urban planning and design. The houses are allotted to families by the leadership of the community, and hence an individual's living quarters are subject to reallocation as the needs of the community dictate, and as the family's requirements grow and diminish through marriage and death.

In the more traditional colony, when a newly married pair are granted living quarters, an allocation is also made of furniture, often sparse, and conforming to a community pattern. Whether this furniture becomes the exclusive and personal property of the married pair is, perhaps, not clear; expectations might vary from colony to colony, and also over time. In general in the newest colonies such furniture is seen as the exclusive property of the couple, and, as we shall see, under certain circumstances they might dispose of some of it (although not flagrantly). Meals are still largely taken in the communal eating-halls, where in fact women are seated apart from men, so that the need for a kitchen in the family's dwelling is confined to preparing light refreshment, especially following the arrival of visitors.

Significant to our discussion is the distinction between goods allocated for ready consumption, in contrast to goods over which the individual has the power of disposition, a disposition which does not necessarily include their immediate consumption. This distinction relates to cash, and also to some noncash goods, such as the less fundamental elements in diet. Thus adult Hutterites would be given an allocation of wine, and families would receive fruit and honey, as well as materials for clothing, wool, etcetera, in a regular ration. This would be allotted to households or to individuals, and the items would be removed to the privacy of the individual dwelling in which, it was expected, they would be consumed, or in the case of the materials, made into clothes by the womenfolk of the household.

Although the regular allocation of these foodstuffs and materials offered Hutterites within the same social category (such as those based on gender, health, and age) equality of access, it did not ensure that the use of these items was similarly equal. Indeed it was inevitably the pattern, recognized in practice in many communities, that different people would use these equally distributed items differentially, so that the idea that a person might dispose of the surplus of a given product that he or she did not wish to consume, was soon apparent. This practice became a "grey area," not formally forbidden, but not openly legitimated. The goods were clearly distributed on the assumption that they would be used, but consumption would not be regulated, only expected.

Thus there was a range of possible behaviour in disposing of items that had formed part of such a communal allocation. A woman might give some material for a blouse that she had received from her colony to her married daughter who would be living elsewhere, since as a norm colonies formed exogamous units. This would not formally be allowed or disallowed. However the donation of material to a daughter would also have other social consequences. Since Hutterite colonies would buy their clothing materials in bulk, there was a uniformity of dress among the women (or the men) of a colony, which was socially desirable since it conformed to the religious ideal of the avoidance of personal vanity. Material obtained by a woman from her mother would probably be of a different quality and appearance from that worn by her fellow womenfolk, and hence the gift would carry with it the chance of relief from uniformity, and thus also a minor assertion of individuality. The demonstration of personal attachments, other than that between husband and wife, was disapproved in early Hutterite thinking, but we observed the increasing acceptance of stronger emotional bonds between parents and children, especially in the younger generation of parents. Few colonies among the *Dariusleut* would now disapprove of the giving of a gift of material by a woman to her daughter, even if the other social consequences of such a gift might still be condemned. We see, therefore, that since the Hutterite family does not have an economic base, the individuals are only able to bestow minor economic benefits through such gift-giving, which in turn leads to a strengthening of the ties between members of the extended family.

There are also certain specific allotments in kind made to individual Hutterites; these include the household items a young Hutterite woman receives towards her dowry, which are kept in a personal chest given to her by the community when she reaches the age of eighteen.[2] These will mostly be soft goods such as domestic linen, which she will be employed in making for her household, and some of which she will be allowed to keep for her future personal use. When a woman becomes pregnant she is given bedding for the coming child, including feathers. If a mother has already had children she may not need the new supplies, and so they become surplus goods which she can eventually sell or barter, and she may retain the proceeds. We might also mention at this point the burgeoning home industry, including quilt-making, down jackets, and other needlecraft which is occurring in Hutterite colonies, and provides items for private sale, often through the conversion of raw materials, or poor quality materials, into saleable goods. Wine, honey, and dried fruit, if available, are also items that an individual may legitimately acquire, but which he or she may not need, and can consequently later trade. Furniture that a family has received from the colony in the past, but which also proves surplus to their requirements, may also be sold to outsiders for cash (usually by the women). Thus it will be seen that there are a number of ways in which a female Hutterite can engage in personal marketing, although usually it is by the conversion of goods into cash.

Perhaps the most striking deviation from the traditional way of life is manifested in the allocation of sums of personal money, which the individual may keep, and be permitted to accumulate. This may be obtained by methods both "legitimate" and "illegitimate" (although these are not categories used by our informants). However as we have already stressed, this boundary is a shifting one. Foremost among legitimate money is a small personal allotment made to all adult members of the colony. One Hutterite community recently raised this allowance to ten dollars per person per month; in others it may be as low as two to four dollars. These personal funds are given without precise specification as to how they are to be used and no distinctions in respect of gender, relative age among adults, or health, are made. Further, it has long been Hutterite practice that when individual members travel on the business of the colony they are given a daily allowance, which with some care may result in a surplus which an individual retains. This may then, for example, be converted into candies, which on return to the colony, will be given to selected children for somewhat surreptitious consumption.

For male members of the colony there is a trend to acquire cash directly. This may be achieved by undertaking minor economic services for their neighbours. Of course this will by no means be on a full-time basis, but Hutterites, with hitherto a good supply of male labour, would often be called upon by neighbouring farmers in an emergency. The service that they performed might be paid for in ready cash, which the persons completing the task would partially or wholly retain. Small items of furniture that a man might make in his spare time could also be sold. Machinery belonging to the collectivity might be loaned, usually with labour to operate it, and the method of paying for this would be somewhat imprecise. These "grey areas" are a frequent source of money for the male Hutterite. One cannot altogether preclude the occasional sale of goods, such as vegetables, correctly belonging to the whole community, but which might also fall in this "grey area" and become the source of individual gain.

There is a further source of personal property, however, that is increasingly being manifested in some of the more "progressive" colonies. This is particularly associated with *rites de passage*, especially marriage. Today many Hutterite couples are given gifts at the time of marriage by relatives from other colonies in particular, and these gifts are always seen as personal property. They will have been purchased by the donors out of personal rather than community funds, generated in ways outlined above. Although the individual items might be relatively inexpensive, the large number of contributing relatives may result in a great number of gifts, so that whole rooms might be furnished, often with consumer items that indirectly conflict with Hutterite principles, such as toasters, dishes, and other cooking equipment

which incidentally also appear to contradict the Hutterite practice of communal eating. The birth of a child, traditionally
treated with a degree of religious indifference due to the rejection
of infant baptism, also now becomes the occasion for the send-
ing of further gifts, although these are not usually on such a lavish scale.

In this chapter we have sought to document the growing practice among Hutterites of setting apart specific articles or products
as private property, belonging to the individual or to the immediate family unit, rather than to the community as a whole. The
consequences of this practice are perhaps of greater social than
economic significance. We believe that they constitute the tangible modification of the earlier Hutterite ideal of communal
ownership. The bestowal of personal gifts necessarily involves
redefining the "community of goods." Redefinitions of the community of goods are seen by us as a continuing process in Hutterite life stretching back to the sect's earliest years and are the
means by which major discontinuities are averted, offering an
opportunity for change without the direct challenging of tradition. Such changes, however, have to occur within the context of
a three generational traditional memory for them to be acceptable.

These processes do not occur in isolation from other social
trends, however. Thus we have identified increasing privatization, although this process may apply to a whole family as
well as to an individual. We have also noted the stronger emphasis on kinsmen, who may be the source of private property
through gift-giving.

Of fundamental importance to our analysis is the recognition
that the process is marked by imprecision and uncertainty.
Flagrant violation of the norms is accompanied by scandal,
which leads to the reassertion of the traditional practice, so that
the process of change is temporarily halted or even reversed.
This is the anthropological reality, which would be concealed if
we simply chose to present a single model of Hutterite society,
analysed in terms of a uniform progression. However, what is
most apparent from our study is the enhanced differentiation to
be found within a single Hutterite colony, a differentiation
manifested not merely in a growing trend away from a total

uniformity in such external matters as dress, but also in visible inequality in the extent to which houses may be equipped with consumer items, in variable practice in minor ways such as the enjoyment of supplements to the food still largely eaten communally, and in differing behaviour towards children, as well as in a variety of views concerning what constitutes appropriate behaviour between parents and children. The diversification that we describe is to be found not only within a single colony, however, but also between different colonies within the same endogamous division (i.e., the *Leut*). Although ostensibly concerned with the acquisition of private property by Hutterites, our study may also have illuminated the role of informal social control in the process of cultural change.

ELEVEN

The Hutterite Economy

Recent Changes and Their Social Correlates

The traditional sociocultural and economic adjustment of the Hutterite colonies in North America has recently come under severe pressure, due primarily to major technological changes in the field of agriculture, as well as to regulatory impositions, largely of a bureaucratic nature, by the state. These pressures have given rise to such social problems as unemployment, as well as to economic inefficiency, and these in turn threaten both the social fabric and the spiritual unity of the community. In adjusting to these pressures, the Hutterites have been compelled to engage in a far-reaching restructuring of their economic system, with concomitant extensive changes in their social structure. The present chapter seeks to analyse these changes in detail, especially through observations in recently established colonies in the eastern part of the State of Washington, and also attempts to assess the impact of these same changes on the future survival of the group.

The Hutterites have been a singularly successful minority group. Its expansion during the past century was, as we have seen, in large measure due to a subtle but well functioning relationship between psychological, economic, and social structural factors. Traditionally, Hutterites have instituted and refined a communal system of production based upon the principle of economic diversification. The grain production common to western Canada and the U.S. formed the economic core around which were organized such activities as the raising of cattle, sheep, hogs, chickens, ducks, geese, and turkeys. The rationale behind this mixed farming was to grow basic agricultural products as efficiently as possible, and then to convert this grain, by way of the digestive tracts of livestock, into products offering a maximum profit.[1] Any surplus of grain was marketed through normal commercial channels. The diversified system of production offered a good insurance against the risks inherent in the cultivation of a single product, and it fitted in also with the Hutterite system of social stratification. The basic division between male and female labour effectively took care of the considerable variety of economic pursuits, whilst the efficiency of the system was maintained by the hierarchical organization based on a gender-determined division of labour.

This traditional system has now come under pressure from three new factors, namely technological change, regulatory restrictions primarily bureaucratic in nature, and the limiting of expansion due to changes in the surrounding farm population.

The principal change in the technological sphere has been the emergence of machinery that reduces the demand for manual labour, with the consequence that the relatively large adolescent labour force that existed in the past is no longer required. Instead of a multi-skilled large work-force that would often be employed on a number of different tasks in the course of the agricultural year, there are now required a few, mechanically competent machine operators, with a sufficient degree of technical knowledge to use sophisticated equipment.

In the bureaucratic sphere there have emerged, more especially in Canada, a variety of government agencies whose principal function is to regulate the production and marketing of such items as eggs, chickens, hogs, etcetera. These boards are seen by Hutterites as having created a rigid structure which reduces their own flexibility, and in some cases has made the continued production of the item no longer commercially profitable. Most of all it has the effect of limiting the productive opportunities.

The trend in the consolidation of farm operations during the last twenty years has been towards larger farms using a complex technology requiring increased capital investment. This process has on the one hand eliminated a great number of marginal farms, and on the other has facilitated a process of economic consolidation for the surviving ones. The elimination of marginal farms affects the opportunities for Hutterite expansion by withdrawing land from the market. A general increase in the price of land, which coincides with the disappearance of the marginal farm, makes expansion much more costly than was the case previously. For a decade and a half, therefore, Hutterites could often expand only into frontier areas of Canada, or into marginal agricultural areas.

How have these factors affected the structure and dynamics of Hutterite society? Regulatory impositions by government agencies or semi-official boards affect certain economic pursuits through the setting of quotas and of standards. Thus the egg production in a particular colony normally depends very much on the available manpower, the capital resources, and the marketing conditions; these factors must be balanced to achieve economic efficiency. But production quotas which are set or refused, for example, by an Egg Marketing Board might interfere with the establishment of such a level of economic efficiency. Demands for certain standards of production might necessitate the installation of equipment which Hutterites might not wish to meet, or which they might find unprofitable. Standards of production relating to the final product might likewise interfere with the overall efficiency of the Hutterite enterprise. Some colonies, for example, might find it more profitable to turn out an average hog rather than attempting to produce a top-quality one. Calling for government inspectors to supervise certain processes might prove to be time consuming and disruptive.

The overall effect of these regulations is to discourage the maintenance of certain operations under mixed–farming conditions. On the other hand these regulations encourage specialization, with the resulting concentration of colony resources to meet the stipulated standards. If such a concentration of resources is attempted, it demands production on a scale that would no longer allow the continuation of the balanced mixed farming. Even where these regulatory impositions are absent, general market conditions tend to have the same effect. The permanency of supply, the maintenance of quantity and quality, and the scale of production are all prerequisites demanded by the agricultural wholesaler and the price structure. When these conditions cannot be met, certain branches of production might run into marketing difficulties which could make their viability questionable.

The trend toward larger farms in the western prairies accelerated after the Second World War, and resulted in the elimination of a great many farmers who for some reason could not participate in this trend. This situation provided a very favourable environment for the Hutterites by making the acquisition of agricultural land possible. During the last ten to fifteen years, however, the trend has slowed down considerably, as more farms have reached a size and level of efficiency which no longer makes them marginal operations. There are, therefore, considerably fewer people willing to sell land, and if they do the prices they demand are much higher than was the case in the past. Hutterite colonies aim at a minimum of 6,000 acres, which few family farms can manage. Tracts of land that come on to the market are usually much smaller than a colony's normal requirement. The probability of assembling more land in a particular locality so as to satisfy the minimum needs of the colony, therefore, diminishes as more farms outside Hutterite control become economically efficient. To acquire land within a reasonable distance from the home base has, therefore, become more difficult over the years. This is especially so for those colonies who have not managed a sufficient accumulation of capital to make rather enticing offers to farmers reluctant to sell. The result is that the bulk of moderately wealthy Hutterite colonies find it more difficult to acquire the landholding that would allow them to branch out after seventeen to twenty years in the traditional way.

How do Hutterites cope with these factors? As has been shown, there are strong indications that the higher rate of natural increase of 4.12 percent per annum has declined to 2.9 percent and is still declining. There is also a considerable drop in the average size of colonies from ninety-eight members per colony in 1950 to 88.4 members in 1977. Such a decline is indicative of a much diminished demand for manpower. By reducing the size of the colony the problem of under-employment has somewhat declined. Although all three main divisions among the Hutterites, the *Dariusleut*, the *Lehrerleut*, and the *Schmiedeleut*, have reduced the size of their colonies, the *Dariusleut* have gone much further than the others by reducing the average colony size to seventy-seven members, whilst the *Schmiedeleut* have a colony size of ninety-two, and the *Lehrerleut* colonies remained as large as ninety-eight members. This suggests that the groups deal with the problem in somewhat different ways.

Whilst it is of course both difficult and extremely risky for an established colony to change its balanced economic operations, newly established colonies are less inhibited by such concerns. It is in these colonies, therefore, that major adjustments to the above-mentioned pressures become visible. A number of recently established colonies of the *Dariusleut* in the eastern part of the State of Washington and in Montana clearly show these patterns of adjustment. At the beginning most of these colonies tried to establish a mixed–farming enterprise; however they soon came to realize that agricultural specialization provided a much more solid basis for survival than did mixed farming. The form of specialization they finally adopted was dictated either by geographical circumstances, as in the case of ranching, or business opportunities in the form of dairy production, the raising of hogs or turkeys, seed potato or large-scale potato production. Each of these modes of production implied a loss of cultural experience that the mixed farming culture among Hutterites had built up over generations, and that incorporated the collective economic wisdom of the sect. In contrast, the new specialization could only partially build on the traditional wisdom. The scope of the operation, and the expertise necessary for its successful implementation, had to be generated within each of the new colonies separately. Such an enterprise demands an active, creative, and risk-taking population willing to discard traditional wisdom, and prepared to tread on new ground. Some of the new colonies openly describe themselves as being "aggressive" in their economic relationships, which is a major departure from older Hutterite values and behaviour.

Accompanying greater specialization we find that there is also required a high degree of economic innovation. In order to achieve good economic returns, and also to avoid competing with neighbouring Hutterite colonies that might also be adopting a policy of specialization, there is a continuing requirement of inventiveness, in contrast to the old pattern of mixed farming, in which change was relatively slow. Such personality characteristics as flexibility and creativity become much more desirable than in the old-style colony, where the only outlet for flexibility lay in the variety of tasks that the general work-force would complete in the course of the season. Both of these new virtues are in marked contrast to the esteem placed on cultural continuity which has hitherto been so characteristic of Hutterite life. These demands are primarily made on the leadership rather than on the rank and file membership, but the relative smallness of the total work-force in a specialized operation makes it probable that the individual will in due time be required to demonstrate and exercise such qualities as well.

Of particular importance is the need for an understanding of the potential advantages of a complex technology. For a successful and efficient enterprise there is a distinct need for a high level of production, to achieve maximum economies of scale, and this in turn requires the use of the most modern equipment to achieve such efficiency. At the same time more attention will have to be paid to the quality of the ultimate product, since to remain in the economic vanguard the colony can no longer be satisfied with achieving a middle-range standard. The highest financial returns accompany highest quality productivity.

We may document these trends by describing a particular new colony which specializes in large-scale potato production totalling annually 45,000 to 50,000 tons which was established ten years ago. It maintains six large semi–trailer trucks for long-range potato hauling and ten large three-axle trucks for medium distances. It receives its seed potatoes from first class producers, some of which have to be brought over distances of four hundred miles; it markets its products to processing firms which produce a variety of potato–based products. The colony irrigates most of its land, and developed a highly sophisticated system utilizing deep wells. It has a number of tractors, four of them of the largest type to be found in the region. It connects all of its moving equipment through a private radio system which alone cost $80,000 to install (although the use of radio and television receivers for domestic entertainment in Hutterite dwellings is still barred). The colony harvests 40,000 bushels of wheat a day at the height of the season, and hauls these products over a distance of twelve miles to its own elevators.

Perhaps the most striking evidence of the changes accompanying such economic specialization is shown by the type and layout of the buildings. The dwelling units are laid out according to a careful and artistic plan, so that they resemble a modern subdivision; the units themselves having the appearance of condominiums. In a departure from tradition these dwellings contain interior plumbing, including several bathrooms, as well as a kitchen unit, although the scale of equipment is still somewhat low since members eat in the communal eating-hall. There are hardwood floors and carpets, and a good, but not lavish, degree of electrical and other fittings. The houses face well-landscaped lawns, maintained by an underground sprinkler system, and planted with flowering shrubs, illuminated at night by street-lighting.

The working environment is similarly changed. In place of the low wooden barns customary in the older colonies, there are precast concrete structures, of the size and proportions of an aircraft hangar, with the most modern facilities including air-conditioning, as well as a small coffee-shop where workers may take light refreshment without returning to the communal eating–hall. While older colonies have fuelling facilities for their trucks and tractors, this colony has a fully-equipped service station with a concrete canopy prominently situated in front of the work area. The maintenance of the equipment is facilitated by a complex of machine shops, including separate sections for welding and tire-maintenance, as well as a large truck-washing facility. All transportation equipment is kept indoors, and is maintained in impeccable condition. Potato-sorting, -cutting, -planting, and -harvesting equipment is kept in such quantities as to enable maximum demands due to variable weather conditions to be met. In contrast, cattle, dairy, sheep, and hogs have shrunk to insignificant operations meeting only the domestic needs of the colony. Similarly the production of ducks and geese is now a minimal operation to satisfy the colony's own requirements.

For the period of the year when there is no agricultural work, the colony maintains a large and well-equipped carpentry shop, in which is made custom built furniture of the highest quality. This is highly priced, and is usually supplied to commercial enterprises which place precise orders for individual units. The materials used are expensive hardwoods, wrought on machinery often imported from Europe. Although a smaller operation than the complex of machine shops, the carpentry enterprise still reflects high calibre planning.

The whole colony has a population of less than sixty people, of whom thirteen are adult males. There were no complaints of these individuals being overworked; on the contrary, when discussing the future viability of the operation, colony members let it be known that they would rather branch out than enlarge the scope of the existing operation. It seems, therefore, that specialization demands only approximately half the population base that was previously required in the mixed-farming economy.

Turning to the effects which such economic changes have on the social structure, it is evident that with the disappearance of such operations as the raising of beef, cattle, and hogs, a number of traditional work and status positions have also disappeared. New jobs, including the maintenance of the new equipment, do not carry the traditional social statuses — their value is derived from the utilitarian nature of the enterprise. There is therefore not only a shrinkage in the division of labour, but also an injection of egalitarianism, since all status is derived from the utility of the operation in the overall economic process. An example might illustrate this point. In time of famine, the Hutterites elected a trusted male to distribute bread among the members of the community in accordance with established convention. Today where bread is plentiful a few colonies still have a breadcutter, who during mealtimes goes back and forth between the tables and the kitchen to replenish the supply of bread. The utility of this job has now disappeared, since the females who serve the meals anyway could easily supply the bread as well. The status of this position nevertheless has been maintained, because only male individuals honoured as exemplary members of the colony would be allotted the appointment to this position.

The shoemaker, who traditionally cared for the footwear of all individuals in the colony, was forced to remain in close contact with them. He would have to repair all footwear, and thereby stood in a service relationship to his fellows. Feelings of generosity and gratitude, but also sentiments of equality and economy, would flow between the shoemaker and the members of the colony. This exchange of sentiments was an important component of the social bonding. New job positions, however, lack this overlay of traditional sentiment. Their utility relates to machinery rather than to people; greater social distance between one individual and another is the consequence. The performance of machine-oriented work is accompanied by long periods of isolation when individuals drive trucks for hundreds of miles alone, or operate tractors in a solitary situation. The radio communication was consciously installed by this colony, not merely because of its efficiency in eliminating delays after breakdown or malfunction of equipment, but also to maintain social contact between individuals who were isolated by the nature of this new work from their fellows. Yet despite the use of electronics, a greater degree of individualization is apparent.

Even among women, who still perform many of their jobs in groups, such as cooking, baking, and cleaning, there is a nostalgic yearning for the evenings spent spinning, singing, and storytelling. Splitting feathers used to be a popular winter activity, which afforded an opportunity for the exchange of gossip between women. In many colonies where these jobs have disappeared, women are very vocal in complaining about the loss of this type of social contact with their neighbours. Since there is no corresponding compensation for these activities, either in reading or through the electronic media, the reduction of such communal discourse is keenly felt.

Hutterites maintain that the religious community and its services demand a minimum number of people to make their rituals psychologically impressive. Since the religious services have become completely ritualized the emphasis is very much on the emotional effects which such rituals have on individuals. As the mediaeval Catholic Church found, such emotional effects can best be achieved in buildings of a certain size, and with a congregation sufficiently numerous. The intonation of a hymn carried by only a few voices does not contain this emotional effect. Therefore Hutterites recognize that small congregations lack certain religious qualities. This feeling is enhanced by the practice of establishing colonies based on one or two families. In the past a community usually consisted of four, five, and up to seven extended families thereby drawing on a number of family traditions all known to each Hutterite. The reduction of family-diversification creates a community which coincides with a close kin-group. This results in the loss of diversified family traditions and in restricted contact, apart from the existing isolation brought about by the three endogamous divisions of the Hutterites.

In the colony mentioned the traditional kindergarten, where children between three and six were taken care of during the working-day, and which was an important instrument of socialization, was discontinued. Instead children between these ages remain in the care of the family, which requires a major shift in the working patterns of mothers in this age-group. This will ultimately have consequences on the uniformity which is such a salient feature of Hutterite life. It should be mentioned that the preacher in this colony, a man in his late thirties, left his community in his younger years and lived for a time in the outside world. He has, therefore, extensive experience with alternate lifestyles, which allows him to make innovations which reflect what he regards as a healthy disrespect for obsolete Hutterite practices.

Equally difficult was the election and training of the German schoolteacher, who having had no previous experience, felt himself to be inadequate for the post. Since there are no training facilities among Hutterites for the German language teacher, the linguistic proficiency of the pupils leaves much to be desired. In fairness to this individual, this is a long-standing problem. The complex farm machinery is maintained through English-language manuals, so that no technical German vocabulary is readily available. Therefore, among the changes from traditional Hutterite practice is the extensive utilization of English instead of their archaic variety of German. The abandonment of German, especially as a medium of communication when discussing matters relating to everyday life, has reached the point that the colony cook is unable to read a German–language cookbook. A person who had accompanied a patient to hospital and was writing to report progress to the relatives in the colony employed English.

Colonies which are as small as forty to sixty persons have some difficulty in electing a full slate of elders. Very often the second preacher becomes redundant. When such a colony branches out, a preacher must be quickly elected, and thereby is deprived of a long apprenticeship in his role as preacher and leader.

Another change that becomes apparent is the shifting of prestige to a somewhat younger group of persons in the economically specialized colonies. The new economy requires that leaders have a technical understanding that is often not possible for those of an older generation, and hence the positions of authority tend to be filled by a younger group of persons, in contrast to the traditional mixed–farming economy where knowledge might often be equated with experience, and hence also with age. There is therefore a perceptible shift in the relative status hierarchy, which works to the disadvantage of the older group.

There are, on the other hand, a number of consequences which seem to strengthen the central authority within the specialized colonies. The disappearance of operations such as the raising of cattle and other livestock also means the disappearance of operations that are partially independent in a financial sense. Every boss of a Hutterite enterprise had to account for his financial transactions every two weeks. This gave each of the bosses a degree of freedom to handle the finances as he thought best. Although ultimately he would be responsible to the manager, he nevertheless enjoyed a degree of autonomy commensurate with his experience. In a specialized colony where many of these positions are lacking, all financial transactions are now conducted by the manager. He in turn employs a chartered accountant who will assess the financial success of the different operations strictly according to profit and loss. On the basis of his advice colonies have eliminated whole operations when their accountant deemed them unprofitable. The accountant, of course, is unaware of the social consequences when his advice is followed. Torn between economic efficiency and social utility, they are most likely to follow the route of economic efficiency as offering immediate economic benefits. The social consequences are only realized much later, and often at a time when the economic process is irreversible.

We might conclude that changes in technology, bureaucratic impositions, and scarcity of suitable land have all induced a number of Hutterite colonies to change from a mixed–farming economy to one involving agricultural specialization. The consequences of such changes are noticeable in a utilitarian transformation of the Hutterite social structure. A great many positions having traditional status are being eliminated, thereby reducing the job and status-positions in the colonies, and requiring fewer personnel to run these operations. The highly complex technology that is being adopted tends to isolate the individual from his neighbours by reducing or eliminating the work-group. There is a certain amount of egalitarianism in running different types of machinery in contrast to the hierarchically organized division of labour in mixed farming.

Each colony is forced to find its own form of economic specialization, subject to local opportunities and conditions. The result is a loss of the traditional agricultural wisdom. We may also expect over time that the commonality of Hutterite experience, previously developed through the common practice of mixed farming, will disappear to the detriment of the solidarity of the sect as a whole. There are, however, no signs yet that colonies that have specialized are in any greater danger of breaking up. At least at this juncture specialized colonies seem to display a degree of economic vigour that draws the individual towards the common centre, and thereby contributes to its unity.

The risk to the Hutterites is perhaps greatest at the point of transition to the new economy. Success depends on the presence, among those changing, of a high degree of inventiveness and independence. These characteristics will not necessarily always be present in sufficient quantity, and when they are not, a colony will probably not be successful. Such failure, with resulting tensions and the visible fruitlessness of social upheaval will all be serious obstacles in the search for new social and economic dynamics. Where these qualities are present, however, new but substantially different units in the form of economically different colonies will emerge. Some of the new psychological and behavioural characteristics of the aggressive economic enterprise may, however, contribute to a reduction in the social distance to the host society, which has hitherto contributed to the isolation of Hutterites.

TWELVE

The Changing Roles of Hutterite Women

Relatively little description, and even less analysis of the roles of women in Hutterite society have so far been published. The reason for this neglect, it would seem, is connected with the strong male dominance that characterises life in this Anabaptist sect, and as a result most of the scientific discussion is taken up with aspects of the life of male Hutterites. To be sure Eaton and Weil (1955) in their study of Hutterite mental health devote some space to the condition of Hutterite women, whilst Bennett (1967: 111-14) as well as Hostetler and Huntington (1967: 30-33) supply some descriptive material concerning various aspects of the world of Hutterite women. Schluderman and Schluderman (1971a;1971b) treat the roles of Hutterite women in the context of child-rearing and child-development, and the bulk of the descriptive ethnographic material on the Hutterites treats women in the context of the family or the division of labour within the various colonies.

This chapter attempts to analyse the role of women in Hutterite society with reference to recent changes that have occurred within that society. The decline of Hutterite population growth suggests that a far-reaching restructuring of Hutterite society is presently under way. These changes, which seem to be correlated with the adoption of technologically more sophisticated, and generally labour-saving, devices by Hutterites, also affect the roles of women within that culture in a substantial way. But over and above these more visible technological changes, there are areas within religion and tradition that are undergoing a more subtle transformation; indeed the changes presently observable in Hutterite society are at the same time both religious and material in character. The effects of these changes on the formal structure of society are so far minimal, but they have already had a major impact on the informal relations in Hutterite colonies.

We shall here attempt to investigate certain religious/ideological changes which have led to the reinterpretation of cosmology and have changed traditional customs and mores. In the second part of the chapter we shall discuss the consequences of certain technological changes upon the life of Hutterite women.

As we have seen in Chapter 10, the social reality of Hutterite life is based on a moving boundary of principle, so that any characterization has temporal limits and validity. The diversity of behaviour is in fact increasing due to the emergence of different forms of economic specialization by individual colonies, which is giving rise to substantial differences in the economic and cultural basis of the individual colonies themselves.

Turning to religious/ideological changes one must remember that the nature of Hutterite religion is structured in accordance with the collective orientation of the society as a whole. As we have already shown, the individual, his work, and his eternal future were all unalterably welded to the state of the total community, and to the extent that he could be saved only if the whole community were saved, he in turn had to do his share to make such communal salvation possible. In his calling the individual carried the burden of saving his neighbours and kin.

The role of women, like that of men, came under this great social pressure, but unlike the men, women were considered morally weaker and therefore in need of men's guidance. One of the early Hutterites writing from prison to his wife expressed this when he admonished her to be quiet in demeanour as becomes a woman, reminding her that one woman's speech was all that had been needed to precipitate the fall of mankind (Gross 1980: 98). The reference is, of course, to the role of Eve in

the Garden of Eden and from there derived the notion in Hutterite theology that women are seen as weaker than men. This
inbuilt expectation of unreliability not only determined the
lower status of women, but on occasion also frees them from
some of the hierarchical constraints which operate for men. The
low estimation of women offers them a permanent role as an
instrument of change with the result that an important number
of new ideas and inventive behaviours originate among the female population of the colony. The guidance of women by men
was not supposed to be oppressive, but in accordance with Christian love and understanding. However, when, as we have seen,
Hutterite society traditionalized and lost much of its individual
fervour and religious consciousness, such understanding and
love were difficult to maintain. A religiously legitimized male
authority relying mostly on forms of social control relegated
women to second-class status. Men could not only claim religious authority over women, but also dominated traditionally
the political and economic structure of the community. For centuries, therefore, it was possible to maintain a practice whereby
Hutterite couples were matched by the preachers, a custom
which only disappeared in the first half of the nineteenth century. Even today Hutterite women routinely marry outside their
own colony. This virilocal residence pattern favours the preser-
vation of the male hierarchy in the community by protecting it
against the competition of incoming husbands.

This religiously supported male authority which legitimized
male/female differentials has recently come under pressure. Although Hutterite religion forms a coherent ideological system,
there are a number of reference points with other fundamentalist Christian orientations whose specific formulations do not remain unnoticed in Hutterite colonies. As we have shown in
Chapter 3 on religious defection, one of these reference points is
the emphasis on Christ as a personal saviour for the individual
believer. God as an individual's personal saviour is somewhat
antithetical to the Hutterite conception of God as the collective
saviour of the community. Hutterites, however, like the rest of
society, find the notion of the individual saviour greatly attractive for psychotherapeutic reasons. Indeed, members of the sect
are slowly and unconsciously drawing more and more into the

direction of this individual conception of God, and it is the Hutterite women who tend to accept this concept more readily than the men. This is understandable, since their socioreligious position of inequality disappears with the concept of a God who is the saviour of all individuals regardless of gender, in contrast to a communal conception of God which retains far-reaching inequalities. The egalitarian component of this religious reference point carries other intellectual attractions for Hutterite women. Faced with problems in child–rearing and child-socialization, there is a tendency to be concerned with individual differences and personal psychological problems. These are traditionally seen in the light of religious doctrine, and solutions are sought in religious theory. Individual concepts of God, in contrast, lend themselves much more easily to psychological introspection than does the collective concept of God of the traditional Hutterite faith.

This indicated shift in the concept of God is, of course, very subtle and progresses slowly. Its immediate effect on Hutterite women is a change in self–perception and self-consciousness. The woman able to communicate with God as her personal saviour finds an outlet by which personal problems can be communicated and explored. This individual process reduces her spiritual dependency on the community where traditionally she would carry such problems to the preacher if she felt at all justified in appearing with personal concerns before the highest authority in her community. Since the latter is not often the case and women therefore see little or no possibility in communicating problems to a source of authority beyond husband and mother (if these are receptive to such confessions), many problems become internalized and remain unresolved. The concept of a personal saviour, whose willingness to listen and to respond is unquestioned, gives women the possibility of coming at least partially to grips with their problems. This mechanism at the same time reduces the woman's dependence on the spiritual authority of the colony, and enhances her self-consciousness and her individuality.

With this newly acquired self-consciousness, long-standing traditional customs and behavioural patterns now can be reinterpreted. There is, of course, no possibility of entertaining separation or divorce; such drastic measures are still outside her reach. There are nevertheless a great number of ambiguous areas where this newly acquired individuality can tilt the interpretation of a custom in a new direction. The following example might illustrate the process: in the cultural definition of health and sickness among Hutterite women, a number of legitimate conceptions existed that to a great extent determined when a woman could consider herself to be ill, how severe her illness was, what kind of advice should be solicited and what kind of medical treatment was to be applied. Although Hutterites hold little or no superstitions in regard to medical sciences, there were ambiguous areas where traditional definitions and medical requirements would confront each other. Whether a woman suffering from some sort of gynaecological disorder should have more children or should terminate her reproductive capacity, was in the past unquestionably answered in favour of the former. The shift in the individual perception of women, as indicated above, tends to tilt the decision in the direction of giving greater consideration to the woman's health, rather than to her continued reproductive capacity. The frequency with which this type of decision is presently made is such that Hutterites generally claim that their women today are much more sickly than in previous generations. In certain colonies the number of women who have terminated their reproductive capacity by surgical means outnumbers those whose fertility is still intact. Such a process is concomitant with the acceptance of a doctor/patient relationship where the advice of the doctor carries greater authority than the traditional religious proscription of the community.

Changes similar to the above can be found in courtship, marriage, education, and in the general life of the community. A further example might be cited; the previous high fertility of Hutterite women indicates that the frequency of intercourse was extremely high (Eaton and Mayer 1954). Some Hutterite women today have learned that "refusing to be nice" to their husbands is one way of having husbands pay greater attention to their concerns. This shift from an unquestioned sexual availability to that of sexual access depending on the behaviour of the male is a pattern of behaviour which simply did not exist in the past.

Perhaps most noticeable is a change in mate-selection. Hutterite women agree that today's females are much more selective and reluctant to enter into marriage than in the past. A great many characteristics regarding the prospective husband, his personality, background, family, and community are considered before marriage is decided upon. This elaborate process not only results in a greater number of Hutterite women remaining unmarried, but also leads to a postponement of marriage to an age-level where more mature judgements regarding the above criteria can be made. This again is a marked departure from the almost automatic entering into marriage at an early age which previously was the practice.

The spiritual sources of change among Hutterite women however must be seen in conjunction with material changes largely caused by the adoption of technological devices. Ever since Hutterites made the crucial decision to adopt electricity, trucks, and tractors several decades ago, the economic unit of the colony was inevitably pushed towards greater efficiency. This efficiency was at once enforced by the general market conditions, and the enormous population increase which made considerable financial demands on the individual colony. In contrast, living conditions for Hutterites remained very austere, so that internal toilet facilities were often lacking in their homes. Hutterites choose to make the visit to the outhouse in weather of -25°C more comfortable by putting a heating lamp into the facility, while at the same time refusing to furnish their dwellings with indoor sanitation. While all productive and community-serving facilities were modernized to the latest standards, facilities for individual convenience were kept in an archaic state.

During the last decade and a half these restrictions on consumption are slowly breaking down. The old living quarters are increasingly replaced by modern housing facilities containing such items as bathrooms, central heating facilities, and floor and wall coverings. A new type of housing arrangement has moved the storage space from the attic to the basement, with the result that the basement facilities became individualized for the family living immediately above; this is in contrast to the open attic facilities shared by a number of families. Such individualized basements almost automatically lead to an extension of the living area into the basement. The result is that the Hutterite family which previously was confined to a bedroom plus the sharing of a sitting-room now virtually comes into the possession of housing facilities resembling a condominium. For women this means an extension of their private sphere and family authority. Men who were accustomed never to take their footwear off when entering the living quarters come increasingly under pressure, simply because a failure to do so creates an all too visible disorder. Modern facilities require new cleaning devices such as floor-polishers and vacuum cleaners, but also soaps and detergents, thereby increasing the variety of products required by the colony. The old-fashioned laundry facilities in the colony and the scheduling of a wash-day for each family have been replaced by the most modern washing facilities constituting a battery of devices as found in a coin-laundry. A change in the pattern of consumption has led to the discontinuation in some colonies of the laborious fruit and berry-picking activities customarily engaged in by the women. Women who, according to tradition, do most of the painting in the colony now do so by using the most modern devices. Twenty years ago a Hutterite woman would try to clean a paint-brush with gasoline because turpentine was too "expensive" to buy; today turpentine and other solvents are available as a matter of course.

There is, therefore, a definite shift from an under-valuation of human effort and labour which was taken for granted, to the acceptance of labour-saving devices. Women are greatly affected by this shift since they traditionally performed many of the activities which were labour-intensive and relatively unpleasant. The milking of dairy cattle, which was a traditional chore for women has been taken over by men with the introduction of technologically sophisticated milking devices. Field work formerly done by Hutterite women has virtually disappeared with the exception of gardening, and much of the work even here is performed by machines.

The work routinely done by women like cooking and baking has been modernized through the utilization of cooking and baking facilities living up to modern commercial standards. The occasional work of cleaning and killing chickens, geese, and ducks is now largely done by machines. The cleaning and sorting of eggs also largely consists of monitoring machines. Sorting and cutting potatoes is still a monotonous activity, but has lost much of its drudgery and its dirtiness. The work patterns of Hutterite women therefore have taken a definite shift from the lifestyle of the peasant to that of a modern farmer. There is now less work to be completed, and this reduced amount is less laborious. The corresponding free time of women is spent in the family dwelling. Toys and playpens for children have appeared where previously there were none; a great amount of clothing that traditionally had to be supplied by the women, such as socks, shirts, and underwear, are now replaced by commercial garments.

Hutterite women have become conscious of their appearance both in dress and figure. A great many women of all ages diet and refuse to eat such foods as potatoes and other carbohydrates. Exercise devices for women appear, although their use is confined to the younger age groups. Most women look at these devices with a degree of approval. Only a few years ago men tended to reject such items by saying "Give them more work, and that will provide enough exercise for them!" Nonvisible cosmetics such as hand and face lotions can be found frequently, although visible cosmetic preparations such as lipsticks, etcetera, are still shunned. Some women have taken to dyeing their hair, and many claim that they will do so instead of allowing it to turn grey. Undergarments are still largely produced by hand; however, patterns to manufacture brassieres have been acquired by some women, and home-made support devices have appeared. The dress patterns, which previously de-emphasized body contours are changing to reveal in a moderate way the shape of the breasts and the waistline. The hemline has moved upwards to expose the ankle, and shoes and stockings are of commercial quality.

The organization of communal female work which was always done by the women themselves has taken on new forms with the disappearance of some collective activities such as milking, etcetera. The principal method of rotating such activities as cooking and baking is still being used; however, the rotational pattern is more organized to the specific convenience of women. Some women prefer to cook for ten or twelve weeks and to be free for the rest of the year. Such an arrangement would allow them time to engage in visiting other colonies for longer periods of time. Short-term jobs such as cleaning a load of fish or butchering ducks and geese are still performed by calling out all women, but the working environment has been made much more acceptable for the individual. Women who detest a certain task are much more likely to be listened to, and men are prepared to take over these activities. After a prolonged period of work, some women demand special rewards like visiting another colony or being allowed to undertake activities of their own preference. The colony authorities are more likely to accede to such demands.

The independence that women enjoy in organizing their own work has led to a situation where the women in a colony as a whole represent a force to be reckoned with. Such remarks as "The women don't like that" or "Our women wouldn't go for that" are frequently encountered among Hutterite men. The male authority in the colony tries to avoid a confrontation with this organized female opinion, and if possible tries to accommodate it whenever possible. Being a "woman's man," that is, coming under the dominant influence of one's wife, still carries a negative connotation, but men who are called such names are much less concerned about it than previously. The official treatment that women receive from men during dining hours, for example, still appears to be somewhat rude and overbearing. But now there are men who complain of having been verbally abused by women, something unheard of in the past.

As we have shown, Hutterite women often engage in home industries with the intention of producing items which can be sold for private gain. Some of the allotment of wool or feathers might be diverted to manufacture pillows or bedspreads which can then be sold to visitors; the money acquired in this way is regarded as private property and will be spent for private purposes. Considerable differences between families in room furnishings, children's dress and care, might be introduced in this way. At the same time these activities provide an opportunity for the woman to take care of her own house and family independently of the supplies allocated by the community. The result is a strengthening of family ties to the detriment of community solidarity. The latter in some colonies has also deteriorated somewhat due to the disappearance of work-patterns that brought women together in the evenings, where they engaged in story-telling and singing, spinning and weaving, and feather-splitting, activities that most women enjoyed immensely. Some Hutterite women complain of being isolated from other women despite the fact that they are engaged in a number of communal working groups during the day. What obviously is of importance is not only the physical proximity of working women, but also the atmosphere that characterizes a given situation. The quiet hours spent together in splitting feathers allowed for communicative patterns that women cannot engage in during the day. As compensation for these missing activities, some women take an interest in popular child psychology and child-rearing, either by reading books or even attending local lectures.

The changes in the role of women as indicated above have not produced any alteration in the formal authority and power structures of the Hutterite colonies. Nor are these changes as yet extensive in all colonies as reported here. The important point in the analysis of this situation is that the sources of change which we have located in an altered concept of God, and a general modernization of Hutterite colonies, cannot be stopped. Hutterites are inevitably locked into the drive for greater efficiency which makes modernization inevitable. Although this drive might moderate if the rate of natural increase continues to drop, there is little possibility that Hutterite colonies might return to a self-sufficient economic system. Religious influences from the outside likewise will continue to have an effect on Hutterites. The religious creativity of Hutterites which had come to a standstill more than 350 years ago has left them with a remarkably coherent and effective ideological system. However, this ideological system is structured to support community concerns and community affairs. With the recognition of individual problems the community has little in terms of individualized treatment facilities to address itself to these difficulties. A Hutterite woman who unsuccessfully tried to commit suicide might be subject to traditional forms of punishment, but the Hutterites recognize that such punishment might not be appropriate nor might it effectively deal with the root of the problem. A Hutterite woman who feels that she lacks certain abilities to interact harmoniously with others might think of turning to a psychologist or her family doctor with her problems, rather than approaching her preacher. The tendency towards individuality on Hutterite colonies which is the result of the changes indicated above stands very much in contrast to the collective ideology and behaviour patterns on which the community rests.

It should also be clear that the changes observed among Hutterite women do not take place in isolation from other ongoing changes in Hutterite communities. The transformation of the Hutterite social structure from a socially oriented one to a technologically oriented hierarchy affects the whole performance of man and woman. Work patterns directed to the operation of machines rather than to work-cooperation in human groups enhance this process. Greater individual isolation and greater opportunities for individual perceptions and actions are the inevitable results. The drive towards individualization has made Hutterites particularly susceptible to religious teachings that offer an individualized concept of God. In several colonies fundamentalist sects have been able to make converts, thereby endangering the integrity of the whole community. The culture therefore is faced with reconciling a much more individually conscious individual with the communal qualities of its social system. This is not a unique necessity for Hutterites but a continuation of what has been occurring for several centuries. It would be wrong therefore to assume that dramatic changes are in the offing. The present situation, however, makes it likely that a number of colonies which exist on the liberal fringes of Hutterite society might not be able to achieve this reconciliation between individual and communal concerns, and slowly drift out of the Hutterite orbit.

PART V

Ethnic Relations

THIRTEEN

Hutterites and Ethnic Relations

On August 12, 1899 the governor general in Ottawa approved a report of the Privy Council saying that:

> The Minister is of the opinion, under the circumstances and considering that the Brethren of the Hutterische Society would appear to be a most desirable class of settlers to locate upon vacant Dominion Lands in Manitoba and the North West Territories, that it is expedient to give them the fullest assurance of absolute immunity from military service, not only to those who have already settled but also to those who may settle in the future.[1]

A little more than two months later the deputy minister in the Department of the Interior wrote to the commissioner of Immigration in Winnipeg, Manitoba:

Ottawa, 27th October 1899

Dear Sir,
    I have your letter of the 12th instant, No. 21,759, enclosing a petition from certain members of the Hutterite

community in which they ask that in coming to Canada they may be assured of certain privileges.

(1)   As to their request for exemption from military service, this question has already been dealt with, and I enclose you a copy of the Order-in-Council authorizing their exemption.

(2)   These people will not be molested in any way in the practice of their religious services and principles, as full freedom of religious belief prevails throughout the country. They will also be allowed to establish independent schools for teaching their children if they desire to do so, but they will have to be responsible for their maintenance themselves. The children will not be compelled to attend other schools if their education is properly provided for.

(3)   The law does not compel the taking of an oath in court by persons who have conscientious objections to doing so, and there is no compulsion as to voting for or holding offices, but the privilege of doing so is generally most highly prized.

(4)   There will be no interference with their living as a commonwealth, if they desire to do so.

(5)   The Dominion Lands Act makes provision for the locating of people as communities and their being allowed to live in villages instead of being required each to live separately on his own land.

(6)   The privileges asked for in the last four sections cannot be more firmly established by any further official document than they are by the established laws of the country, and the members of the Society in question may rest assured that the statements made above are of as full value to them as they could be made by an order of the Governor-in-Council or any document of that nature.

Yours truly,
(signed) Jas. A. Smart
Deputy Minister

These two documents spell out the privileges under which Hutterites were admitted into Canada. They are the preconditions for a successful maintenance of this sociocultural system and were insisted upon by the sect throughout its history.

Exactly twenty years later, Canada's minister of Immigration and Colonization, J.A. Calder, wrote to one of the Hutterite elders in South Dakota who inquired about the possibility of migrating to Canada.

Ottawa, September 15, 1919

Dear Sir:

I am in receipt of your letter of the 6th instant to the removal of the remaining members of your community to Canada. I have noted carefully all you state respecting the separation of members of your faith, and can appreciate your feelings and wishes in this regard. However, I must advise you that after the most careful consideration of all the fact and circumstances, the government concluded that it would be inadvisable, owing to the general feeling prevailing throughout Canada, to continue to permit certain persons to enter Canada because of their custom, mode of life, habits, etc., were such as to prevent them becoming readily assimilated.

These persons included Doukhobors, Mennonites, and Hutterites. We have had so much trouble in Canada in connection with school and other matters in the colonies and communities of these people that their neighbours and people generally insist that no more should be permitted to come.

If in the future this decision should be reversed, it will depend largely, if not entirely, upon the conduct and mode of life of those of your people now settled in Canada. Unless they are prepared to become Canadian citizens in the truest and best sense of the term, and unless they are ready to assume all the obligations of citizenship including military service if called upon, it is extremely doubtful if any government in Canada would be prepared to admit them.

I trust I have made the situation quite clear. Should you desire any further information, or in case you wish to place any further facts before me, I shall be pleased to hear from you.

Yours very truly,
J.A. Calder
Minister of Immigration and Colonization

Privileges bestowed on Hutterites at one time were revoked at another. Canada's official policy which had granted exemption from military service and similar matters, changed into its opposite when these privileges were taken to the task during the First World War.

It is interesting to note that at the time when the last letter was written only one Hutterite colony had settled in Canada and this one colony existed for less than a year. The minister therefore could hardly have referred to first hand knowledge about problems encountered with Hutterites. In fact what he must have referred to were problems associated with Doukhobors and Mennonites. Of these the Doukhobors had culturally and socially little in common with Hutterites and insofar as it concerned the Mennonites, history has rendered its judgement. The hostilities encountered by this group during and after the First World War were unjust, unjustified, and nothing but the result of a nationalistic hysteria that vented its resentment against a conveniently situated and harmless social group. Of course the minister was well aware of the fact that Hutterites had experienced the same nationalistic hysteria in the United States and the major reason why they attempted to migrate to Canada was the death of two of their young men inducted into the U.S. army and dying as the result of torture while refusing military service. As later events showed, particularly during the Second World War, a patriotic-minded population resented Hutterites on national and cultural grounds. The German origin of Hutterites, particularly their use of the German language and their sociocultural isolation, created an atmosphere of suspicion. There was also a feeling of deprivation by those who thought they were carrying the burdens of war and citizenship while they alleged that Hutterites gained materially at their expense.

As it turned out, Hutterites immigrated to Canada anyway and by the end of he 1920s most had settled in Manitoba or Alberta. In response to an inquiry by one of the last colonies to move from the U.S. to Canada the mayor of the town of Raymond, Alberta wrote in 1934:

The Hon. John E. Brownlee   Raymond, Alberta
Premier of Alberta   Mar. 3, 1934
Edmonton, Alta.

My Dear Mr. Brownlee:

I have been asked by representatives of a Hutterite Colony to express to you my personal attitude toward the entrance and location of the Rockport Colony near Raymond and to give you my opinion as to what the sentiment of the District is.

We personally have lived as neighbours to a Colony for a number of years and have found them to be good neighbours. They pay their bills and taxes promptly and are honourable in their business dealings.

I have not found any group public sentiment against the entrance and location of this Colony near Raymond. Their entrance will be a decided advantage to the vendors and to their creditors.

Yours truly,
W. Meeks
Mayor, Town of Raymond

The Lethbridge Board of Trade sent the following telegraph to Ottawa:

Brig.-Gen. J.S. Stewart M.P.   Lethbridge
Parliament Bldg.   March 14, 1934
Ottawa, Canada

The Board of Directors of Lethbridge Board of Trade are of the opinion that the Department of Immigration should grant the admittance of about one hundred Hutterites to settle in the Raymond District. Stop. The admittance of these people will mean the disbursement of large sums of money to a great many individuals also to the Sugar City Municipality and Provincial Government. Stop. These people have furnished evidence that they will be selfsustaining and able to pay their taxes promptly.

Lethbridge Board of Trade
per. Pres.
Sec.

The inspector of schools in the Lethbridge area wrote to the Premier of Alberta the following letter:

The Hon. J.E. Brownlee   1108-7th Ave. S.
Edmonton, Alta.   Lethbridge Alta.
                                      Jan. 12, 1934
Dear Sir:

At the request of the Hutterite Brethren of Southern Alberta I am testifying to the efficiency of the schools in the Colonies where public school districts have been organized.

As the official trustee of these districts I have been responsible for the selection of teachers and the maintenance of their schools during the year. The leaders of these Colonies have always co-operated with the Department of Education in the schools and have invariably supported their teachers.

When the isolation of the children in these schools is considered their attainments in the English branches is all the more remarkable.

Incidentally it should be mentioned that in one of the Colonies all unemployed boys and girls must attend school during the winter months — this by order of the manager of said Colony.

All of these Districts are sound financially. They pay their taxes promptly. In the Hutterite District of the

Lethbridge Inspectorate all obligations to banks, teachers and school supply houses are regularly made at the end of each month.

During the inspection of these schools I have never witnessed mentally deficient children. In fact the Hutterites have the proud boast that since their arrival on this continent only one instance of such is on record.

I believe that if the present system of Official Trusteeship is maintained over the Colony schools, we shall secure as good results for them as in the ordinary ungraded schools of the Province.

Your obedient servant,
Owen Williams
Inspector of Schools

Eight years later in the middle of another war, the Alberta Legislature passed the "Land Sales Prohibition Act" which prevented the purchasing of land by Hutterites. Because the 1942 Legislation referred to enemy aliens as well as Hutterites, it was disallowed and consequently re-enacted with reference to Hutterites only.

There has been a roller-coaster policy in regard to the immigration and presence of Hutterites in Canada. When the country was in need of hardy immigrants willing to settle the prairies they were welcomed with open arms. When they insisted on utilizing the original privileges they were granted during the First World War they became undesirables. When it became known that they would pay their taxes and generated business during the Depression they again were looked at in favourable terms, only to be officially restricted and unfairly regulated when they, as committed pacifists, stayed aloof from the nationalistic sentiments of the Second World War. Hutterites were caught in the squeeze of being accepted by Canada on economic grounds and rejected on nationalistic emotional grounds. The contradiction between these two categories certainly did not make for enduring relations between the sect and Canadian society.

This relationship took on new forms when the Second World War marked the end of the West as a pioneer area. The drought had finally ended and technological advances in agriculture together with improved market conditions created entirely new conditions compared with those prevalent during the dirty thirties. Farms consolidated into larger units. Land became scarce and a great many individuals whom the Depression and the war had driven off the land returned and attempted a new beginning. These new conditions changed the outlook on Hutterites drastically. No longer was it of great value to pay taxes or to give an economic stimulus to a depressed area. In fact everybody was most eager to get into the act and share the boom of the postwar prosperity. Hutterites now were looked at as a group that prevented returning veterans from taking their rightful place in society — a place which they thought they had risked their life defending.

The "Land Sales Prohibition Act" which was to expire after the war therefore was replaced by "An Act Respecting Lands in the Province Held as Communal Property." The most important sections of this act read as follows:

> 6- (1) No colony hereafter established and no branch of a colony and no person acting on behalf of a colony as trustee or otherwise, shall purchase, agree to purchase, attempt to purchase, lease or otherwise acquire any land or enter into any contract or agreement which directly or indirectly may result in the vesting of title or the right of possession of land in a colony or in any trustee or other person on behalf of a colony or in the acquisition of land by a colony or any branch therefore within forty miles of any part of the communal property held by an established colony.

The maximum amount of land to be held by any Hutterite colony was regulated by subsection two:

> 6- (2) No such acquisition shall be made of land exceeding in area sixty–four hundred acres or of land which when added to the lands already held by the colony

makes their total acreage in excess of sixty-four hundred acres.

In fact this act stipulated that *any* land offered for sale and lease to a Hutterite colony anywhere in the Province of Alberta must first be offered for sale under the provisions of the Veterans' Land Act of 1942 and such offer had to remain open for a period of sixty days (Section 8-).

The immediate postwar era launched the ethnic relations of Hutterites as those of an invading minority. The demographic expansion and the exclusive agricultural preoccupation of the group invariably sent it on a collision course with those sectors of the Canadian society that occupied the same ecological niche. Hutterites are a minority unlike any other ethnic group in Canada. They represent a subculture on the one hand and a society on the other. This society maintains a complete set of institutions serving its members from the cradle to the grave. Although some of these institutions, education and the economy for example, are interrelated with those prevalent in Canadian society, the totality of Hutterite institutions and its particular management form an alternative to the norm at least in regard to those engaged in the business of agriculture. Hutterites do not intend to walk the road of "anglo-saxon" conformity; they represent an alternative lifestyle which in the last resort is a challenge to some conventional values, norms, and behaviours. Although this challenge has failed to attract converts, as very few outsiders permanently join Hutterite colonies — the essence of the Hutterite challenge is traceable to the cultural and economic success of the group. Among the most threatening of these factors are superior agricultural organization, resource utilization, and demographic expansion. The Hutterite challenges in these areas are formidable indeed.

A society encountering the threat of an invading minority is able to face such challenges only under very special circumstances, if at all. Primary among these would be a high level of tolerance, which in turn would require cultural self-esteem and economic security. In an ethnically diverse region like western Canada cultural self-esteem has developed only very slowly. National cultural symbols and policies are still being questioned as the flare–up of the Western Canadian Independence movement demonstrated; Canada's multicultural policy, if it had any effect at all, managed to spread the feelings of ethnic marginality even to those groups who previously thought they represented the dominant cultural entity. Cultural equality it seems levels out on an equal sharing of cultural insecurity.

Economic security was always problematic in the agricultural sector of western Canada and will be so for the foreseeable future. The business of farming includes a great deal of risk inasmuch as weather conditions can eliminate the best of human efforts in a few hours. Frost, hail, and drought form an unholy trinity and have left a deep feeling of insecurity among many farmers. In addition there are the unstable market conditions for western Canadian products. Hutterites seem to be all but oblivious to these cultural and economic problems. The relative isolation which they maintain in regard to their communities guarantees them a high degree of cultural self–determination. Economically they are opportunists in the sense that they combine the efficiencies of their communal organization with the technological standards and marketing practices of their host societies. They in fact have the best of two worlds: cultural security through the maintenance of their own institutions, including the community of goods, and economic security through successful participation in the agricultural economy of western Canada.

It is true therefore that Hutterites have an advantage over the family farm. Whether this is an unfair advantage or not is another question. In fact that question cannot be answered without referring it to someone's point of view. And this point of view usually is heavily infused with self–interest. The Hutterite threat as an invading minority finds its foremost expression in the threatened lifestyle of the family farm. Changing economic conditions in the prairies have facilitated the emergence of rival structures to the family farm. Corporation farms and gentleman farms as well as Hutterites are challengers to the family-farm organization.

All of these can be seen as invading minorities; although the most visible are the Hutterites which, due to their high birth rate and economic success rate, have replaced part of the farm population during the last fifty years. Such a replacement of the majority by an invading minority made it impossible for western farmers to adopt another possible position — that of ignoring the group. Such a response would only be possible with respect to ethnic groups that do not grow, and therefore fail to pose a threat to the majority or parts of it. The growth of the Hutterite population and its increasing share of the land resources in western Canada do form a threat and this threat as we have seen is at once cultural and economic.

It is therefore understandable that the preconditions for a high level of tolerance toward Hutterites — cultural self-esteem and economic security within the western farm population — have not grown to the point where they would wipe out anti-Hutterite sentiments. It would be wrong to dismiss the anti-Hutterite sentiments as expressions of prejudice born out of ignorance and bigotry. Although there is no shortage of these when individuals or groups attempt to express their anti-Hutterite feelings, the underlying cultural and economic causes are real and must be addressed as such. The usual position of sociologists to condemn ethnic prejudice as evil, irrational impulses employed by people in search of scapegoats, attempts to locate these attitudes in the psychological make-up of individuals who, in one way or another, suffer from psychological maladjustments. Whatever the explanatory power of this theory might be in other cases, its application to the Hutterite problem in western Canada is of a very limited utility. We are dealing with an ethnic struggle over scarce resources. And this struggle unquestionably has resulted in the elimination of parts of the western farm population, which in defense of its position is fighting back with all the political, attitudinal, and economic means that it can muster, including unreasonable and irrational forms of prejudgements. The invasion of a majority by an economically successful and culturally cohesive minority is one of the most difficult ethnic problems to deal with. It is probably one of the oldest social problems that man has faced in his evolutionary history and it might very well have played a major role in man evolving the way he did. This is not to say that it is a good thing to have or that one can do nothing about it. On the contrary, it means that one must deal with it in the culturally reflective manner with which man, having evolved to the point that he has, must deal with all his problems.

Accurate information about the population growth of Hutterites, evaluated and removed from the emotionalism of anti-Hutterite sentiments, is a beginning. Hutterites cannot go on growing forever they way they have done for most of the last century. No human or animal population has ever done so. There must be a point of inflection and our chapter on the decline of Hutterite population growth contained in this book plus the postscript to the demographic section clearly show that a significant decline has taken place. Soon more detailed and more comprehensive data will be ready for publication by a research team consisting of Drs. Edward Boldt, Lance Roberts and myself. These data will allow us to see the invading threat of this minority in a more factual light. But it cannot stop here. Ethnic tolerance means first and foremost acceptance on the emotional level as well. Society it seems is not only a system of law where relations between individuals and groups are determined by "rights" as seems to be the trend of the last decade or so, but it also constitutes a moral order that is unwritten. The pursuit of group rights has led to important changes in government policy and is bound to have long range effects. The abolishment of the Communal Properties Act through the Alberta Bill of Rights is a demonstration of this sort. The point I am trying to make is, however, that exercising group rights in society is not synonymous with participating in the moral order; it is probably no more than a necessary precondition for such participation. Hutterites have the unquestionable right to live as they do and shy away from any involvement in the moral order of the larger society. But in view of the conflict that exists, it is questionable whether it is wise to do so. An in-group attitude among Hutterites which can be interpreted as indifference toward the rest of society is ill–advised and dangerous. Group selfishness is as reprehensible in a moral order as is selfishness among individuals. Ethnic tolerance means first and foremost the probability of any group being accepted by and included into the moral order of society on an emotional level. This does not imply assimilation but accommodation and above all mutual understanding. What are the preconditions for accommodation and understanding between Hutterites and farmers in western Canada? On this level of the moral order, society must be given an opportunity to relate to the sect in some meaningful way. Whether one person might be proud of such hard–working people; whether neighbours feel they are helped by Hutterites; whether the intellectual sees in them a demonstration of his or her society's tolerance; there are countless ways in which this moral relationship can be established.

There is on the part of Hutterites a trend to recognize this necessity to become more open toward the rest of society, to get involved in the moral concerns of society to the extent that such involvement does not endanger their own cultural existence. All this is possible but requires flexible and intelligent leadership, in which the sect unfortunately is lacking to some extent, no matter how economically efficient such leadership might be. From the religious-ideological point of view, greater societal involvement would require a reformulation of the age–old concept of "separation from the world." Hutterites have always lived in this world and have adjusted to the conditions of the world in which they existed at any one time. There is nothing new about a pragmatic reformulation of this concept. During the last decade most Hutterites have modernized their colonies and in the process have thrown out their native material culture to be replaced by stainless steel utensils and vinyl floors. This unfortunate loss of material culture goes unnoticed by leaders and membership alike. It is propelled by a relentless drive for efficiency and has destroyed work groups, prestige hierarchies, and status expectations. The cultural dangers from these forms of modernization are much greater than any moderate attempt to participate in selected societal affairs of their own choosing. There is an enormous struggle within the sect over exactly this question. And it can only be hoped that with the passing of a rigid, uninventive and basically scared older leadership, younger men will emerge who do have the intelligence, insight, and authority to reformulate the place of Hutterites in a quickly changing society. But Hutterites of course are not the only ones who need changing. A sober reflection on how this sect has been treated in the past should teach us a number of valuable lessons about ourselves, our motives, and our behaviour. The relocation of the

Japanese and the confiscation of their property provide examples along the same lines. Cultural enlightenment is an upward struggle to discover the humanity which is common to all of us. North America got under way in this direction but it has still a long way to go — as has every nation and society. Accurate information about Hutterites and the establishment of moral relations with them does not resolve the basic cultural and economic conflict. True enough. But these positive steps alter the conflict, moderate it, and make it one more social problem that can be handled by reasonable policies, mutual accommodation, and restraint.

NOTES

Introduction

1. Karl Peter, "Social Class and the Conception of the Calling: A constructive revision of Max Weber's hypothesis," M.A. thesis, University of Alberta, 1965. The sociopolitical motivation of Hutterites and their orientation toward earlier communal social structures destroyed by feudalism are extensively treated in this thesis. There is also an account of the militant movement in the Tyrol under the leadership of Michael Gaissmaier.

1 The Survival and Institutional Evolution of Hutterite Society

1. The first community ordinance appeared in the 1560s and regulated the educational institution (*Schulordnung*). It spelled out the educational philosophy of Hutterites and formalized parent-child relations as well as teacher-pupil relations. During the following century all crafts and household activities of Hutterites were similarly regulated including the amount of food and drink allocated to various individuals. As a rule these ordinances were read once a year to the assembled community members.

2 The Certainty of Salvation

1. The term "psychological sanction," first introduced by Talcott Parsons in his translation of "The Protestant Ethic and the Spirit of Capitalism" (Weber 1958: 97) is a somewhat infelicitous choice of words. Unfortunately Weber was not consistent in the German terminology he employed.

3 The Contemporary Dynamics of Religious Defection

1. Obtaining accurate figures is a sensitive and difficult undertaking, sensitive because the issue of defection is not one that Hutterites like to discuss, and difficult because a complete count would necessitate a visit to virtually each of the 250–plus colonies scattered across three provinces and four states. This was not possible under the circumstances, and we therefore resorted to a poll of Hutterite informants representing each of the three kinship groups, including some highly placed and well informed leaders. On this basis we were able to determine that the problem of religious defection is most severe among the *Schmiedeleut*, who also happen to be the most progressive and loosely structured group. Approximately 150 individuals (out of a total 9000 plus) are estimated to have left the *Schmiedeleut* on religious grounds during the past five years. For the *Lehrerleut* our estimate is seventy (out of 6300 plus) and for the *Dariusleut* eighty (out of 6500 plus). As noted above, these numbers (three hundred defections out of a total population of 21,800 plus, affecting approximately fifty colonies out of a total 250 plus) do not appear to be particularly high in absolute terms; but when compared to Eaton and Weil's (1955: 146) total enumeration of only 123 permanent defections for the period 1918-1950, the Hutterites' concern becomes clear. Leaders typically describe the recent spate of religious defections as a "wave" sweeping through their colonies and which, among the *Schmiedeleut*, shows signs of getting out of control.

2. During the course of our research it was discovered that some Hutterite preachers are beginning to interject, extemporaneously, personal comment and opinion into their sermons. This is a very recent development, and its significance for the issues we have raised is not yet clear.

3. One might speculate that the attraction of evangelical Protestantism for Hutterites represents a renewed search for *Gelassenheit*.

4. The individualization and liberalization that is occurring on Hutterite colonies may also be related to the fact that the Hutterites are now enjoying a period of calm in their relations with the host society, more so, perhaps, than at any previous point in their turbulent history. If the Hutterites are regarded as a defensive society then it may well be that a lack of external threat eventually translates itself into internal disintegration (Boldt 1980).

5. Radio and television are still not openly tolerated, although there is one Canadian colony that has recently allowed T.V. sets in the homes of its members, at least temporarily. More frequently these (particularly radios) are secretly acquired and used by younger members without offending their elders.

6. One special case of "semi-permanent visitor" deserves special mention in this context, and that is of the English school teacher. The Hutterites maintain their own schools, but the curriculum and teacher must meet provincial and state requirements. Since the Hutterites do not as a rule keep their children in school beyond the legal leaving age, most of the teachers are University-trained non-Hutterites. As such they have a unique opportunity to influence not only their students but older members of the colony as well. There have been occasions where this influence has presumably

taken the form of religious persuasion of the kind we have described (Mackie 1975).

7. The processes we have described in large part apply to at least two of the three groups of outsiders who have emulated and adopted in part Hutterite beliefs and practices. These groups, which are still in existence today, are the *Arnoldleut*, or Society of Brothers, and the *Juliusleut*. They initially sought out Hutterites, who cooperated with them and assisted in establishing them as nonethnic Hutterite communities. The subsequent relationships between the Hutterites and these groups have been complex. Suffice it to say that some Hutterites left their own colonies to join these groups, thereby precipitating a break in relations. These events, therefore, can also be regarded as a form of religious defection brought about by Hutterite efforts to win converts. (For a fuller discussion of the *Arnoldleut* which concludes before their recent reconciliation with the Hutterites, see Whitworth 1975: 167-209). A third group, the Owa community of Japan, was recently formed as the result of a Japanese scholar coming in contact with Hutterite theology. This group, however, is extremely small, and although Hutterites render it economic aid, there are only few, and sporadic, personal contacts. The psychological effects, which an apparently successful conversion of Japanese individuals to Hutterite beliefs brings are demonstrated in Hofer's account of the Owa community (Hofer 1980).

6 Problems in the Family, Community, and Culture

1. The study of life histories and biographies is not a major methodological device among contemporary sociologists, but earlier sociologists found such material extremely useful in the study of social conduct. Studies such as Thomas and Znaniekl's "The Polish Peasant in Europe and America" and Shaw's "The Jackroller" made significant contributions to the understanding of human action. As pointed out by Howard Becker in the 1966 edition of Shaw's book, life histories reveal useful information in at least three important areas of human conduct: (1) They reveal the point of view of the actor; (2) They elaborate on the sociocultural context to which the actor is responsive; (3) They reveal the sequences and the interconnections of past experiences and situations in the life of the actor.

    The methodological problems associated with the study of life histories are authenticity, accuracy, and representativeness. In the present study, the first two problems were overcome through the author having the opportunity to check his data against those collected through participant observation. From the literature it is further evident that the woman's description of life and routine activities is highly representative of conduct in Hutterite communities. But this is of minor interest to the author. The real task is to select from this autobiography those crucial descriptions which provide insights into problematic areas of the sociocultural life of Hutterites, 'and to present them in their logical, religious, and sociocultural connectedness. To do so required drawing on additional information not contained in the woman's autobiography. Nor is this analysis meant to present a definitive statement of sociocultural problems among Hutterites, but it is being put forward as hypothetical, awaiting further confirmation or refutation.

7 Psychophysiological Typologies

1. There are some minor variations in the current Hutterite pronunciation of these names, so that the forms we give here are approximations rather than a precise phonetic transcription.
2. The inbreeding coefficient is defined as the probability that at a given locus an individual has two identical copies of an allele present in an ancestor common to both the individual's parents.

9 The Decline of Hutterite Population Growth

1. The breakdown of data according to different time periods is prone to introduce distortions which might be interpreted as contradictory. Ryan (1977) for example reports the establishment of twelve new Manitoba colonies for the period 1970-1975 given a high rate of annual increase of 4.5 percent. From the end of 1964 to 1970 however only six new colonies were established at a rate of 2.71 percent per year. From 1960 to 1965 ten new colonies were established in Manitoba at a rate of 5.59 percent per year. Since our argument is based on a time period from 1964 to 1977 a corresponding observation in Hutterite expansion should cover the same time period. If, therefore, the high increase of expansion 1960–1965 is neglected the rate of expansion of Manitoba Hutterite colonies from 1964 to 1977 has decreased very much in line with the decrease in population growth.

10 Changing Attitudes and Practices

1. Rideman's life and work has been summarized in Friedmann, 1970.
2. This age may vary to as low as fifteen in some colonies.

11 The Hutterite Economy

1. For detailed descriptions of the mixed–farming economy among Hutterites see Bennett 1967 and Ryan 1977.

13 Hutterites and Ethnic Relations

1. This and the following letters are taken from Zieglschmid (1940: 621ff).

BIBLIOGRAPHY

Bendix, Reinhard. 1962. *Max Weber: An Intellectual Portrait*. Garden City, N.Y.: Doubleday.

Bennett, John W. 1967. *Hutterian Brethren: The Agricultural Economy and Social Organization of a Communal People*. Stanford: Stanford University Press.

Bettelheim, Bruno. 1961. "The Challenge of Youth." In *Fertility and Survival*, edited by Alfred Sauvy. London: Chatto and Windus.

Boldt, E.D. 1976. "Acquiescence and Conventionality in a Communal Society." *Journal of Cross–Cultural Psychology* 7: 21-36.

———. 1978. "Structural Tightness, Autonomy, and Observability: An Analysis of Hutterite Conformity and Orderliness." *Canadian Journal of Sociology* 3: 349-63.

———. 1980. "The Death of Hutterite Culture: An alternative interpretation." *PHYLON* 41: 390-95.

Boldt, Edward D., and Roberts, Lance W. 1980. "The Decline of Hutterite Population Growth: Causes and Consequences — A Comment." *Canadian Ethnic Studies*, no. 3.

Clark, P.G. 1973. "Dynasty Formation in the Communal Society of the Hutterites." Ph.D. dissertation, University of British Columbia, Vancouver, B.C.

Coser, Lewis A. 1974. *Greedy Institutions: Patterns of Undivided Commitment*. New York: Free Press.

Deets, Lee Emerson. 1939. *The Hutterites: A Study in Social Cohesion*. Gettysburg: Times and News.

Diener, Paul. 1974. "Ecology or Evolution? The Hutterite Case." *American Ethnologist* 1: 4, 602-18.

Diener, Paul, and Robkin, Eugene. 1978. "Ecology, Evolution, and the Search for Cultural Origins: Question of Islamic Pig Prohibitions." *Current Anthropology* 19(3): 493-540.

Eaton, Joseph W. 1952. "Controlled Acculturation." *American Sociological Review* 17: 333-40.

Eaton, Joseph W., and Mayer, A.J. 1954. *Man's Capacity to Reproduce: The Demography of a Unique Population.* Glencoe: Free Press.

Eaton, Joseph W., and Weil, Robert J. 1953. "The Mental Health of the Hutterites." *Scientific American* (December): 189.

————. 1955. *Culture and Mental Disorders.* Glenco: Free Press.

Franz, Guenther. 1956. *Der Deutsche Bauernkrieg.* Darmstadt: Gentner.

Friedmann, Robert. 1961. *Hutterite Studies,* edited by Harold S. Bender. Goshen, Ind.: Mennonite Historical Society.

————. 1970. "A Hutterite Census for 1969: Hutterite Growth in One Century, 1874-1969." *Mennonite Quarterly Review* 44 (January): 100-105.

Friedmann, Robert, and Mais, Adolf. 1965. *Die Schriften der Hutterischen Taeufergemeinschaften.* Hermann Boehlhaus Nachf., Graz-Wien Koeln. Gerth, H.H. and Mills C. Wright, eds. 1958. From *Max Weber: Essays in Sociology.* New York: Oxford University Press, A Galaxy Book.

Gross, Leonard. 1980. *The Golden Years of the Hutterites: The Witness and Thought of the Communal Moravian Anabaptists During the Walpot Era, 1565-1578.* Studies in Anabaptist and Mennonite History No. 23. Scottdale: Herald Press.

Gross, Paul S. 1965. *The Hutterite Way.* Saskatoon, Sask: Freeman Publishing Company Ltd.

————. N.D. Private correspondence.

Hofer, Joshua. n.d. *Japanese Hutterites: A Visit to Owa Community.* Elie, Manitoba: James Valley Book Centre.

Hostetler, John. 1965. *Education and Marginality in the Communal Society of the Hutterites.* Cooperative Research Project, OE 2-10-131; Project No. 1683. The Pennsylvania State University & U.S. Department of Health, Education and Welfare.

Hostetler, John. 1974. *Hutterite Society.* Baltimore: The Johns Hopkins University Press.

Hostetler, John A., and Huntington, Gertrude Enders. 1967. *The Hutterites in North America* (Case Studies in Cultural Anthropology). New York: Holt, Rinehart and Winston.

Hruby, Frantisek. 1935. *Die Wiedertaeufer in Maehren.* Leipzig: Heinsius.

Kanter, Rosabeth Moss. 1972. *Commitment and Community: Communes and Utopias in Sociological Perspective.* Cambridge: Harvard University Press.

Kautsky, Karl. 1897. *Communism in Central Europe in the Time of the Reformation.* Translated by J.L. and E.G. Mulliken. London: T. Fisher Unwin.

Klassen, Peter James. 1964. "The Economics of Anabaptism, 1525-1560," Studies in European History, Vol. III. The Hague: Mouton.

Klaus, A. 1887. *Unsere Kolonien.* Odessa: Odessaer Zeitung.

Kraybill, P.N., ed. 1978. *Mennonite World Handbook.* Lombard Ill.: Mennonite World Conference.

Kretschmer, Ernest. 1936. *Physique and Character: An Investigation of the Nature of Constitution and of the Theory of Temperament.* Translated by W.J.H. Sprott. New York: Cooper Square.

Kurczynski, Thaddeus Walter. 1969. *Studies of Genetic Drift in a Human Isolate.* Ph.D. dissertation, Case Western Reserve University, Cleveland.

Lorimer, F. 1958. *Culture and Human Fertility.* United Nations Educational, Scientific and Cultural Organization. Berichthaus, Zuerich.

Mackie, Marlene. 1975. "Defection from Hutterite Colonies." In *Socialization and Values in Canadian Society,* Vol. 2., edited by R.M. Pike and E. Zureik. Toronto: McClelland and Stewart.

Mange, Arthur P. 1964. "Growth and Inbreeding of a Human Isolate." *Human Biology* 36: 104-33.

Mannheim, Karl. 1936. *Ideology and Utopia.* New York: A Harvest Book, Harcourt, Brace, and Company.

Martin, Alice Opaskar. 1969. *Recurrent Founder Effect in a Human Isolate: History and Genetic Consequences.* Ph.D. dissertation, Case Western Reserve University, Cleveland.

Mead, George Herbert. 1934. *Mind, Self and Society.* Chicago: University of Chicago Press.

Peter, Karl. 1965. "Social Class and the Conception of the Calling: A Constructive Revision of Max Weber's Hypothesis." M.A. thesis, University of Alberta, Edmonton.

_____. 1967. "Factors of Social Change and Social Dynamics in the Communal Settlements of Hutterites, 1527-1967." Ph.D. dissertation, University of Alberta, Edmonton.

_____. 1980. "Rejoinder to 'The decline of Hutterite Population Growth: Causes and Consequences'." *Canadian Ethnic Studies* 12, no. 3.

Peter, Karl, and Peter, Franziska, eds. 1980. *Der Gemein Ordnungen 1651-1873.* Reardan, Wash.: Espanola Gemeinde.

Reid, Russell M. 1973. "Inbreeding in Human Populations." In *Methods and Theories of Anthropological Genetics,* edited by M.H. Crawford and P.L. Workman, pp. 83-116. Albuquerque: University of New Mexico Press.

Ridemann, Peter. [1542] 1950. *Account of Our Religion, Doctrine and Faith.* Translated by Kathleen E. Hasenberg. London: Hodder and Stoughton.

Ryan, John. 1977. *The Agricultural Economy of Manitoba Hutterites.* Toronto: Carleton Library 101.

Sauvy, Alfred. ed. 1961. *Fertility and Survival.* London: Chatto and Windus.

Schluderman, Shirin, and Schluderman, Edward. 1971a. "Adolescent Perception of Parent Behaviour (CRPBI) in Hutterite Communal Society." *Journal of Psychology* XXIX: 29-309.

_____. 1971b. "Maternal Child rearing Attitudes in Hutterite Society." *Journal of Psychology* LXXIX: 169-77.

_____. 1975. "Personality Development in Hutterite Communal Society," Paper delivered to Canadian Ethnic Studies Association, Winnipeg.

Shaw, Clifford Robe. 1966. *The Jackroller: A delinquent boy's own story.* Chicago: University of Chicago Press.

Sheldon, W.H. 1944. *The Varieties of Temperament: A Psychology of Constitutional Differences* 2nd ed. New York: Harper.

Steinberg, Arthur G., Bleibtrau, Hermann K., Kurczynski, Thaddeus W., Martin, Alice O., and Kurczynski, Elizabeth M. 1967. "Genetic Studies on an Inbred Human Isolate." In *Proceedings of the Third International Congress of Human Genetics*, pp. 267-88. Chicago, 1966.

Thoman W.I. and Znaniecki F. 1927. *The Polish Peasant in Europe and America.* New York: Alfred A. Knopf, Inc.

Vana, Lucille Ripley. 1974. *Maintenance of Genetic Polymorphism in an Inbred Human Isolate.* Ph.D. dissertation, Case Western Reserve University, Cleveland.

Vayda, Andrew P., and McCay, Bonnie J. 1975. "New Directions in Ecology and Ecological Anthropology." *Annual Review of Anthropology* 4: 293-306.

Weber, Max. 1904-05. "Die Protestantische Ethik und der Geist des Kapitalismus," *Archive fuer Sozialwissenschaften und Sozialpolitik,* Vols. XX and XXL.

————. 1920-21. *Gesammelte Aufsaetze zur Religionssoziologie.* 3 vols. Tuebingen: J.C.B. Mohr.

————.1958. *The Protestant Ethic and the Spirit of Capitalism.* Translated by Talcott Parsons. New York: Scribner.

————. 1961. *General Economic History.* Translated by Frank H. Knight. Collier Books BS 13. New York: Collier.

————. 1965. *The Theory of Social and Economic Organization.* Translated by A.M. Henderson and Talcott Parsons. New York: Free Press.

Weeks, John Arthur. 1977. "The Genetics of Fertility in a Human Isolate." M.Sc. thesis, Case Western Reserve University, Cleveland.

Weiss, Mark L., and Mann, Alan E. 1978. *Human Biology and Behavior: An Anthropological Perspective.* 2nd. ed. Boston: Little, Brown.

Whitworth, J. Mck. 1975. *God's Blueprints: A Sociological Study of Three Utopian Sects.* London: Routledge and Kegan Paul.

Zieglschmid, A.J.F., ed. 1943. *Die älteste Chronik der Hutterischen Brüder: ein Sprachdenkmal aus frühneuhochdeutscher Zeit.* Philadelphia: Carl Schurz Memorial Foundation.

————. 1947. *Das Klein-Geschichtsbuch der Hutterischen Brueder.* Philadelphia. The Carl Schurz Memorial Foundation, Inc.